PRAISE FOR BLACK LOVE SIGNS

"Thelma Balfour has written a droll, entertaining travel through the astrological universe . . . on the black hand side."
—Vern E. Smith, author of *The Jones Men*

"Easy, enjoyable, informative reading!"
—Jamie Foster Brown, publisher of *Sister 2 Sister* magazine and editor of *Betty Shabazz: A Sisterfriends' Tribute in Words and Pictures*

"All signs point to great fun and keen insight, thanks to Thelma and her work in *Black Love Signs*."
—Sybil Wilkes, co-host of the *Tom Joyner Morning Show*

Praise for *Black Sun Signs*

"Cosmically informed and culturally specific."
—Leslie Lockhart, *Quarterly Review of Books*

"A sexy, slangy, chatty book, written with a twinkle, and a wink."
—John Beifuss, *The Commercial Appeal*

Black Love
Signs

Also by Thelma Balfour

Black Sun Signs

THELMA BALFOUR

ATRIA PAPERBACK

New York   London   Toronto   Sydney   New Delhi

Black
Love
Signs

An Astrological Guide
to Passion, Romance,
and Relationships
for African Americans

ATRIA
PAPERBACK

An Imprint of Simon & Schuster, Inc.
1230 Avenue of the Americas
New York, NY 10020

First Atria Paperback edition February 1999

ATRIA PAPERBACK and colophon are trademarks
of Simon & Schuster, Inc.

For information about special discounts for bulk
purchases, please contact Simon & Schuster
Special Sales at 1-866-506-1949 or
business@simonandschuster.com.

The Simon & Schuster Speakers Bureau can bring
authors to your live event. For more information
or to book an event, contact the Simon & Schuster
Speakers Bureau at 1-866-248-3049 or visit our
website at www.simonspeakers.com.

Designed by Judy Wong

Manufactured in the United States of America

3 0   2 9

The Library of Congress has cataloged the Fireside
edition as follows:

Balfour, Thelma.
Black love signs : an astrological guide to passion, romance, and relationships for
African Americans / Thelma Balfour.
p. cm.
"A Fireside book."
1. Afro-American astrology. 2. Astrology and sex. 3. Love—Miscellanea. 4. Mate selec-
tion—Miscellanea. I. Title.
BF1714.A37B25 1999
133.5'089'96073—dc21   98-33240 CIP

ISBN 978-0-684-84783-2

ACKNOWLEDGMENTS

To my family:

My husband, Gabriel, for supporting me through my many career changes.

My two sons, Erin and David, and my stepson, Gabriel Jr.

My granddaughter, Alexia Nicole.

My sisters, Levennette, Adrienne, Laurie, and Lisa.

My two aunts, Dr. Agnes Lattimer and Camille Lattimer, for their never-ending support.

My nephew Damion Breathett and my cousin Holly Jones.

My niece, Cheryl Hudson, for her enthusiasm and legal counsel.

My nephew Cedric Hudson, who assists with public relations and marketing needs.

Special thanks, in alphabetical order, to:

Gwynette McDonald Blackburn for her support and assistance with this project.

My agent, Marlene Connor, whose levelheadedness and calm keep me focused.

Dawn Daniels, my editor, whose enthusiasm, professionalism, and youth inspire regularly.

Yvonne "Bonnie" DeBose and Virginia DeBose, two sisters who are like my sisters.

My newest goddaughter, Evangeline Louise Heath.

Peggy Hill-Heath, my friend, whose name I forgot to include during the first book, and for that I am truly sorry.

Pauline McDonald for her upbeat spirit and for allowing me refuge and privacy during the writing of this book.

Peggy McKenzie, my friend and colleague, whose continuous support keeps me afloat.

Minister Shirley Prince, who keeps me in the spirit and encouraged.

Dr. John Rankin Jr., my dentist and friend, whose expertise in computers saved me a small fortune.

Denise Suggs Rixter of Rixter, Tate & Associates, whose marketing and public relations skills never cease to amaze me.

Ida Louise Scott, my college roommate, whose friendship I continue to cherish.

Venita Steppe-Smith, who keeps me tuned in and up to date on the latest computer Web sites, e-mail addresses, and the like.

Deanie Parker, my former boss and mentor: Thanks for lending me your computer after mine crashed a week before my editing deadline.

Roxie Gunter Singers of Friendship Baptist Church.

Sandra Vaughn, friend and mentor.

And all of you who responded and took the time to complete surveys and participate in interviews, I thank you!

To my father, Limuel Lockard, who died recently—a man of great genius who did it "his" way. I love you.

To my aunt, Thomasine Lattimer Jones, and my two cousins, Michael "Busta" Jones and Bernard Cassell Goss, who all died within the same year. I miss you terribly!

CONTENTS

INTRODUCTION

This book, *Black Love Signs*, is a continuation of my first book, *Black Sun Signs: An African-American Guide to the Zodiac*. *Black Sun Signs* was very successful, first and foremost, because of the enormous support it received from the black community. Black people are no different from anyone else in wanting an astrology book about themselves. *Black Sun Signs* is a book about astrology and how it relates to the African-American experience. It's also a book about us, about our culture, our parents, our grandparents, our friends, relatives, and lives. And it was a book whose time had come.

As I was conducting interviews and sending out questionnaires to hundreds of people for the first book, one thing became abundantly clear to me: Everyone is looking for that all-important soul mate. And both men and women seemed to be willing to dump their present companion or spouse to be a part of what they consider a fulfilling, exciting, and fun union with a person yet to be found.

I knew that an additional book would be in the works soon. And after talking to the masses, I decided to write one that was strictly dedicated to love, romance, and sex—because according to all those who responded, these three areas of a relationship are the most important.

After *Black Sun Signs* was published, I went on tour to promote my book and meet my public. The question I was asked most often, other than "Who am I compatible with?" was "What signs will do what sexually?" The women I talked to wanted to find that sexually uninhibited man—that man who would and could appreciate their creativity in bed. In fact, the only group who didn't sound off were the pets!

The women complained that they were sick and tired of having to "play dead" during sex and pretend that they knew very little about the sexual experience. One sister commented that women, just like men, have had a life before the newly developed relationship begins, and men should respect that.

For the most part, women felt that the brothers were living in the Dark Ages. The gap between what men and women were allowed to do, sexually and in relationships, was continuous and widening even though the sisters were taking control of their lives, in both their careers and sexual matters. But when it came to actualizing the concepts about sex and romance for women, the disparity between the sexes was overwhelming.

For example, one sister said that when she showed some creativity in bed and had the brother hollering and beggin' for mercy, after the encounter was over, he'd want to play Twenty Questions! He'd ask with an air of disdain, "Where did you learn that?" or "Do you do that with every man you meet?" Go figure.

The brothers were also in da house with their complaints. Most commented that they weren't mind readers. Some brothers commented that when the female isn't satisfied from a physical, emotional, or sexual standpoint, it's only fair to let the brother know what's up. Said one brother, "They want total ecstasy, yet I have no idea what turns my lady on, initially. We have to work at it. But don't blame me if you don't see stars at first during sex!"

Further, the brothers said that they were victims of their upbringing. "When I was in college and a teenager, there wasn't any mention of being sensitive," a forty-year-old brother said. "The only thing I was told by my father was 'Go get it, son.' These kinds of things need to be overcome gradually, over time. Don't expect me to have a blueprint on being great, wonderful, and sensitive without some kind of ground rules or information!"

Another brother complained that, yes, there are new rules in the dating game. But who pays and when should be addressed. "The payment for dinner should be equal if that's what we decide to do. But don't expect me to pay if or when we go to an elegant restaurant and you're only paying when we go for fast food!"

Then there were gay men who commented that I didn't include them in the first book, and of course, they were hot under the collar about it. They said that I needed to include them in my new book. One gay Taurus disagreed with my assessment of the Taurus man in the first book. "The section on the Taurus woman seemed to fit me better than the Taurus man," he said. "Okay, fine. No problem," I said. My philosophy is, Whatever works.

Initially, I became interested in astrology only after a friend gave me a book on the subject and told me to read about my Virgo husband, who, I felt, was very complex and hypercritical of me. After seeing his behavior in black and white, I was sold. Reading about his personality clarified a lot of areas in our marriage for me. I also realized that his hypercritical nature had very little to do with me because he would criticize a signpost. I am a natural skeptic. If it is not rational, I have trouble believing it. But I am willing and eager to be entertained. Get my attention and I might listen. Astrology got my attention when I read about my husband.

After reading my first astrology book, I took my questions to the masses and found that when I asked a Virgo if he was a neat freak, he responded in the affirmative nine out of ten times. When I asked the Scorpio if she was a control freak, she hedged a bit, but eventually came clean and admitted that she was indeed. When I talked to Aries people about ranting and raving constantly, they tried to offer (still ranting and raving, of course) justification for why they yelled and screamed so much.

Astrology is certainly not a cure for all of life's struggles, twists, and turns. It's merely an innovative and fun way to determine compatible mates, career paths, and overall general personality traits. It's human nature for people to be interested in finding out about themselves—black folks are no different.

And, whether we like it or not, astrology is all around us. How many times have you heard the question "What's your sign?" Most folks hear the question in some sort of social setting. The question can serve as an icebreaker and a way to talk to people when you're kickin' it at a party, hoping to meet that all-important soul mate. Trying to impress that sister with what you want her to think you know about astrology. Nodding your head when the sister responds and says, "Pisces." It's all a part of the game— the games people play. Like you actually know what it all means. Yeah, right.

But from a subliminal standpoint, we are inundated with the psychic hotlines, the 1-900 numbers and the novice predictors of the future. Therefore, the image and concept of astrology are ever-present. But what do we really know about the phenomenon called astrology? Usually it's what we hear other people saying, like "Girl, Scorpios are mean." Or "You don't need to deal with Geminis 'cause they're moody and two-faced." But aside from all that we hear and think that we know, what *does* it all mean? When asked, "What's your sign?" some of you who are trying to be cute will say, "Dollar sign." But what does it really mean to be, say, a Gemini?

It means that Gemini is an air sign and one of the twelve signs of the zodiac in this astrological approach. Astrology is the study of the planets, including the moon and the sun, to determine how and what effects the changing positions of the planets have on human behavior. This book will give you a basic understanding of astrology and a window into the hearts and minds of the people you love so you can have a better appreciation of the differences in our personality and makeup. Folks, what goes on in the heavens has a direct bearing on what's going on down here!

How many times have you seen a full moon and couldn't take your eyes off it? How many times have you been totally invigorated

by the sun? That energy from the sun, the moon, and the other planets is compelling, and so is the energy that people give off, both overt and subtle. It's unmistakable. I dare you to put it to the test and pay attention to those around you. Pay attention to what's going on and the vibration you're feeling from all of the interaction and energy that others give off! And once you're truly indoctrinated, your next comment will be *"Wow!"*

ASTROLOGY CAN
ENHANCE YOUR
LOVE AND
IMPROVE YOUR
ROMANTIC
AND SEXUAL
RELATIONSHIPS

Astrology can help you find that all-important person, that soul mate, the love of your life. I know some will say, "I don't care what the sign is—there are jerks in all twelve signs." So true. But before you write off this whole concept, read further. I too was the skeptic. However, once I started to pay attention to the various signs, talk to people directly, and discover personality traits all on my own, I began to think, hey, there may be something to this. And there was— for me, anyway.

The point of this section is to let you, the reader, know what's up with *Black Love Signs:* how you can use this book as a reference, an owner's manual, or simply for information about the twelve signs of the zodiac in general and the gory details of sex, love, and romance.

Writing this book was interesting to say the least. The response was overwhelming from both the men and women. But what was most interesting to me was the differences in perception between men and women about what makes for good romance, sex, and love. Take one couple that I interviewed, first separately and then together. Initially, the man told me he liked to make love for at least two hours. I mentioned his comments casually to his companion, not for verification, but in conjunction with another question. The female promptly corrected me by saying that the two hours included dinner, listening to music, and bathing. Thank you very much!

Some of the interviews were, of course, over the top, but I believe that many of the responses were strictly for shock value. Of course, my goal was to keep my poker face on because, after all, I thought I should be in control of the situation. But many times I wasn't at all, so I would simply leave the room for a minute, holler out aloud, compose myself, re-enter the room, and resume the interview.

For the purposes of this book, the Sun sign aspect of astrology, the most noted and popular portion of the zodiac, will be examined. The sun is the central most important celestial body; therefore, your Sun sign is the most important aspect of your birth chart. (Your birth chart is determined by the position of all the planets at the time of your birth.)

The sun moves around the earth each year and travels through all twelve signs of the zodiac. The Sun sign is the astrological sign that the sun is moving through at the time of your birth. For instance, the sun will move into the sign of Aquarius on January 20 and exit on February 18, so anyone born between January 23 and February 18 is known as an Aquarian, the sign of the water bearer.

From an astrological standpoint, the Sun sign controls your personality, style, general demeanor, and outward appearance. For example, if you're a Sagittarian, you are usually prone to casual dress and an over-the-top sense of humor. Therefore, you may be attracted to members of the opposite sex, or in the case of gays or lesbians, who have a great sense of humor, for instance, Cancers—and they to you. But generally, Sagittarians and Cancers are not compatible. The initial appreciation for making everyone laugh may be what draws these two together, but little else will hold their attention. Cancer is a water sign and Sag is a fire sign. And the water sign will be quick to put out the flame of the fire sign. In other words, water and fire don't mix.

Here's how the mix works. There are twelve signs of the zodiac, and these signs are divided into the four elements of the universe: earth, water, fire, and air. The earth signs are Capricorn, Virgo, and Taurus. The water signs are Cancer, Pisces, and Scorpio. The fire signs are Aries, Leo, and Sagittarius. And the air signs are Aquarius, Gemini, and Libra. Each element—earth, fire, water, and air—also reveals tidbits about the twelve Sun signs. Now consider these elements for a moment. We don't need a Ph.D. from the School of Astrology before we can pick up juicy and illuminating clues about a person's behavior.

Earth signs: Taurus, Virgo, and Capricorn. You're down to earth, practical, and cautious. Basically, you're always the same—predictable, reliable, grounded. (Ground-ed, ground, earth—get it?)

Fire signs: Leo, Sagittarius, Aries. Like the element of fire, you're unpredictable, feisty, aggressive, impulsive, and hard to control. (To put it more bluntly, it's going to be your way or no way at all!)

Water signs: Cancer, Scorpio, Pisces. In reality, people generally love to be close to lakes, rivers, oceans, and ponds. If you're a water sign, people love to be close to you because you're reassuring, emotional, intuitive, soothing, and nonthreatening.

Air signs: Gemini, Libra, Aquarius. If you're an air sign, you're independent, aloof, analytical, intriguing, and very hard to keep up with. You must have freedom. Like air itself, you cannot be contained, harnessed, or backed into a corner. If this happens, you'll simply disappear.

From a practical standpoint, earth and water signs make beautiful mud together. And fire and air make a bonfire that's hard to put out.

Here's the breakdown of the Sun signs:

> Aries (March 21–April 19)
> Taurus (April 20–May 20)
> Gemini (May 21–June 20)
> Cancer (June 21–July 22)
> Leo (July 23–August 22)
> Virgo (August 23–September 22)
> Libra (September 23–October 22)
> Scorpio (October 23–November 21)
> Sagittarius (November 22–December 21)
> Capricorn (December 22–January 19)
> Aquarius (January 20–February 18)
> Pisces (February 19–March 20)

Compatible mates:

✴ Aries works best with Sagittarius, Leo, Gemini, and Aquarius.
✴ Taurus is compatible with Virgo, Capricorn, Cancer, and Pisces.
✴ Gemini is more suited to Leo, Aries, Aquarius, and Libra.
✴ Cancer is better with Pisces, Scorpio, Virgo, and Taurus.

The four signs listed within each group are also compatible and interchangeable. In addition to Cancers, for example, Scorpios are compatible with Virgo, Taurus, and Pisces.

And please, please, please don't send those cards and letters declaring that you and your husband, boyfriend, girlfriend, or partner of twenty years are not listed here as being compatible. I didn't say all of this astrology business is foolproof. I'm simply saying that this method will enable you to leap over some of the many frogs before you meet the prince or princess of your dreams.

Your opposite sign is generally about six months from your birth date, or directly across from your sign on the circular horoscope. The following signs are opposites:

Aries–Libra
Taurus–Scorpio
Gemini–Sagittarius
Cancer–Capricorn
Leo–Aquarius
Virgo–Pisces

If you pay attention to astrology or know the birth date of your companion, you will probably realize that you're constantly meeting your opposite and the encounters are usually quite interesting. The conversations are stimulating; there's definitely chemistry. As you're trying to emphatically leave this courtship, exchange, date, or whatever, you'll constantly get this "Wait a minute, baby" plea. The magnetic attraction is so deep that the two of you won't be able to accept that the relationship ain't working! And you'll spend most of your time making up. But on the real tip, you know that after the morning after, reality sets in. You need to give it up and you know it!!!

Understanding astrology may clarify a few issues and help you bring closure to a relationship or make it blossom. But if homeboy or homegirl is certifiable, then astrology or numerology or the psychic hotline won't help. Use common sense, and get the hell out of Dodge City while there's still time!

Here's how to use *Black Love Signs*. At the beginning of each chapter the positive and negative love traits for that sign are listed. But bear in mind that when I list "kinky" or "S & M" as a negative trait, this is open to interpretation. By and large the concept of what is negative or positive is all relative. It's really up to the reader to decide what's negative or positive.

Each chapter includes an overview of the sign and then some general information about both the man and woman and how to attract these creatures that we assume you can't live without!

Next is the Guide to a Love Connection, which includes a breakdown of the sign with the eleven other signs. This section cuts to the chase: Before you even start reading all that "stuff" on the man or woman you're planning a life with, it tells you whether you should even bother reading further.

The Romance section for each sign is next. This section is a quick study in how to be romantic. You may already be romantic, but just in case you need some help, and need it quick, fast, and in a hurry, you can turn to this section.

Then comes the Sex section—presumably the most popular section. Here's where to find out what your companion will and will not do.

After you've recovered from your long, sweaty hours in the sack, you can check out Money Matters, Pampering Tips, and Gift Ideas for your companion. You've definitely got to keep the groove going, so pay attention to these sections!

Once you've determined what all of the commotion is about with your companion, then you'll see tangible results. And I do mean *tangible:* She or he won't want to leave your side.

Black Love Signs will also save you and your partner some embarrassing moments. For example, if you like swinging from the chandelier and she doesn't, some foreknowledge about her sexual leanings may help you keep the egg off your face. So chill out, and enjoy the book for what it is—an exercise in fun!

P.S. One area I overlooked was that fine Lord-have-mercy-motor-scooter mate, where there is no rhyme or reason why you are in the relationship. Don't ask me for an explanation—that's a whole other talk show!

We talked so much about sex, romance, and love that I forgot to mention one other important issue—safe sex. Hopefully, being adults, we all know what safe sex is all about. It's called using a condom (the male or female variety). No matter what the astrological sign is, sexually transmitted diseases are an ever-present danger. So listen up! Protect yourself. I wanted to include a condom in every book to bring home my point. However, I didn't want the *context* of the book to be overshadowed by the *content*. So in two words—Be safe!

ARIES

(March 21 to April 19)
SYMBOL: THE RAM

Positive love traits: Passionate, sensual, spontaneous, insatiable lover, and one of the stars of the freak show.

Negative love traits: Selfish, sadistic, impatient lover; kinky, master-slave inclinations.

Ruling planet: Mars is associated with initiative and courage.

Word to the wise: The faint of heart need not apply. Ranting and raving are a way of life for the ram.

When you first meet Aries people, you won't have any trouble recognizing them. They're usually the ones in the room talking and laughing the loudest, telling a story, including every gory detail. If you've got all day to listen, that's fine. If you don't, no matter. All they need is an audience of one to continue. You'll find Aries people where the action is, provided they're not at home resting up for the next adventure. They love sports, horseback riding, theater, poetry readings, listening to or performing music, and any other outlet where there are hordes of people.

Their ruling planet is Mars, which means they're cheerful, enthusiastic, and gung ho about everything in which they're involved, including a budding or impending relationship with you, provided that they're interested. If you catch their eye and they're interested, both men and women go in for the "kill" early and don't waste precious time. While you're stalling and thinking about it, they're already planning their next move.

If the Aries isn't interested, then I would suggest not trying to force the issue. Aries people have definitely been known to be pretty blunt. And believe me, they will tell you in no uncertain terms that initiating a date or a conversation is an exercise in futility. The conversation will go like this: "Baby, I wish we could have a relationship, but you're kind of too slow for me. You don't want to do anything, but you call me all the time. I just can't have that. You need to find something else to do."

Aries is the first sign of the zodiac, and these rams expect to be first in everything they do. And that also includes having your undivided attention. The symbol is the ram, an animal that is very aggressive and able to climb to great heights. Now if you plan to soar with the eagles, uh, excuse me, rams, you better read further.

The ruling planet of Aries is Mars, which is associated with initiative and courage. One thing you can count on with an Aries, they are never thin-skinned when it comes to taking chances and trying new ideas. For example, an Aries saleswoman discovered that a friend owned several commercial lawn mowers for maintaining lawns of companies and apartment complexes. The Aries sister convinced her friend to start a lawn service business. She put the marketing plan together and wrote the sales pitches and ended up getting clients for the company. But unbeknown to the Aries, her friend had a drug problem, and instead of providing the lawn service for customers, he stayed home most days with his crack pipe. Undaunted, the Aries sister contacted several other companies. And now she's marketing director for a number of lawn service concerns.

The element for Aries is fire, and like the element, Arians are bold, hot-tempered, and hard to control. With these rams, there will also be a lot of ranting and raving going on. They simply can't help it. In an effort to make their point, their voices automatically go up at least two levels. When the noise starts, just ignore it, and don't take it personally.

For the most part, these fire signs are loners. Getting to know an Aries may be difficult sometimes. They feel very comfortable with themselves. They can also be totally self-absorbed and preoccupied with whatever they're about. If you point out that the ram is selfish, he readily agrees. But that doesn't mean he's going to do better. They mean well, but they can't help it. An Aries key word is "self," meaning whatever the situation is, the Aries should be the first considered. For example, an Aries man who was acting like Scrooge before Christmas would not accompany his Cancer wife to the woods, chop down an evergreen, and play the total Christmas scene with her and his stepson. When his wife came on with the flood of tears, Mr. Ram was unimpressed. His only retort was "I am not going because I don't feel like it. I don't care if you're crying. Now cry, cry, cry!"

With both the men and women of this sign, it's going to be their way or the highway. These fire signs are very demanding, domineering, and opinionated about most things. A Scorpio wife said her Aries husband was a blockhead about most things, unless it was something he wanted to do.

Physically, Aries people are quite striking. They're usually medium tall to tall. They have larger than average heads, with lots of hair. If you look a bit closer, there's probably a scar or mark from some accidental injury. Both the men and women have broad shoulders. They have an unmistakable charm and a winning smile.

Arians are the cheerleaders of the zodiac. They're usually charged up about most projects that they start and never finish. They can be wonderful, too—but they have to want to be. So don't frustrate yourself with questions like "How could he say that to me?" or "She was supposed to bring the paper goods for the party and she didn't show up!" Charge it to their heads and certainly not their hearts.

THE ARIES MAN

When you first meet this brother, the first thing you'll notice is his confidence. He definitely does have a sense of style. But many Aries men wear outdated clothing. This brother may even show up in a leisure suit or bell-bottom pants. They simply don't take the time to shop for clothes. They can usually think of a million and one things to do other than the mundane and boring task of shopping. It's only when they're standing in front of the closet, trying to determine what to wear to a club or some other function, that they realize that they haven't been shopping for months—even years. His mate is on the sidelines, doggin' the brother out and saying, "I can't help you find anything. Every time I want you to go shopping with me, you don't have time, and you know you don't want to spend any money on clothes."

Besides, Arians feel that clothes don't make the man because they feel like their unmistakable charm, sense of adventure, and bedroom maneuvers are basically all that they need.

These brothers, whose sense of adventure is ever-present, are attracted to women who are independent thinkers and those sisters who want a sense of adventure in their lives no matter what their age. For example, your ram may decide impulsively that he wants to photograph you in the nude, with the trees, grass, and setting sun as the backdrop. While you're protesting all along the way, he will reassure you by agreeing to undress as well, as he's taking pictures of you in all of your "every which way but loose" poses. Much to your chagrin, the photos will be pleasing to the eye and create for you an off-the-cuff sexual sense of yourself. Chill out, you may enjoy the experience.

If you are a clingy type and want to know the Aries brother's every move, well, I suggest you move on to another section of the book. If you're a homebody, you're going to be home alone. You won't ever know his every move because half the time he doesn't either. Aries brothers will want, and encourage, you to do your own thing.

A Libra literary agent who had a platonic relationship with an Aries man, or so she thought, overheard him mention to someone else that his girlfriend nagged all the time. "I realized after a while that he was talking about *me*. It was the first I had heard that I was his girlfriend." Well, now.

The Aries brother invented the power of persuasion. While you're trying to collect yourself and figure out whether you're going to agree to the initial date, the brother may be at your door demanding to talk with you. You had better be careful. One of his favorite lines is "I'm on my way over there!" Besides, he knows that if he can simply have an audience with you, it will be all over but the shouting.

Since he's at your door demanding entry, you've probably passed the test. Aries men are attracted to women who are independent thinkers and those sisters who want a sense of adventure in their lives. He simply doesn't plan to see or be with you every day of your life. Even if you're married to an Aries, he will have a room that he considers his domain, complete with porno movies, old sports tapes, his favorite music, and old pieces of furniture from his college days or stint in the military.

As husbands or lovers, they will never give you a dull moment. He will sweep you off your feet with cards every day, phone calls, and information about what's in store for the week. Your only requirement is to be ready, willing, and able for this nonstop roller-coaster ride. For example, you may get a call on your job from your eager Aries announcing that the two of you will go out of town with his college roommate. The Aries agreed to drive his room-mate's car back home because his friend was leaving for overseas in two days. Of course, the drive is fifteen hours one way. And never mind that he wants to stop along the way to have sex, whether indoors or out. And you'll be expected to help drive, cajole his room-mate, and have sex with the ram, too. Don't forget, you must be enthusiastic. And so it goes.

The Aries brother demands the direct approach. "Are we in a relationship?" he will want to know. "If we are, well, when are we going to bed?" During the initial phase of the relationship, if you don't plan to deliver, don't accept an invitation to his apartment. He will interpret any flirting or teasing as an open invitation. He'll put on a few erotic videos and charm the pants, or dress, right off you. The Aries man will overwhelm you with his philosophy on relationships, his approach to courtship, and his over-the-top antics in the bedroom. And if you're still around after *that* scene, well, you may be able to hang in for the long haul.

His enthusiasm for any new relationship is similar to a boy with a brand-new toy. He'll approach the courtship as though you're his first and only love. But if it doesn't work, he'll be off again writing more poems for his new lady love with the same passion and commitment he once had for you. When the relationship is over, he's the first to say good-bye. He'll probably be the first to know it's over, too.

On the other hand, if he's in the doghouse and hasn't been as attentive, he knows exactly how to get your attention. You may get a card and stuffed animal with a note of apology in your mailbox. Or he may show up at your house with a full meal that he prepared himself, along with wine and a single rose. After the meal, of course, he'll clean the kitchen. He'll then declare that he's your sex slave, offering himself as dessert.

Oh, by the way, his memory about details is not very sharp because he's usually involved in too many projects to keep up with all the promises he's made. The best approach in dealing with an Aries and his empty promises is not to rely too heavily on his involvement during any special occasion. For example, don't put Mr. Ram in charge of disc-jockeying for the family reunion or the surprise party for your cousin. He may show up when it finally hits him, two hours later, after you've made several frantic phone calls, paged him (he probably left his pager on the dresser), or filed a missing persons report with the police.

Whenever he arrives, he's going to be the life of the party. But save yourself some frustration. Also, ladies, save your breath, this Aries is only going to do exactly what he wants to do. Don't take it personally. The fact that he didn't show up at all or showed up at the eleventh hour has very little to do with you. This same scenario could be played out at a family wedding, church banquet, or his best friend's bachelor party.

Oh yes, Aries brothers are extremely jealous. They figure you have no reason in the world to be flirting shamelessly with another man when you have him. Your Aries will boldly walk right over to you while you're talking to Mr. All That and demand an explanation. Although he was showing all thirty-two teeth when Miss Miniskirt Mama approached him, he'll still want an explanation from you, and with a quickness!

THE ARIES WOMAN

Remember the word to the wise at the beginning of this section of the book? Well, take heed. The Aries sister is very aggressive, independent, and domineering. Although she demands a lot, she gives much more in return. If you're a wimp, quiet, nonaggressive, or insecure, you're going to be miserable in a relationship with Miz Ram. When a man meets a challenge like the Aries sister, he's bound to be intrigued and amused by her devil-may-care attitude and bold confidence.

During the initial encounter, this sister will get right in your face, make eye contact, not waiver in her boldness, and dare you to cross the line into her territory. Her bold demeanor should give you an inkling of what's in store, namely adventure, intrigue, and spontaneity. The Aries woman wants to feel secure in knowing that her man is a take-charge kind of person because if the man doesn't, she definitely can and will.

A courtship with a lady ram will definitely be a challenge. First off, the initial interest is going to be slow-going. But if you decide to make the first move before knowing that she's interested, you may get your face cracked. All you have to do is ask. She will definitely tell you if you're getting warm. Aries people have to create the challenge, so playing hard to get is the best strategy. For example, an Aries female was told by her Aquarian sister that a fine new Aquarian brother worked at the local service station and she should go take a look. When Ms. Aries saw what she described as a 100 percent Mandingo-looking brother, she was definitely interested. He acknowledged by calling to her, "Hey, hot rod." Within a time span of about an hour she was back to fill up her mother's car, then her dad's car, and finally her neighbor's car. Although she was totally interested, she didn't accept a date with him until he had asked a fourth time.

Don't try a short and sweet relationship with an Aries sister because they want a long-term commitment in and out of the bedroom. None of this bim-bam, thank you, ma'am routine. For example, an Aries college student who was a resident adviser allowed a boyfriend into her room during a visit. Shortly boyfriend number two came a-callin'. But because she was an RA, she explained to number two that she had a distraught student in her room whom she needed to console. He believed her. She didn't really feel too guilty about the encounter because, as the Aries put it, "He was no angel himself." This brother was a card-carrying member of the Bim-Bam Club. Her true allegiance was to boyfriend number one, who was attentive and willing to spend quality time with her.

When an Aries sister finally falls in love, she'll shout it from the rooftops. Her zest for life carries over into love relationships. She will support you all along the way, offering words of encouragement and support. She'll give you her undivided attention and expect the same from you. She will shower you with gifts, organize impromptu meetings, arrange weekend getaways, and keep you guessing, not knowing what to expect. You'll love every minute of it. She will demand that you be monogamous. Actually, with this energetic ram, you'll be too exhausted to have a relationship with anyone else. This sister plans to keep you occupied. Consequently, when you make a date, you need to get some rest, rest, and more rest if you plan to run this race!

The race will include early-morning breakfast, followed by lunch in a down-home diner on a dirt road off the interstate, and a walk through the wooded area behind the diner. "Dessert" may commence right on the spot in the woods—so have your condoms handy. And even though you've spent the entire morning and afternoon with her, expect a call from her later that evening, asking what you're doing. *Please* don't let her know that you're soaking your feet from today's activities. Tell her that you're ready to take in the dinner and the play that she's already made reservations for.

The wrath of an angry Aries is serious business. Take the case of an Aries insurance claims adjuster in Georgia whose boyfriend went away for the weekend with his parents to celebrate their anniversary. Sounds innocent enough—except the boyfriend married an old girlfriend during the weekend celebration and didn't bother to tell the Aries sister until after spending the night with her. Ms. Ram had her revenge, though. She called the boyfriend's new wife, told her that they had spent the night together, and also told her that Mr. "Devoted" Husband wanted to continue his sexual relationship with the Aries.

In another example, an Aries woman caught her companion in bed with another woman. Her Aquarian mate had gone to the Aries cousin's house for a rendezvous. "I kicked the door in. He tried to run and close the next door and I kicked it in too. And the wood door cut his arm from the force of my kick. I went in and saw what I wanted to see and I left. But the fear in his eyes told me what was happening." The Aries sister is jealous: If you're her mate, all eyes should be on her. She's not insecure about the relationship. Her key word is "self," meaning she is the one.

Although Aries sisters have the appearance of being aggressive and from the school of hard knocks, they're really very vulnerable and need attention and reassurance. (You really wouldn't know it from all the ranting and raving they do.) They particularly abhor inattentive behavior. If her mate is only half listening as he watches the football game on television, then she may stand in front of it, pull the plug out of the wall, or even pitch the TV if it's small enough. If in fact she's feeling unappreciated and the two of you are driving along in the car, she may suddenly grab the steering wheel, swerving the car into the next lane to get your attention. This fire sign can and will resort to extreme behavior if she feels you're not listening.

One skeptical Aries sister met a Virgo brother who was a little reserved and quiet. Her immediate reaction was that he was too slow for her. But after the first kiss, Mr. Virgo announced that he wanted to take her to his hometown to meet his parents, and she has been smitten ever since. Sometimes, it's just the little things.

Sincerity and a honest approach rank real high with the Aries woman. And strutting around like Mr. Penis is not going to cut it. "While I was at a party," an Aries executive assistant related, "this guy was telling me how good he could be for me with persistent determination when all the while his lady was sitting in the next room. And he wasn't all that!" Knuckleheaded braggadocios are a turnoff.

Guide to a Love Connection

Aries and Aries

When you've got two domineering people or two blockheads or two rams locking horns, well . . . both Arians want to be the star of the show and therein lies the problem. The key word here is "self," which means, for both, see me, take care of me, and validate me. And that philosophy is fine if you don't have two Arians in the mix. There's little peace because both are prone to rantings and ravings constantly. So the neighbors will complain a lot. In fact, when there is peace, the other one is probably asleep or not around. These two will spend most of the time kissing and making up, which will have them purring and on autopilot. But the turbulence is far too frequent and too exhausting to keep this pair together for long. And *puleeze,* I hope these two are not working together or have some common space that they share frequently. Lord, help us . . .

Aries and Taurus

Speaking of locking horns, the ram and the bull are both too headstrong to be good companions to each other. Aries is impulsive and spontaneous and loves to go with the flow. Taurus is slow, steady, and organized, and simply will not make a move without some contemplation first. Aries is constantly flying by the seat of her pants without a net, annoying cautious Taurus to no end. Both are highly sexed. But the lady bull doesn't like all of that kinky stuff in bed, whereas Aries is the master of raw, no-holds-barred sex. His bedroom antics are just like his life—full of reckless abandon. This will frustrate Taurus, who simply cannot understand such behavior. A word of warning to the Taurus: In order to maintain your sanity, you must control the checkbook; Aries' philosophy is "Money is meant to be spent."

Aries and Gemini

Well, now, this relationship can work in and out of the bedroom. Both are creative, imaginative lovers. From head to toe, no area is taboo for these two. Both are versatile and love trying new things at a moment's notice, including sex out under the stars or in a hot tub. With Aries, it's anything goes. Gemini isn't intimidated by the Aries' need to dominate. For when Gemini wants to be assertive, his mental agility will take over. While Aries rants and raves, Gemini will simply sit quietly and wait for the storm to dissipate. Then Gemini will calmly ask, "Are you finished?" Of course, this approach infuriates Aries. But the fight usually ends quickly. This relationship could even blossom into a good marriage, provided both can stay focused long enough.

Aries and Cancer

The Aries-Cancer mix is definitely on between the sheets. And you can bet, Aries, that you've dealt with many Cancers over time. The answer to the question of whether the two of you will make it is still No! Not only no, but Hell, no! Cancers are far too sensitive for tactless, know-it-all, my-way-or-the-highway Aries. Aries means well. He just has to have his way—or at least he has to believe he's in control. In this relationship Cancer will constantly be licking her wounds from the unintentional stabs of the Aries personality. The long-lasting making-up sessions cannot heal past wounds or lessen future hurt. Pass on this one.

Aries and Leo

Leo must have lots of attention. Aries must be praised and acknowledged for innovation, courage, and spontaneity. These two are both fire signs, and they are not turned off by the other's aggressive behavior. During the physical encounters (not fights, but bedroom) Aries takes the lead and provides Leo with the rollercoaster ride of a lifetime. Leo, although turned on by sexual creativity, won't be amused by over-the-top S & M or extreme role-playing encounters in bed. As long as the attention is on the Leo instead of the sex toys, movies, and other enhancements, the Aries will have no problems. This pairing will work nicely if the temper tantrums are kept at a minimum. Some controls should be kept on the credit cards and checkbook, however. The controls certainly won't exist with these two. Financial planners, are you listening?

Aries and Virgo

Aries is far too outrageous, sexually and in general, for prudish and careful Virgo. Although Virgo will swing from the chandelier eventually ("eventually" could be years), Aries will be long gone before Virgo musters the courage to match Aries' appetite for sex, adventuresome spirit, and zest for life. Virgo doesn't like surprises or spontaneous fun. With Virgo all things must be planned, thought out, and executed in a systematic manner. Aries would never sit still long enough for all that preparation. Aries' motto is "Just do it!" They do have mutual respect for each other, but that alone won't hold a relationship together. The two are so ill matched, both will heave a sigh of relief when the liaison is over. But the loudest sigh will come from the Virgo!

Aries and Libra

The birthdays of these opposites are approximately six months apart, and the saying that opposites attract definitely applies here.

They camp out in the bedroom. That's where they better stay in order for the relationship to last. The energy level sexually is so high, the two simply can't get enough of each other. The problem is, as with most opposites, the physical connection won't offset the troubles in all the other areas of the relationship. Aggressive, loud Aries is a bit much for peace-loving, calm Libra. Aries is messy. Libra is a neat freak. Aries is disorganized. Libra is methodical. Aries has little interest in clothing. Libra is a clotheshorse. The ongoing squabbles will drive a permanent wedge into the relationship.

Aries and Scorpio

Sexually, this coupling has no problem. Each has a strong sexual drive that compliments the other. But once the bedroom aerobics are over, this relationship is an exercise in futility. This toe-to-toe matchup will be interesting at best. Scorpio won't back down from your take-charge attitude, Aries. Both want to control the relationship and make all of the decisions. Scorpios love the daring type—but while Aries is off involved in some act of courage, Scorpio is feeling neglected and sulking at home. Aries' outgoing nature and many projects create insecurity and jealousy in Scorpio. The arguments and fights continue to disrupt the foundation of this somewhat shaky relationship. If you want a booty call, just for sex's sake and nothing more, this is the ticket.

Aries and Sagittarius

The flame burns eternal for this pairing of fire signs. All systems are go, provided Sagittarius can keep the tactless comments to a minimum and Aries can minimize the incessant "I" talk about his wonderfulness. The conversation between these two is stimulating. Aries is knowledgeable on a variety of subjects, and Sag has an insatiable appetite for knowledge and higher learning. Aries is the aggressor in the bedroom, but that won't turn off the wariest of Sagittarians. Sag will bring humor, spontaneity, and excitement to the party—to Aries' delight. These two are social butterflies and party animals and keep each other entertained with their offbeat sense of humor. Both have explosive tempers. The kissing and making up last much longer than the fights, however.

Aries and Capricorn

The ram and the goat both have horns, and the similarity ends there. Aries' proclivity to the bizarre and freaky has controlled, conservative Capricorn running for cover. These two have very little in common, aside from their stubbornness. Aries couldn't care less about style and dress. Capricorn will not be seen in public with the ram if his appearance isn't updated, upscaled, and neat. That means, Aries, no polyester bell-bottoms, leisure suits, or Nehru jackets. Fat chance. Aries is impulsive and restless. Capricorn is grounded, calm, and controlled. Aries' sexual motto is whatever, whenever, wherever. That approach will never do for the serious Capricorn. Sex will be on certain days, at certain times, and ordered like the rest of the Cap's life. The respect and admiration that they have for each other will not sustain a relationship, not even a short one.

Aries and Aquarius

This twosome can work, but several conditions must be met. Aries will not be able to control and dominate. Aquarius, though faithful to a mate, absolutely must have freedom and not be backed into a corner by the constant demands, declarations, and pontifications of the ram. There is definite chemistry here. Aquarius loves the take-charge attitude of Aries. The connection continues in the boudoir. And the sex is on! Yes, m'am. Aquarius will be impressed and entertained by the Aries' bedroom antics. These are two of the "stars" of the freak show. They do it all. Aquarius' friendly but aloof behavior keeps Aries wondering what his next move should be. Word of advice: Stop trying too hard, calm down, and take it step by step. Believe me, this relationship is worth working for on both parts.

Aries and Pisces

From a physical and erotic standpoint, the hand has met the glove. The freak show was created and produced by this pair. Aries loves to dominate and control. Pisces loves to feel protected and admires the take-charge attitude of Aries. Both are amorous and take great pains to please the other. The champagne flows, the role-play of master-slave finds these two putting a creative twist on what's already considered to be off the beaten path. Now that all of the physical stuff is out of the way, this relationship will take extra care and feeding. In order for the relationship to work, Aries has to calm down, curtail some of the ranting and raving, and pay closer attention to Pisces' needs and less to his own. Oh, by the way, Pisces, you won't be able to get out of the relationship until the Aries wants out. The ram is relentless.

ROMANCE AND THE ARIES

If you're planning a romantic evening, day, or night with an Aries, you need a checklist. Aries people love to talk and talk to those who have something relevant to say. Because they are so versatile, a romantic evening could include anything from watching videos at home to a candlelight dinner and even sex under the stars. All of your encounters with your Aries companion will be fun and spontaneous, with plenty to do and no time to be bored. The Aries' stamina is relentless.

Both the men and the women of the sign go in for the kill early. A romantic day begins with breakfast with homemade biscuits, followed by a leisurely walk or sex. Then lunch, followed by a movie or browsing through a bookshop or antique store. Then dinner and later possibly a lecture by Louis Farrakhan or some cool jazz. An Aries will always want plenty to do. She doesn't want to be bored, not even for a minute.

Initially, the encounter with the Aries will be to wow you with flowers, fun, frolic, and poetry to get your attention. But the attention span of an Aries can be very short. And once you get used to wining and dining and all of the attention, after the newness wears off, you may feel like you've suddenly been abandoned.

For example, the initial courtship that one Capricorn human resource director experienced was a whirlwind of roses and cards, but after the marriage it gradually stopped. The Capricorn wife, never to be outdone, complained constantly, demanding that her Aries husband remember to send roses and other acknowledgments on anniversaries, birthdays, and the like. To call a truce, her husband came up with an idea: Each week, one or the other would plan a romantic outing for the two of them. Aries began with an intimate candlelight dinner at an elegant restaurant. Aries definitely knows what to do in the romance department, but the point is, will he keep it up?

Once the rules of the games are established, Aries is good to go. But don't start a new game with different rules and forget to tell the ram or you've got trouble. For example, an Aries woman from Atlanta met her Virgo companion through a mutual friend. But the Virgo was on the rebound. After the couple courted for eight months, he spent Thanksgiving weekend with the ex-girlfriend's family. Of course the lady ram saw red and wanted to kick ass and take names. But her point to her Virgo mate was that he should have let her know what the rules were. Were they seeing other people? Was he going to be faithful to her or to the ex-girlfriend? Did he want to end the relationship? The philosophy of Aries is, if you don't know the rules, you can't play the game.

Age is rarely a consideration for Aries. The Aries brother might date someone who's twenty years older without giving it a second thought. This brother will look at this difference in a very philosophical way. If he's in his early twenties, he'll be able to learn a few tricks of the trade. He won't have to concern himself with birth control, and she probably won't be insecure about the relationship, worrying and calling him every minute. The Aries sister loves the tenderonis. As one Aries administrative assistant from California put it, "A mixture of adventurous and student works for me." They like nothing better than to teach or enjoy the energetic spirit of the youth of America.

A Scorpio woman recalled the initial romantic turn-on with her Aries companion's approach. "His honesty got my attention and he was open, very open. He told me his whole life story on the dance floor during two dances." Although she was impressed, the friend of the Aries had to remind the ram of how Ms. Scorpio looked because he couldn't remember. But he was pleasantly surprised when they later got together.

One Aries sister describes her most memorable romantic encounter. "Ten A.M. is my favorite time of day. My mate and I are out walking. We stop and sit and reminisce over how we have arrived at this point in our love life." For the Aries, intimate talks are a number one priority in the relationship. Arians, though very talkative, want a meaningful exchange and honesty about their concerns and yours, too. This is how you get their attention. They want to get inside your head and find out what's really on your mind. You won't have any trouble guessing about them, because they'll tell you in a straightforward manner.

The pure romance for the Aries is that you're ready for flying by the seat of your pants whenever she comes up with an idea. That's true romance for them. Adventure, laughs, sharing information, saliva, and each other's food without any thought to anything but each other. That's the kind of romantic exchange this fire sign wants. And rams want it when they want it—like yesterday!

One thing that's very important to Aries is giving them their props. You must pay attention to his long, drawn-out, detailed stories, rub her feet, remember his favorite wine, her favorite food.

On one occasion, an Aries met a would-be companion and ended up in a long-term relationship. She boldly stated, "After the relationship began, this Aries man was the only person who could undress me and screw me with his eyes, even in a crowded setting." Whew!

SEX, SEX, AND MORE SEX

GETTING THE GROOVE ON . . .

If by chance you happen to enter the bedroom of the Aries, the dilemma probably is that you may not have decided to knock the boots with homeboy and he's already swinging from the chandelier. Remember the Aries Word to the Wise at the beginning of this chapter: "The faint of heart need not apply." Of course this means in the bedroom, too!

With an Aries, for the most part, you can save the melodrama of creating atmosphere and aphrodisiacs. Trust me—they don't need them. They feel that they are all the enticement or enhancement that's needed. Once they're about to get it on, they aren't really interested in the expensive lingerie, candles, and sexy food. They simply don't have the patience for all that stuff. When they're ready,

they're ready. The main point is, *you* better be ready. It will definitely be time out for the games people play: no hemming and haw-
ing or reluctance on your part.

Okay, boys and girls, let the sideshow, or better yet, the freak
show begin. Arians waste very little time when it comes to affairs of
the heart, the boudoir, or any other interest. Now that you've become a curiosity to her, it's time to step up to the plate. The time for
indecision is over.

One Pisces woman, who felt she was pretty sexually liberated,
ended a relationship with her Aries writer companion because she
felt that from an erotic standpoint, the encounters had gone into
overdrive. When he would call, she would protest about seeing him
again. But while they were still talking on the telephone, a courier
service would deliver an oversized smoked sausage–shaped chocolate penis sent by her Aries lover. In short, or in long, uh, excuse
me, if you're trying to leave a liaison with an Aries, it won't be easy.

When Aries people want you, they're definitely up for the challenge. Actually, it's a turn-on. One Aries brother, who shared a
long-distance relationship with his companion, would constantly
send her porno videos in the mail, along with letters outlining that
he was going to apply the video antics to her. A costume that strik-
ingly resembled what the woman in the video wore would also be
included. And when these two finally got together, he would do
just that and more. But in the meantime before the bodies met,
these two would enjoy phone sex, complete with moans of ecstasy.

These fire signs are hot to trot. And you will enjoy hotter-than-
July sex. All of the preliminaries, including hot telephone sex, are
the efforts that your Aries creates to make the sexual occasion a
memorable one. Not only will the sexual encounter include talking
dirty, it will also include a total undressing with her eyes, love
notes, and even erotic moans and groans on your answering machine. I hope you're getting the picture.

While you are trying to resist an all-day date by trying to beg
off because of your appointments, the Aries, who generally looks at
any no as a yes, will commence recounting all of his erotic tales
about what's going to happen when the two of you finally get together. Mr. Aries will be very graphic about licking your back, bit-

ing your clitoris, or using a sex toy in the anal area. You'll be so anxious that you will begin rescheduling your appointments on the spot and set a time for the rendezvous.

An Aries insurance adjuster commented that she usually waits and lets her companion take the lead until the relationship is familiar and her companion feels comfortable. Then the sky's the limit! Aries people are usually in the no-holds, or no-holes, barred category. When it comes to sex, their energy is boundless. It's that same energy that carries over into the rest of their lives. They have a zest for living and loving.

They will even write you poetry. But be careful—you might also find yourself in a fictionalized version of all that's gone on before. For example, an Aries brother took pictures of all of his conquests. The women were usually in various stages of undress, posing in sexually explicit positions. Keepsakes like panties were also in his inventory.

But whatever you're into sexually, your ram will take it to the next level. So be flexible and open to trying new things. And even if you're scared to death, never let him see you sweat!

Remember Annie Mae, the character opposite Richard Pryor's in *Which Way Is Up?* Annie Mae, dressed in leather and boots, jumped on Pryor's back, which made his chin thud and his body collapse on the bed. She then rode his back and stuck a vibrator in his rectum before Pryor knew what hit him. Of course, his eyes bugged out! This is the scenario you can expect from a lady ram.

There aren't any specific sexual positions with the Aries. But for the male of the sign, the man on top is preferred. For the Aries woman, it's just the reverse. This way she can ride it until she's exhausted. Both enjoy doggy style and oral sex from that position. So there are no limits here. Aries people will try just about anything once for the sheer adventure of it. If you're dealing with an Aries man, you'll find yourself in the wheelbarrow position with your head on the floor as your Aries mate enters, holding your legs up around his hips. The sixty-nine position is also to Aries' liking.

And while you're considering the sex, you need to start thinking about sex with an additional partner, sex toys, and any other enhancements the Aries is interested in. Biting is also high up on the list. They will bite you, caress you, spank you, and do anything that strikes their fancy. It's called joy and pain. But you just never know with them.

And if by chance you go out of town with her, well, you had better get your rest because you'll be spending most of your time in bed, either begging for mercy as your Aries tries one new maneuver after another or simply trying to get some rest between rounds two and three or three and four, whatever the case may be. It's hard to keep up, and you'll be hard-pressed to keep up as well.

EROGENOUS ZONES . . . SOME PHYSICAL, SOME NOT

The erogenous zone for Aries is the head area. Any touches, kisses, caresses, and licks to this area will create the reaction you're looking for. The Aries person is even turned on by the sounds he hears, including music, talking dirty, and stimulating conversation. Aries people want all of their senses aroused.

A striptease is always pleasing to the eye of the Arian. But be careful, the dance may end abruptly as the Aries is so turned on, she simply can't wait any longer. But they're usually the first person ready for the entree, and then the dessert. Patience is not a virtue of theirs. A good kisser is a big-time turn-on. Like the Cancerian, they love that deep soul kissing with full use of mouth, tongue, and even teeth. They have that art down to a science.

If you want the ram to charge, try head massages, kissing and blowing in their ears, and nibbles to their lobes. When you're whispering sweet nothings, your warm breath brushing the outer ear, your ram will be ready to ram, uh, excuse me, to roll. But be warned: Don't play with the Aries, man or woman, unless you plan to deliver. Once you work on the aforementioned with your Aries, there's no turning back.

If you want the ram to stand up on his hind legs with passion, massage his temples and sideburn area before approaching his ear. In the case of the woman, comb her hair, scratch her dandruff, or massage her scalp—then run for your life.

Aries people love to be pampered and cared for because they

are the babies of the zodiac. They love to be spoiled. As one Aries woman put it, "Being attentive turns me on, along with candles, music, ice-cold sheets, and good pillows."

Keep it interesting in the bedroom. Aries' favorite sex toy is you. Wearing a wig, a costume, or a totally different look also turns them on because it gives them the illusion that they're having sex with a different person.

Aries people are also voyeurs. Their voyeurism can carry over into the boardroom, onto a crowded street, and even into an aerobics class. The Aries man may be aroused by the movements of the aerobics instructor, paying attention to the vulva imprint on her bodysuit. During aerobics?! They love to imagine what's beneath the sarong skirt, what's below the elastic waistband of those Calvin Klein briefs, what's behind that peekaboo blouse with little hints of sexuality peeking through.

And because they can't stand being bored, having sex anywhere but the bedroom excites them. The Aries would be the person who would have sex in the bathroom of a jumbo jet, 30,000 feet over the Grand Canyon. She would even like to have sex with her companion in the parking lot of the grocery store while waiting for her mother to shop. Nothing to it—wear loose-fitting clothing, drop Mom at the supermarket, pick up her companion, a hand towel, condoms, and even a bottle of wine, and go at it while Mom counts coupons in the grocery store.

For the Aries man, the biggest surprise and the biggest turn-on for him are to bring an additional female partner along for a special occasion like his birthday. But you need to make it clear to Mr. Aries that this behavior will not be included in what's to come. (No pun intended.)

PLAIN OL' SEX AND NOTHING MORE: WELCOME TO THE FREAK SHOW

Of the twelve signs of the zodiac, there are those who participate in the freak show, those who sit on the sidelines, and the stars. Aries is one of the stars. In fact, Aries is probably one of the creators.

With this in mind, you know that your ram is in the anything-goes category. I won't belabor the point about what Aries will do.

It's simple: They will do just about anything short of death in the sexual arena.

With Aries, sex for sex's sake is definitely a possibility, but it's all in how you approach it. It's got to be unique. And you need to have some noteworthy attributes, such as skintight jeans, a spandex dress would help, along with a detailed explanation of why you approached her in the first place. Hey, you might be on to something. If you're given an opportunity, well, you better make it good. There won't be any second chances here.

Don't be surprised if while you're out of town, he suggests that the two of you visit a fun place to shop for sexual enhancements that he forgot to bring along on the trip. And if by chance you see him over at the bulletin board filling out a card to get callbacks on threesomes, don't freak. He will probably take the liberty to fill out a card for you as well. If you're not interested in such notions, never fear, he'll simply find someone who is. For the Aries it is definitely about his or her sexual gratification. He definitely aims to please, but if you're too squeamish about elevating yourself to sexual heights that you've never before experienced, then that's your problem. With this sign, it's on like a pot of neck bones.

MONEY MATTERS

If you're looking to have a nice nest egg, pension plan, or retirement home with an Aries, think again. The best you can hope for with an Aries is to be situated near a body of water, like a man-made lake. Aries people love to fish and sit on the banks of a lake. And you'll have to adjust to whatever they deem is needed to have a serene retirement. So don't figure on having a lot of money.

In the beginning of the adventure, his zest for life and investing in new projects will basically deplete his resources pretty readily. If he feels that a good deal is in the works, he will draw out his IRA (at least half of it) to invest in some foolproof scheme, endeavor, or whatever you want to call it. Of course, you won't know about it until the project goes belly up and he needs your financial help. There's no point in wringing your hands, threatening suicide, or killing him with your bare hands. What's done is done. Sorry.

On the other hand, you have to admire the Arian's courage.

That's one thing Aries people have plenty of, along with a pioneering spirit. And their attitude will be "Since the ram has the plan and courage, someone will have to have the financing." You must bring something to the party, you know.

If you're planning a life with this fire sign, you need to have a Swiss bank account that only you have access to for emergencies like the aforementioned. The investment portfolio needs to be in your name, and the Aries should have access only in case you are no longer in your right mind. In that case, you won't care. Money passes through the hands of an Aries like water. If you want to have money now or in the future, you need to keep up with the checkbook, pay the bills, save for a rainy day, and keep the Aries as far from the bank as you possibly can. Your financial planner, his parents, your children, and the college registrar's office will all thank you.

Aries are daring and courageous types who feel that they must live life on the edge. I know you're thinking, "Not with my money," and that's a valid point. But when you decided to take on Aries, you saw all of the signs and you paid no attention.

Now, regarding spending money on you, well, yes. But if you're married, it will all come out of the same pot. And if you're single and going out on dates with an Aries, you'll need to have some money with you at all times. He may lose his wallet, leave it in the car, drive right by the bank, or forget his ATM password.

If you have a toddler and feel like you want to start saving for the baby's college tuition, well, you need to set up the fund without letting your Aries spouse know. They simply don't see the need to save for a commitment that's eighteen years in the future. Their attitude is to cross that bridge when they come to it. Meanwhile, there's this new car, boat, or riding lawn mower, time-share mortgage, cabin in the woods to consider first.

PAMPERING TIPS FOR ARIES

* The Aries wants your undivided attention. She wants you to be in her pocket most of the time, attending to her whims and needs.
* When he tells you that you're not spending enough time

with him even though you might see each other five to seven days a week, try to do better. (I guess you could add another day to the week to satisfy him.) That's pampering to an Aries!

✲ A spa weekend will get the Aries' attention. Aries people are generally moving in twenty different directions and must have stress relievers.

✲ Aries people are the babies of the zodiac. Feeding them, bathing them, or stroking them always works. They'll purr like a kitten.

✲ Washing her hair, massaging his temples, and scratching her scalp as she lies with her head in your lap scores big with the ram.

✲ Prepare a down-home dinner of ham, neck bones, greens, and corn bread. Watch him devour it and then have you for dessert.

✲ Constantly telling an Aries how wonderful she is has a soothing and calming effect on your ram and will score major points.

✲ Aries people love to fish, ride horseback, hike, and camp. Renting a cabin away from the phones, the faxes, and the pagers will be a welcome relief.

✲ Surprise her with a manicurist who takes her show on the road.

✲ Surprise him with a trip out of town that he and the homies can enjoy!

GIFT IDEAS FOR ARIES

✲ Season tickets to their favorite sports games are a winner. Aries are real sports fanatics.

✲ A signed and numbered print will always work. It can hang in his undecorated apartment. He'll complete his decorating tasks eventually. . . .

✲ Tickets to a vacation spot that offers adventure, fun, and frolic always work for the impulsive Aries. Warning: You may not leave the hotel room, however!

✱ Aries people are in desperate need of a makeover. They're notorious for wearing outdated clothing. Give her a surprise makeover from head to toe!

✱ Try an out-of-the-way weekend camping or fishing trip, complete with horses roaming the hills.

✱ Hiking boots, fishing equipment, or any gifts related to their favorite pastime, which is usually the great outdoors, is a sure bet.

✱ Aries are also animal lovers: A rottweiler puppy for the man or a golden retriever for the woman will have you competing for the ram's affection.

✱ Books on tape for the busy Arian would be better. This ram won't sit still long enough to read a book.

✱ Prince or Puff Daddy concert tickets are good. Give your Aries companion a CD or cassette tape of the aforementioned too. Your ram will be singing your praises.

✱ You may be squeamish about bungee jumping or hang gliding, but your Aries would delight in such a gift. Just let her know you're not part of the package!

TAURUS

(April 20 to May 20)
SYMBOL: THE BULL

Positive love traits: Arduous, passionate lover, confident
partner, conventional and methodical lover.

Negative love traits: Routine approach to sex without
much fanfare, prone to anal sex, an insatiable sexual
appetite.

Ruling planet: Venus is associated with feelings and the
power to love.

Word to the wise: If you don't want to be introduced to the
rage of the Taureans, don't mess with their money.

People born under the sign of Taurus are down to earth and practical and rarely act on impulse.

Their ruling planet is Venus, which is associated with the power to love and acquisitiveness. Most Taureans are collectors and pack rats. Generally, they will keep the twenty-year-old high school cheerleader uniform, the football letter jacket, the banquet program honoring a former teacher, and even the wedding dress, carefully preserved for a granddaughter. Overall, Taureans are prone to long, long relationships. Their devotion and loyalty, when they're in love, are unmatched by most signs of the zodiac.

Taurus people have a tendency to stick and stay even if the relationship has lost its spark. For example, a Taurean teacher was determined that she would stay in a relationship with her husband of ten years. The couple had two children and appeared to be happily married, but her husband was sullen and moody and rarely communicated with her in anything but an accusatory manner. She vowed

to stay, never really acknowledging how unfulfilling the relationship was, saying, "It's too dangerous out there now to be dating
again. Besides, there's nobody out there anymore. Everybody's married." They finally divorced, but only because he pursued it.

You'll find Taurus people at home in their peaceful surroundings. They revere a good, stable home life, a solid career, marriage, a
sense of permanence.

Although the term "homebody" aptly applies to Taureans, they
enjoy church activities and sporting events, and you might even
find them at "happy hour," meeting coworkers after hours at a bar to
support another coworker-musician who's playing his first gig.
They also enjoy hanging out with friends and family members at
social functions or simply kickin' it.

The symbol for the sign of Taurus is the bull, which means
stubborn and strong-willed. Taureans definitely won't be pushed or
prodded into any uncharted waters. It ain't happening until they
decide to move on it—which could take a lifetime. Dragging the ol'
feet, literally and figuratively, is something that the bull does without much effort.

Taureans have an unusually strong but ever so gentle nature.
That's why everyone loves a Taurus. Taurus people are the main-
stays of the zodiac. Whatever their disposition is when you meet
them, it won't change over the long haul. You can count on a Taurus
to remain on an even keel. But when their security is threatened,
then you've got problems. For Taurus people money means security. Security means peace of mind and a clear sense in knowing
that loved ones will be taken care of. They fiercely protect that
which means the most—family, friends, loved ones, and home.

Taurus is an earth sign, which means that Taureans are down to
earth, practical, and cautious. Basically, they're always the same—
predictable, reliable, grounded. (Grounded, ground, earth—get it?)
Taurus people even enjoy gardening—doing a little landscaping,
gettin' down in the dirt, pulling up weeds, and the like. It's relaxing
to them.

Both men and women of the sign have a keen eye for good
taste—more so with the women when it comes to detail, style, and
home furnishings. The men are so extremely masculine, they leave
a lot of the domestic stuff to their wife or companion. Both want

and will create comfortable, lavish, and sometimes even exquisite surroundings for themselves. They know exactly what they need to make themselves comfy at home.

Although the men don't feel pressed to dress in the latest fashions like some other signs, their practical nature will determine very early that if there is only X amount of money to be spent for pleasure, then their companion or wife should be the recipient.

Taurus women will be dressed to the nines, but they do a lot of bargain hunting. Nothing delights a Taurus sister more than finding a good sale on quality merchandise. These sisters go in for designer purses like Chanel, Louis Vuitton, or Prada; they look at the purchase as an investment. They know that they will have the purse for a lifetime or as long as the style lasts.

One point to note: Taurus people can definitely go completely off if they believe a person is taking their kindness for weakness. On the rare occasions that it happens, run for cover.

THE TAURUS MAN

This man can definitely rock your world. He is the personification of manhood and manliness. The Taurus brother is one of the most laid-back signs of the zodiac. He's the mainstay of the zodiac, the person everyone depends on. You're obviously thinking about dating a Taurus or you wouldn't be reading this section. There's something about being around a Taurus man that automatically makes a woman feel secure. Know this: You'll simply have to share him with his many female friends, admirers, and family members.

For the Taurus brother, affairs of the heart, like the rest of his life, will be approached with a slow, methodical analysis and practical approach. He is in search of a companion for the long haul. Consequently, the process must be a long, arduous task.

If you're trying to catch this bull, leave all of the smoke, mirrors, bangles, beads, and hoopla at home—or better yet at the retail store. If not, he'll be so preoccupied with what's underneath the layers of makeup and getup, the date will be a total bust. This Taurus brother wants a real woman. You don't have to show up in jeans or a long floral dress and an apron like Aunt Bee on *The Andy Griffith Show*, but he wants you dressed in a mild, down-to-earth manner. The sky blue fake-nail claws with matching contact lenses and Marge Simpson–style hair are not needed here.

The Taurean male won't be the loudmouthed roustabout, swilling beer and trading war stories; he will be the laid-back brother somewhere in the background taking it all in. He'll be checking out the scene, flirting subtly, making eye contact, and sending over drinks anonymously. Don't misunderstand—Mr. Bull can accommodate those sisters who are interested only in the one-night stand or the intimate weekend for two. He's a passionate, sexy creature and his motto is "Aim to please," no matter what the circumstances. Further, the one-night-stand sister may have a change of heart after a night of knockin' boots with the bull.

As husbands, Taureans are devoted to their spouses. He will buy expensive gifts of jewelry and the finer things in life. He wants the very best for his loved ones. He will definitely want to be in charge of the checkbook, however, to curtail any needless or sporadic spending. For how else will you be the recipient of those lovely gifts? He's the money man, you know. Your home will be decorated as you want, lavishly or moderately, but he will draw the line at sorority colors, pink and green or red and white for the rooms that the two of you share, like the den and bedroom.

When a Taurus brother falls in love, he becomes giddy and playful and he'll want to spend his every waking hour in bed with you. Not that he will want to have sex most of the time—he simply feels that true intimacy is achieved when both parties are in a horizontal position. Hmmm.

The Taurus brother is a shining example of persons or situations not being always what they seem. At first glance, you may be turned off because of his clothing. Many sistas are road-weary when it comes to relationships, and preconceived notions are rampant when it comes to what a person is wearing. Although the Taurus brother's outfit may not be polyester, it may be a close first cousin. Don't despair. He will be well groomed, but he won't be dressed to the nines. So what do you want, a man who spends all his money on clothes or a man who has money to spend on you? Besides, if clothes mean that much to you, that's an area that can be changed.

Any woman with the Taurus man is going first-class. He may hedge when it comes to outfitting himself or buying toys for himself, but his companion will be treated like royalty. For example, a Taurus brother who had recently gotten a lucrative job as a reporter for a morning newspaper refused to buy a new car. His old car, which he'd had since his days at a small-town weekly newspaper in Mississippi, wouldn't go in reverse. His girlfriend was mortified after she found out. But he simply made a point of remembering never to create a situation in which he'd have to drive in reverse. Years later, the couple has three cars.

With a Taurus, there's always a plan, especially when it comes to mo' money. The philosophy here is, the more money he can save by not buying the most expensive clothes, the bigger the nest egg that he will share with his mate someday. He's a builder, not only figuratively, but in reality too. But like his personality, which is even-tempered and calculating (with dollar signs dancing in his head), he will build the relationship and the future in a slow, systematic manner.

Taurus brothers don't like to play games. You can expect the straightforward approach with them. If there are problems or concerns that haven't been resolved, the Taurus must talk it out. For example, a Taurus man and his Pisces companion enjoyed a strong relationship during college, but it ended and they went their separate ways. Ms. Pisces got married and then divorced. After her divorce, she wanted to rekindle the liaison with Taurus. But during this ten-year period, Taurus had accepted the fact that he was gay and told her so openly, saying, "You're now single and now I'm gay." Ms. Pisces didn't feel betrayed because what they had felt for each other previously was genuine.

The Taurus brother may even correct your English. They're not big on ebonics. On speaking the queen's English one Taurus brother put it this way: "I find myself correcting people who don't speak English correctly. I do it in a straightforward and quick manner. My grandmama taught us to speak correctly. And if my great-great-grandparents learned how to speak English by reading the Bible and studying the alphabet when they were sixty and seventy years old, [other people] need to take advantage of [learning the language]."

One point worthy of note: Taurus doesn't have a long list of requirements for companionship. Their needs are simple. They want someone who is sincere and honest, with a good heart. Even the weight issue is not a problem because Taureans have a tendency to be overweight sometimes. They love to eat, cook, laugh, and cuddle at home while they enjoy you! Not necessarily in that order.

THE TAURUS WOMAN

Taurus women are very independent thinkers. They are not prone to listening or tolerant of a potential companion orchestrating their lives, thank you very much.

Taurus women are devoted to a fault. Even if her man is married, the approach that he'll be one day single or divorced is enough for the Taurus woman to hang in there, provided his attention is exclusively with her when he's not playing house at home.

The Taurus sister has very specific ideas about or requirements of the man in her life, specifically, and of the relationship in general. The Taurus sister may even make odd requests, like "Can you grow a full beard, because beards really turn me on?!" When you're out on the first or second date she may even ask, "How do you feel about oral sex?" This may break your face, but Ms. Taurus is simply making mental notes about your personality and what the limitations will be in the boudoir. Her motto is "If you don't know, then you better ask somebody!"

She will want her man to be well dressed. If he doesn't know how to dress himself, she'll be more than happy to accompany him shopping. And brothers, the Jheri curls—or as one Taurus put it, the scary curls—must go. There are very few unreasonable requirements that a Taurus places on her mate. But being honest and giving her the attention she feels she deserves are top priorities.

When you first meet this down-to-earth creature, she'll be curious about you and she may flirt a little. During the introductions, you need to be a tad creative, but above all, be honest in your approach. She may smile and have an exchange, but this relationship is not going anywhere fast. Don't come on like a Mack truck. And they don't like to be smothered with attention either. They expect to be complimented when they're dressed or some thoughtful act is executed, but they will be skeptical if you go on and on about it.

You won't have any trouble finding her. The Taurus sister will more than likely be surrounded by the brothers as they ooh and ah over her voluptuous body, her confidence and genuine earthiness. She may allow you to buy her a drink, but don't expect her to sit and hold your hand the entire night because of one drink. She has to spread her charm around, you know. One Libra sister called her Taurus sisterfriend the social coordinator because everywhere the two of them went, Ms. Taurus knew most of the men.

The Taurus woman downplays her ability to attract men, for the most part waiting for them to come to her. And they do. The Taurus sister gets her share of attention and plenty of it. For example, a Taurus manager saw an old flame she hadn't seen in years in the grocery store. The former boyfriend put his arm around her while whispering and putting his tongue in her ear. Of course, Ms. Taurus was enjoying this, but unbeknown to her, her Scorpio boyfriend had seen the two of them. The lady bull tried to explain, and desperately turned down the invitation of Mr. Scorpio to knock the brother's teeth out.

The Taurus sister would be a fine catch for any man. She's a very independent person with an uncanny determination to succeed. She's not the kind of woman to work in the home. She faces life head-on and wants to have her "own" money. If she is a housewife who works in the home, she definitely has to find ways of creating income for herself, separate from the household.

And the Taurus sister doesn't want you asking her for a lot of in-kind favors. One Taurus sister ended a relationship with a brother who wanted to keep her cell phone and Cadillac while she was out of town—like those items were toys. That affair ended about as quickly as it began.

If you finally muster enough nerve to ask the lady bull out on a date, the evening will be so simple and unpretentious, you will probably ask yourself why you were so reluctant in the first place. She's got a great sense of humor, and will even relate the story of what happened on her last date, saying her date took her to his mother's, then his brother's, and then to a drive-in. The brother never saw one frame of the movie because he was all over her. Of course, she never saw him again. But the reason she's telling the story is twofold: The first point is that she doesn't want that to happen with you. And the second point is to show you that she has a sense of humor, and she's not too rigid, and she hopes you can relax.

A sure bet for a Taurus woman is a nice dinner at home or at your place or at a restaurant, along with dancing, a movie, a walk, or all of the above. She also loves music, and she will have all of the latest up close and personal music to set the mood.

Although the lady bulls are not as slow to move into a relationship as their male counterparts, the Taurus sister can determine more readily if a date has potential. After she determines she wants a relationship with the brother, she goes after him. Lady bulls are full of self-confidence, and that can be somewhat intimidating to men. In addition, the Taurus sister will expect her man to know about the art of making love. If he doesn't, he needs to be in a teachable frame of mind. If he's neither, well, he's history.

As wives and lovers, Taureans are very accommodating, loving, and attentive—and they will expect the same in return. Taureans want open and honest relationships. Lying or being secretive and manipulative will forestall any progress with this bull. Taureans don't lick their wounds; they simply tell you in no uncertain terms what their feelings are. For example, if you as the mate or husband want to go to a Super Bowl party without her, well, that's fine. Not to be outdone, she'll call her friends over at the spur of the moment and create a party herself—or she just may not be home when you arrive. She's not the type to sit at home watching the clock, hoping you will grace her with your presence. It ain't happening here.

The Taurus sister can and will create a haven for you that you will rarely want to leave: good food, good conversation, and semi-lavish surroundings. But if you do leave, don't expect her to be sulking when you get back, ready to play Twenty Questions. She has a life, too, and she can definitely live it to the fullest. This is certainly not a threat of any kind because at some point the Taurean will make her feelings known. The lines of communication definitely have to remain open.

One noteworthy point: These bulls are stubborn. They will not move on love, relationships, or any other area until they're ready.

Guide to a Love Connection

Taurus and Aries

The ram and the bull will butt heads, lock horns, and make each other miserable. Not in the bedroom, of course. But after they all but kill each other, who wants to have sex? These two aggressive people are strong-willed, and both are determined to run the show. There are very few compromises that they are willing to make in the relationship; hence there's no real relationship. Both have insatiable sexual leanings. Aries is the star of the freak show, while Taurus is the traditional type of lover. A booty call every now and then is the only real reason for these two to ever come together.

Taurus and Taurus

The potential complication is that these two are too slow and cautious to act impulsively, so there won't be any unplanned trips to the Caribbean. Taureans must be prodded into most endeavors that require an abundance of money. This union will be plagued by the ever-looming question "Where is the money coming from?" or in 1990s lingo, "Show me the money!" Taureans are homebodies and possessive of the other. In all honesty, there's nothing to be possessive about. Both are loyal, faithful, and guarded about most things. The problem is that because they are so much alike they really have a tendency to bore each other. This pairing will be a ho-hum one except when it comes to bedroom matters. Each has a strong sexual appetite. Therefore, neither will have a problem with telling the other that foreplay, in this instance, is *not* a musical group.

Taurus and Gemini

This relationship will take far more work than each is willing to give. Taurus is an earth sign, grounded, reasonable, careful, and stable. Then enters the Tinker Bell of the zodiac, Gemini, airborne, flitting from one corner of the room to the next, but never remaining still to absorb much conversation, contact, or plain ol' understanding. Taurus, with all of the tact he can muster, will be compelled to try to tame and harness all of the unbridled energy of Gemini. This sign of the twins is really two people. For Taurus, it's going to be difficult enough to deal with one Gemini, not to mention two. Gemini will find stay-at-home, meat-and-potatoes Taurus a bore—good-hearted, but a bore nonetheless. To bother with anything but a friendship would be a waste of time.

Taurus and Cancer

Home, hearth, harmony, and help to each other are the adjectives that would describe any relationship between these two. These two soul mates have found each other. Taurus is a homebody and so is Cancer. Cancer loves to cook and Taurus loves to eat. Taurus is the strong, silent type and that suits the damsel-in-distress Cancer. Cancer's mood swings are met with support from the even-keeled bull. Both hoard money and spend it carefully, unless the bull is spending it on his lady love. Sexually, Cancer will show the traditional bull a thing or two, to Taurus's delight. Both have hearty sexual appetites. The only thing missing with this couple is the violins playing in the background.

Taurus and Leo

From a physical standpoint, there's lots of history. The lion and bull can go toe-to-toe when it comes to the boudoir. Through the years, this twosome can't seem to stay away from each other; the chemistry is awesome. But over the long haul, that's where it ends. Leo sits on her throne and wants Taurus as one of her subjects. The bull will have none of that. Taurus simply cannot understand what all of the fuss is about. Taurus, a stubborn, frugal, grounded type, won't give in to Leo's over-the-top whims and impulsive personality. Leo will buzz-saw through Taurus's carefully accumulated savings, much to Taurus's dismay. Leo's taste for filet mignon contrasts with Taurus's inclination toward the pot roast of life. Forget the dinner plans and a life together.

Taurus and Virgo

At least these two won't die of terminal boredom as they plod slowly through life together. Theirs is a happy and fulfilling relationship, and all systems are go with this union. These two are too much alike for words. They are both earth signs, which means they are both slow, methodical, cautious, down to earth, basically home-bodies. This pair will watch a lot of videos, do a lot of reading, and enjoy other nonstressful activities that they can do at home. Each is devoted and faithful to the other. Virgo, the worrier, will be reas-sured by stable, steadfast, and reasonable Taurus. Virgo's dedication to Taurus, family, and work will support the need of the bull to be acknowledged for the drive, goals, and strong foundation that he brings to this pairing. For most of those on the sidelines, the rela-tionship's a sleeper. But who asked you?

Taurus and Libra

Both are charmers of the zodiac. Libra is the social butterfly with an outgoing personality and a sassy, in-style dress and other enhancements, like the latest in cars. Taurus is the strong, silent type with a quiet power that's hard to resist. When the two come together, the sparks are hot. But once the twosome emerges from the bedroom . . . oh well. Libra will be bored by Taurus's stay-home, lackluster life. For Libra, life's a beach; this includes the nude beaches, the muscle-shirt-clad honeys, or anyone who will take no-tice. This approach will infuriate Taurus, who will demand and ex-pect devotion and a stay-at-home partner who only wishes to please. Libra will determine that the bull must have just arrived from the planet Mars! And there won't be any alien unions!

Taurus and Scorpio

These two opposites are so magnetically drawn to each other that they could sniff each other out at a crowded party. Sex between these two is more steamy and passionate than between most oppo-site combinations of the zodiac. A sexual encounter with a Scorpio, according to one woman, is like having sex with a person who knows he's about to be put to death! Whew! Basically, for this cou-ple to sustain a relationship, they would have to live their lives in bed! Both are stubborn, jealous, obsessive, and strong-willed. And with two dominant people, the stress and tug-of-war between them can put too much strain on the relationship—not to mention the box spring.

Taurus and Sagittarius

One thing's for sure, Taurus won't be bored with free-spirited, energetic Sagittarius. Cautious Taurus merely wants to stay at home and chill, but restless Sag will have none of that. These two are drawn together physically, and romping in the bedroom suits them just fine, but once they emerge from between the sheets, the trouble starts. Sagittarians want to fly by the seat of their pants. This attitude of throwing caution to the wind will drive the careful, steady bull crazy. Taurus's possessive ways won't set too well with Sag, who refuses to be controlled. Both are ambitious and goal-oriented. Trouble is, Taurus is building a security base for the future, whereas Sag's motto is eat, drink, be merry, and spend money, for tomorrow we die. Need I say more?

Taurus and Capricorn

This pairing never leaves home except to go to the job or to school. Their home is their sanctuary. Both are earth signs and have a lot in common. They are practical, determined, and goal-oriented and plan to have serious nest eggs one day. Sexually, both are conventional lovers who want very few surprises in bed. Both have lots of friends and are very popular socially. A great date for these two would be a nice dinner at home, followed by an evening of movie videos and popcorn. They may appear boring to some, but they're in sync with each other. This can be a great relationship or a happy, fulfilling marriage.

Taurus and Aquarius

This couple will need prayer in order to survive this turmoil-filled relationship. Taurus is stable, methodical, practical, and a homebody. Aquarius is impulsive, unpredictable, disorganized, and a free spirit. And neither is interested in changing. Taurus's jealous tirades when Aquarius wanders off without a word will alienate Aquarius. Aquarius's indifference to the bull's stay-at-home need for security will drive these two to battle. The area that they can agree on is the bedroom. Both are highly sexed; but the Aquarian's freak-show approach to bedroom antics will annoy Taurus, who is a conventional lover. This one is doomed from the start!

Taurus and Pisces

These two are in this relationship for the long haul. Generally, they can be soul mates and perfectly suited for each other, but here's the poop: Taurus's steady, strong, and dedicated demeanor helps Pisces to overcome indecisions and insecurities about career paths and life overall. Earthy Taurus keeps Pisces from dreaming dreams and rarely facing the here and now. Pisces, one of the most creative bedmates, takes cautious, standoffish Taurus to new sexual heights. Pisces craves romance, with waves washing up on the shore as the backdrop. Practical Taurus finds these longings silly and childish. Both must be tolerant and patient if they expect the togetherness to last. Each has qualities that can be beneficial to both.

ROMANCE AND THE TAURUS

Now that you've gotten the attention of the Taurus, which was somewhat of a feat in itself, you're halfway there. Now it's time to determine what the requirements are on the romance tip.

First of all, when Taureans determine that they want to take an encounter with you to the next level, you won't be disappointed. They are definitely into taking their own sweet time with making arrangements for dinner, at either a nice restaurant or the home headquarters. In any case, the preparation and time they put into the planning and execution of the date will have you impressed. When they are interested in a person, attention to detail is essential. Everything has to be just so.

Although Taureans are not prone to impulsive behavior or melodrama, they definitely can appreciate enterprising efforts on the part of would-be suitors. A Taurus from Memphis commented that one of her most memorable approaches to romance was when a clerk at the post office memorized her name, address, and phone number as she paid for stamps by check and showed her driver's license as identification. He called her later that evening and asked her out. She was definitely impressed that he had tracked her down.

Now, the romancing is just as important as the relationship. Having a sense of humor is an asset that you need when dealing with a Taurus. Taurus people have a great sense of humor and they love to laugh. A sense of humor scores major points with your bull.

A Sagittarian over-the-road truck driver kept his Taurus companion in stitches by telling her tales of a long-distance driver. "Baby, I was scared of the 'lot lizards,' because I didn't know if they had a gun and were gonna rob me or or what." "Lot lizards" is what truckers call the brazen prostitutes who knock on the drivers' motel room doors and truck windows to offer a host of services. By the way, the driver was 6 feet, 2 inches and weighed 240 pounds.

They love the great outdoors (maybe not while the lot lizards are out and about). A picnic under the big blue sky while the golden retriever romps in the park is a great date for the Taurus. Walks in the woods, camping, and even home-style gatherings or daytime parties are to their liking. Love notes turn Taureans on. For them, it's gratifying to know that they're being thought about.

Taureans are the meat-and-potatoes people of the zodiac. They don't have long lists of do's and don'ts; they simply want your undivided attention and the assurance that they are in a monogamous relationship. Romance for them means not only wining and dining, but being there: being at his side during a crisis or picking up her children if she's working late at the office. Intimate talks, communication, and honesty rank very high with Taurus people. They simply cannot stand people who they feel are not being honest and open about the pertinent areas of their lives. For example, a Taurus attorney ended a relationship abruptly after her companion asked her to marry him when he was already engaged to someone else. Go figure.

A Taurus wants to know everything about you in order to make a credible assessment about the relationship. He's nosy. He'll want to know about your family, church affiliation, job status, marital status, friends, enemies—the whole ball of wax.

The Taurus person loves food and fine dining. Eating is a sensual experience, just like sex, and Taurus wants the total experience. If you're invited to a Taurean's house for dinner, then you're in like Flynn. Their abode is sacred to them, and very few people can enter without showing credentials. So, hey, an invitation to their house for dinner is a sure bet for the fun and frolic to follow. They also love music, with the lights down low and Maxwell, Luther, D'Angelo, or any other balladeer singing softly in the background as the two of you get to know each other. Their needs are simple: They enjoy quiet evenings and stimulating conversation.

One of the biggest turnoffs for Taureans is a discussion of money before a date. Their inclination would be to ask you why you are concerned about money that is not even yours in the first place.

Actually, with a Taurean the romantic approach is part of the total sexual experience. If she agrees to go back to your place after a romantic date, then clean sheets are a must. Aromatic candles set the mood, and a good bottle of wine rounds out the package.

One Taurus man came up with a way of assessing whether a would-be companion was interested: If the person looked back at you once, it was probably only curiosity, but a second glance represented cruising, which meant possible interest, and if they looked three times you knew you had them.

For Taurus, a ball game or other sporting event can be a romantic outing. Taureans are not pretentious in the least. In fact, they have a certain disdain for social climbers and nose-in-the-air types.

A Taurus man remembers meeting a woman at a black-tie function. A conversation began, and as they talked, they discovered that neither one had a business card on them—which impressed them both. (For the most part, Taureans are turned off by business card–carrying knuckleheads, especially those whose cards are embossed and include long, insignificant titles.) They later went to a jazz club for a while, then back to her place, where they talked for hours and kissed the night away. No pressure for sex, simply each enjoying the company of the other. (It helped that both saw their dentist regularly, since they were both aware of all of the intricate details of the other's mouth.)

A Taurus store owner met his Sagittarian mate at a liquor store. She was coming out as he was going in. He made an about-face and followed her to the car. He begged for her number, declaring that he wasn't a former inmate or a drug pusher, and she complied. The two married six weeks later. "I knew it was right, and I couldn't let her get away," he said. During the wedding reception at her house, every time he would pass her, he would kiss her on the mouth. Awwww . . . isn't that sweet?

Romance for the bull includes the simple things of life. A lot of money doesn't have to be spent, but a lot of time does. Walking through the autumn leaves, sitting by the lake, reading each other stories, listening to music, enjoying the great outdoors, and gazing at each other in appreciation is mostly all that's required for a Taurus.

Just remember, a Taurus wants you in da house present and accounted for! If you're not, you better have a damn good reason!

SEX, SEX, AND MORE SEX

GETTING THE GROOVE ON . . .

When it comes to the Taurus libido, which is higher than most, the bulls are very direct about what they want in a sexual partner. And if you're not up for a long, involved sexual encounter, skip the after-dinner drinks. But if you're receptive to a night of fun, passion, and pleasure, get some rest before the pillow talk begins. You're going to need it.

Taurus people are so serious about getting the sexual act down to a science, you might even want to consider a show-and-tell kind of presentation before the actual foreplay begins. Basically, we're talking about a heart-to-heart talk about sexual turn-ons and turnoffs for you both. Hopefully, this maneuver will save some time, and some face, too. For example, a Taurus computer programmer would invite his companion over for an evening with no thought of having sex that night, but simply to discuss pleasurable areas of his companion's body in a practical, matter-of-fact way. While listening to music (clothing optional), the Taurean brother would touch a part of his partner's body and ask his partner to rate how the touch felt on a scale of 1 to 10. During this approach, they would both make mental notes about the action and save a lot of frustration during the inevitable visit to the bedroom.

"Every orifice," one Taurus repeated to himself over and over. "Every orifice of the body will be kissed, touched, stroked, and caressed, either manually or orally." There won't be a dull moment in this bull's pasture. With Taurus people, you're involved in the tried and true. Forget about threesomes, S & M, and what a Taurus considers bizarre behavior. It ain't happening here. And if you're involved in over-the-top sexual leanings, that's okay between two consenting adults. But you need to break out the checklist of do's and don'ts in the bedroom with Taurus so that there won't be any misunderstanding.

Sexy underwear is also a turn-on for Taureans. The Taurus man loves to buy frilly lace bras, sexy, skimpy teddies, and crotchless panties for his woman. The woman prefers bikinis and even French-cut briefs on her man. If at all possible, leave the boxers with the Tasmanian devils print at home in the drawer.

As lovers, they plan for a memorable encounter. Sex is rated right up there with eating and breathing. In other words, it's highly pertinent to their lives and overall well-being. They are passionate, sincere, and extremely concerned about *your* pleasure, to the exclusion of their own. When you're pleased, so are they.

The Taurus man wants passion, passion, and more passion. The Taurus woman wants foreplay, foreplay, foreplay, and passion. Although oral sex is definitely a turn-on for both, it's not the living end. One Taurus woman proclaimed, "Oral sex is okay. But I like the meat, the entree, the best. If you eat it, you're going to have to screw it, too."

A Taurus from Tennessee said the most memorable way anyone ever got his attention was when a coworker sent a pair of her panties through the office mail and said in a note that she was attracted to the bull. "Boy, what a turn-on," he explained. That maneuver got his attention!

Oh, by the way, the Taurus sister will tell on you if your bedroom skills and agility are sorely lacking—or you may never hear from her again. It will probably be both.

One gay Taurus from Virginia said the biggest turnoff for him is a person who is unattractive. "I ain't having no double-bag action up in here. That's when you have to put a bag over his head and your head too, in case there are breaks because the brother is so ugly. If they are ugly and arrogant, there's no sense in coming in this direction."

The Taurus man is the strong, sensitive type. That's a turn-on for any woman. They pride themselves on being sensitive to the woman's needs. They love those intimate talks and that heart-to-heart exchange that's rare but very meaningful when it happens.

They want to understand their partner completely. And they pay attention.

He likes a straightforward approach to sex. No smoke and mirrors. You won't be able to swing from the chandelier with this down-to-earth sign. But what he lacks in creativity, he makes up for tenfold with his ability to hang in there (no pun intended) when others fall short.

A Taurus college student decided she was going to have sex with the campus hunk. Although he was muscle-bound from head to toe, that's where all of the sensual stuff ended. Once they met between the sheets, it was a fiasco, commented the Taurus. "I couldn't wait to get in bed with the brother, but when I did, his penis was teeny-tiny. And he didn't know what to do with what little he had. He laid his penis on top of my abdomen and just lay there. I wanted to yell, stick it in, fool, but I didn't."

Actually, it would have been better for Mr. Jock to have admitted that he was inexperienced. His honesty with the lady bull would have been all that was needed. And in this instance, it wouldn't have been all over campus. Just kidding!

In many cases, however, if the sexual encounter is a disaster, meaning the Taurus female didn't believe you knew what you were doing or the Taurus male felt you were trying to run the show, you may get a reprieve.

If you're planning on springing a new and daring maneuver on a Taurean (oral sex is basically as daring as it gets with bulls), you need to position the move so that the bull believes it was her idea. Taureans are stubborn. For example, a Taurus sister was given some K-Y jelly in a little gift pack, along with candles, incense, and perfume. Of course, she was delighted to get the gift pack, but this was her companion's way of saying he wanted to introduce her to anal sex, so he brought some jelly along to make it bearable. "By whose standards?" she wanted to know, leaving his house and not looking back.

Once you have a sexual encounter with a Taurean, you will definitely want to make plans to see that person again. If you were truly able to get the groove on, well, you'll be invited back. If not, there won't be one word mentioned about future encounters. If I were you, I wouldn't ask why, because tact is not really a virtue with Taureans either. They try to be tactful, but they do call it like they see it. So if the technique is not the bomb, remember, practice makes perfect.

EROGENOUS ZONES . . . SOME PHYSICAL, SOME NOT

The neck and throat area are the erogenous zones for Taureans. A tongue flicker to the trachea area and kisses to the back of the neck send the bull charging. Any touch in the area, intentional or unintentional, arouses the Taurus. Even when you're dancing, if you reach up and put your arms around the Taurus brother's neck during the slow drag, you have arousal. If you don't want any titillating teasing, don't go near the neck. You'll find yourself in a horizontal position and wonder how you got there.

As one Taurus woman explained, one of her biggest turn-ons was when her man was simply waiting at home for her after a stressful day at work with a glass of wine, full body massage, good conversation, and sex, sex, sex!

Scents and odors can turn a Taurus on as well. The Taurus sisters are in search of real men with real scents. Not body odor, where the person rarely bathes, but the slight hint of muskiness after her companion has had a long day at work or in the yard.

Porno movies, sex toys, and a little masturbation are acceptable forms of sexual behavior for these earth signs. But warning! You need to check with Taureans first for what they consider bizarre sexual conduct. Talking dirty, along with intimate talks, is high on the list too. Remember, the Taurus plans to have the total sexual experience, so you need to learn the whole story.

One Taurus man said his most memorable encounter was after he and his companion watched a porno movie; she performed a striptease and many of the actions shown on the video, adding her own creative twists. For example, the video included fellatio, and his companion also put his testicles in her mouth.

Kissing is also high in the ranks with Taurus people. And if you don't know how to kiss, you need a crash course. Don't despair—they'll teach you. Ear nibbling and whispering sweet nothings are a turn-on. In short, any activity near or on the edge of the neck area sends them over the edge. As long as you're teachable, there will be very few problems. For Taurus, all of the preliminaries must be in place. Good food, soothing music, great conversation, slow dancing (hopefully, you won't be stepping on toes), and the rest will be history.

Don't try to rush this experience; the turn-on for the Taurean is knowing that this experience will probably go on through the night and the next day. Don't plan to be in a hurry. For Taurus, the art of lovemaking can't be rushed.

For the Taurus man, the thought of more than one partner is a big turn-on. The heterosexual Taurus brother would want the additional party to be a woman. Although bisexuality is not a total impossibility, the Taurus man has to exude his masculinity—so more than likely another man wouldn't be in the mix.

For the Taurus woman, a ménage à trois could be to her liking. She is constantly seeking ways to heighten her sexual pleasure. Everybody loves a Taurus, so the lady bull might very easily find herself in the mix with an additional person, either male or female. Don't be boring. If you don't know what you're doing, have a sense of humor about it and it can be worked out. The Taurus believes that all behavior is learned, including sex, so look at this encounter as a learning experience.

PLAIN OL' SEX AND NOTHING MORE: WELCOME TO THE FREAK SHOW

Of the twelve signs of the zodiac, some signs are the stars of the freak show. Taurus people, for the most part, watch from the sidelines.

Taureans love being at home enjoying the domestic scene. But never fear—Mr. Bull can take his show on the road and visit your crib. A 31-year-old Taurus man dated a 21-year-old Virgo and every Saturday morning washed her laundry, folded the clothes, prepared breakfast and served it to her in bed, then performed sexual aerobics, including oral sex, until the Virgo sister was at the point of passing out from exhaustion. Well, all righty, then.

Sometimes you can even catch them in a because-I-know-you-need-it-but-I'm-not-really-attracted-to-you sexual encounter. Such was the case with a young adult from Arkansas. Taurus and his two buddies had gone to see three girls, one of whom was overweight. The girls refused to have sex with any of them unless one of them had sex with the overweight girl. The Taurus agreed to be the sacrificial lamb.

The freak show won't be like any freak show you imagine. But yes, a Taurus wants sex all the time—so having sex just for the sake of having sex is very appealing to the bull. Both the men and women of the sign are sexually driven. If a sex partner can't be found, masturbation is oftentimes an option. If they happen upon a person who is appealing to them sexually, then they may just go for it. They certainly wouldn't be turned off if someone said, "I saw you from across the room and you were so sexually appealing to me. I was wondering if you would like to rendezvous sometime, no strings attached." The answer could very well be "yes" or "Let me think about it." In either case, you're still in the pajama game.

Money Matters

Money is very important to Taurus people, who will save and manage even from the smallest of paychecks with an expertise unmatched by most. And they, like the Gemini, plan to have it in abundance one day. "Show me the money" had to have been coined by a Taurus because money is their watchword and their preoccupation most of the time.

Taurus people are very easygoing until somebody messes with their money. Then you've got problems, and I mean big ones! They don't mind lending a friend money or going to the aid of a family member during a financial crisis. But if they learn that you've had custom drapes made or bought a new stereo without handing over the dough first, they may even show up at your job on payday and demand that you hand over what you owe. And that's it, you won't be able to borrow money from them again. Unless it's for a funeral—your own.

Taurus men are not preoccupied with material things; they're more practical in their approach to having a lot of stuff. They do, however, want their homes, where they spend most of their time, to be comfortable and outfitted with the trappings that they prefer: computer, stereo, television, and the like.

This sign will readily save for a rainy day or any other day. Money is security, and security means peace of mind and comfort to the practical bull, so investing in mutual funds, stocks, bonds, and retirement plans will be a familiar refrain.

If you're married to a Taurean, she will want to set up a college fund for the children even before they're born. Taureans cherish their children. They are definitely the doting parents, and creating some source of financial support for their loved ones is a foregone conclusion for them.

If your child is a Taurus, he'll be the child who will want a paper route. She'll want to work in a grocery store so that she can have some control over the money that she generates. At an early age they are responsible children when it comes to working for pay. They will dutifully report for work on time, save, and count their money at the end of the week (one of the simple pleasures for them). As parents, you won't know how much they have, but you will see the evidence in the form of gifts for the family during the holiday season.

There will be very little impulsive spending. You won't have to be concerned about having a secret bank account to hoard money in—your bull will be doing most of the hoarding. If there is some foolproof investment project under way, the Taurean will be the first to call in the accountants, the investors, the attorneys, and all the players to determine if he should invest. If the bull decides to invest, you can bet that he has examined this initiative from every angle, and then some.

In short, you don't have to worry about the spending and investing habits of Taureans. They have covered all their bases because they had the incentive when they received their first paycheck. They knew way back when that they wanted to have it, hoard it, look at it, revere it, savor it, and, last but certainly not least, spend it.

PAMPERING TIPS FOR TAURUS

❋ Plan a getaway weekend with CD player, wine, and books in tow. Your road-weary bull will be most appreciative.

- A Taurean's home is his castle, so much of the pampering needs to be executed in his favorite place—at home. Creating a romantic setting with candles, music, and great food always works.
- A picnic in the country with rolling hills, barns, and silos as the backdrop will have your bull grazing and feeling relaxed. Simple yet thoughtful gestures are small ways to pamper her.
- Taking care of what the lady bull considers "men things," like getting her oil changed, tires rotated, or hedges trimmed, will get her attention every time!
- For the Taurus man, preparing a Dinty Moore feast is all that's required. Both men and woman have hearty appetites and love soul food fare.
- Arrange a full body and foot massage for your Taurus companion. After the masseuse leaves, follow up with hot oils and a bath. Then watch out!
- Taureans are practical and down to earth, and they appreciate sensible pampering. Find a baby-sitter—then a little champagne, some Chinese food, and each other.
- Plan a week-long vacation and leave the children and dog at home. But your Taurean must have input; he's too practical to simply get up and go!
- Afternoon delights can work, too. Not sex, necessarily, but quality time spent together away from the daily routine.
- A date with a hot tub in a hotel room is all the pampering that's needed sometimes.

Gift Ideas for Taurus

- Taureans love jewelry. Necklaces, dangling earrings, bangles, rings, and bracelets are ideal.
- Taurus people are avid readers. Curling up with a book by the fire at home is a favorite pastime for the bull.
- Although Taureans have expensive tastes, buying an elaborate gift like a gold watch or diamond ring could be a bit much for Taurus, initially.

❉ Give your Taurus a coupon that entitles him to one full day of whatever he wants during a 24-hour period. Nine times out of ten, it will probably be a romantic evening with sex, sex, and more sex.

❉ Gifts for the home like small lamps, crystal, or candleholders are on the mark for the Taurus. They love semilavish surroundings.

❉ The other major part of their lives is spent at work. So a small CD player with her favorite jams can work nicely; a clock radio or a clock for the office wall is also good.

❉ A daily journal or Bible engraved with her name will be received with heartfelt thanks.

❉ Scents turn a Taurus on. Her favorite perfume or his favorite cologne is a great gesture. Buying the fragrance you want to enjoy on your bull is fine, too. Make sure it's not High Karate or White Shoulders!

❉ Have an African outfit made, preferably from original fabric from the motherland; Taureans love handmade clothing. It can't be "Bama," however.

❉ A print, sculpture, or original artwork will be greatly appreciated. If it's signed by the artist, all the better.

❉ Symbolic gifts that represent some phase of the relationship work well, too: a rose for a rose, charms for a charm bracelet denoting the courtship, or a congratulatory plaque for a special milestone are all good.

Gemini

(May 21 to June 20)

SYMBOL: THE TWINS

Positive love traits: Unconventional lover, confident partner, and one of the participants in the freak show.
Negative love traits: Distracted lover, kinky, a penchant
for ménages à trois.
Ruling planet: Mercury is associated with intellect and
the brain.
Word to the wise: Mysterious and private, Geminis are going to allow you to know only just so much about
their personal lives.

Geminis are the communicators of the zodiac. With these air
signs, you won't have to worry about any awkward silence because
they talk incessantly. All they need is someone who will listen, including the bus driver, the mail carrier, the salesclerk, or the street
sweeper.

Gemini people can be found just about anywhere. Their outlook
on life knows no bounds. Gemini people love the spotlight, so you
may find them center stage, singing or reciting poetry. This young
brother could even be in the pulpit preaching his first sermon. The
Gemini sister could be one of the finalists in the Miss Illinois con-
test. Anywhere there are throngs of people, you'll find a Gemini
somewhere in the middle of the happening.

The ruling planet of Gemini is Mercury, which is associated
with intellect and the brain. Geminis are intelligent and well read
and pride themselves on being knowledgeable about a variety of
topics. Consequently, dummies need not apply. Also I suggest that

you go shopping first: You're going to have to be dressed—they will insist.

Geminis must analyze and examine everything from all angles. While you're looking twice at the Gemini brother at your office or the Gemini sister whom you were thoroughly impressed with at a mutual friend's house, this air sign has already assessed whether to pursue a relationship with you.

These mentally agile people are usually two steps ahead of the game. When the Gemini brother initially saw you in the workplace, he was already making a mental note about whether a date, a conversation, or a telephone call would be in the works. The answer was probably yes, so it really just boiled down to determining the right moment to ask you out. He must be discreet, you know. For if this courtship or date is a disaster, then he must have someone else waiting in the wings. But he doesn't want it to be known that he has asked out more than one person in the office. He's definitely into his privacy and doesn't want to be the subject of any office gossip, real or imagined.

You're probably thinking, "If this brother is that paranoid, why bother?" He's not paranoid—it's just the way he operates. Discretion is the law of the land for these mental creatures.

The symbol of the Gemini is the twins, so you're actually dealing with two distinct personalities. This is why they're in perpetual motion. Their dual personality finds them with two jobs, two homes, two hobbies, and sometimes two companions. One side of her personality has her involved with humanitarian projects or business interests. The flip side may include endeavors in the arts, music, sculpture, or painting. Gemini people have great eye-hand coordination, so they usually are quite proficient at playing a musical instrument, carpentry, typing, painting, or any task where manual dexterity is required.

One of the problems for a Gemini is the ability to hang in there and be counted on for the long haul. Geminis might stick around for a while if there is some excitement going on. But their ability to hang in when there's a lull or things get boring is sorely lacking. Geminis are loyal and have the ability to bring any friend, companion, or acquaintance out of the doldrums with their quick wit or storytelling ability. But the question is, how long will they stay around?

These air signs have problems when it comes to how much time and labor it takes to complete their many projects, promises, and appointments. Their heart is in the right place, but these elusive people have too many irons in the fire to give quality time to any one endeavor.

Geminis are usually slender, rather tall people, with long, willowy arms and distinctive-looking hands. They're usually dressed in the latest fashions with that fresh-creased look. She's the sister who irons her T-shirts and sheets. The men's hairstyles can range from dreads to the bald look, permanents, braids, or texturized look. The women usually cut their hair short because they're moving too fast to sit all day at the hair salon. The hair salon they frequent will do it all: nails, feet, hair, hosiery, and clothing.

In case you're tired of trying to track down the Gemini, there won't be a problem. Geminis love change and new situations, so moving on to a new companion, or a new city, is something Geminis look forward to. They will be out of there before the fat lady can clear her throat.

THE GEMINI MAN

If you're interested in a Gemini man, you're in for the challenge of your life. First and foremost, you've got to get this brother's attention. That will be a major feat in itself because he's always in perpetual motion.

When you first laid eyes on him, chances are (if he was sitting still) that it was at some social function, in the workplace, or at choir rehearsal—or the brother just may have been entertaining his homeboys at the crib. Lucky for you that you decided to come along with a friend; otherwise, it would have been hard to see this brother in action or even to have any time to determine if you liked what you saw. I bet dollars to donuts you loved what you saw.

The scenario with a Gemini at his house is quite impressive. Of course, he's going to have *all* of the gadgets, including keyboard in the corner, computer games, CD player, and big-screen TV. The stereo system is rigged so that the sound from the TV comes directly through his 3-foot-tall speakers, creating the movie theater effect. He's wearing the latest style. He's ordered food in and the spirits are flowing. And of course, you're sitting on the leather sectional and you're falling in love. Hold up. Wait a minute!

The Gemini brother is the consummate entertainer. All of the trappings are very impressive. (I didn't say that they were all *paid* for.) But here's the flip side of the coin. The Gemini is the sign of the twins, which means a dual personality, and he will be a challenge to keep up with. Yes, this particular evening, the charm is turned up high and he is the perfect host. But the next encounter that you have with Mr. Wonderful could be totally different. He may be sullen, quiet, and moody—or all three. His temperament, moods, and general outlook run hot and cold—thankfully, not at the same time.

When the cold spell hits, leave him alone. Save yourself some frustration and don't bother to ask what's wrong. Your concerns and questions will be an exercise in futility. Don't take it personally because if you do, you will constantly be licking your wounds. This brother will reappear later in the week, happy-go-lucky, with barely any recollection of what happened or the reason for his mood. He will probably ask, "What mood?"

You won't be able to believe what a class act this brother is; he'll pour on the champagne, roses, and poetry. He's good to go, as long as you can find him. But don't expect to see your Gemini until you see him. He won't even call his mother on a regular basis unless he's constantly reminded. He usually has two jobs or a part-time gig, playing with a band or the gospel choir or disc-jockeying. So all the quality time that you'd hope to have may end up being empty promises. For example, an Aquarian marketing director started seeing this Gemini photographer. The two had officially been seeing each other for about two months—but they'd had only two dates, a lunch date and an invitation from Ms. Aquarius for him to come to her party. He called all the time, but usually en route to a photo shoot or some other assignment. I guess he felt that checking in was a clear sign of being interested. You see, you may be in the Gemini's thoughts, but he ain't always in da house!

Sometimes a date with your Gemini might include his taking

you to a black-tie function where he's working as well. He sees nothing wrong with having you help collect the invitations at the door, as he comes over intermittently to you, smiles, says a word or two, and retreats back to his labor-intensive work. He'll then ask you at the end of the party, "Wasn't this a great party?" Of course, for him it was great because it was a successful job on his part, but for you . . . well, just get used to it.

The Gemini brother has the capacity for love, and when he falls in love, he puts all his energy in that direction—for as long as he's interested. That's the key here. The relationship will be fun—lots of outings and adventures peppered with impromptu trips out of town. However, because of their dual-personality traits, Geminis can also be el cheapos. They do have expensive tastes, and they know how to purchase the finest that money can buy. But sometimes you'll be expected to treat them as well. Geminis are usually preoccupied with money because they must save their money and invest it for early retirement.

Remember, this brother is an air sign, which means he's independent, aloof, analytical, intriguing, and very hard to keep up with. And if you happen to be married or considering marriage to the sign of the twins, you should know by now that the liaison will be anything but boring.

Even if you're in a long-distance relationship, your Gemini will send cards with money inside, call constantly, and try a little phone sex, too. When he wants to talk to you, he'll simply pick up the phone day or night. He has to do this when he has the opportunity.

When you don't hear from him in a while, you'll be totally intrigued by the excuses he can come up with on the spur of the moment. For example, instead of saying, "I forgot and I'm truly sorry," he will give 101 reasons why it wasn't his fault. He'll let you know that he would never intentionally hurt you by not showing up. The biggest problem with a Gemini man is his inability to keep up with his keys, appointment book, or pager. He'll tell you that on his way over to your house, he ran into his college roommate, whom he hadn't seen in ten years. The two of them started talking and homeboy persuaded your Gemini man to stop by his mother's house. Gemini gets to the mother's house and she's cooked a full-course meal and the rest is history. Oh, well.

Oh, by the way, Geminis are sticklers for neatness. The clothing you wear doesn't have to cost a fortune, but having a sense of style is important to them. He looks at his companion as a reflection of him. If by chance he picks you up for a date and you're dressed a bit too casually for the dinner-theater outing he planned, he may change directions in midstream and the two of you may end up at the bowling alley instead. He's very tactful and he wouldn't tell you that you were more appropriately dressed for a football game. He'd simply suggest that the two of you go somewhere else. You get the picture.

It's also a good idea to be well read and have a working knowledge of current events. Geminis are very intelligent people. Your appearance and his ability to get inside your head are two very important areas for you to concentrate on. For example, if you tell him you're in college and you're planning on becoming an engineer, he may jokingly ask you to spell the word.

Intelligence rates higher than looks in their book. And a variety of looks, like different color contacts, braids, hair weaves, and any other enhancements, is fine with the Gemini. The Gemini seeks variety in his life, and offering him different looks keeps him guessing about what he can expect from you so he doesn't get bored.

THE GEMINI WOMAN

The Gemini sister is the sassy one, the charmer of the zodiac. The brothers perk up when this air sign decides to turn on her irresistible charm. She's the one-of-a-kind sister whose mind is always spinning on how to improve herself or manipulate a situation to get exactly what she wants. And most of the time she succeeds! The Gemini sister could write a how-to book on getting what she wants, but unfortunately, she's not giving away the tricks of the trade.

The Gemini sister is constantly in a mental and intellectual tennis match with herself. The ever-looming questions are always in her mind: "Should I take this job, go on this trip, or go out with this guy?" She can even be preoccupied by what color top to wear the next day or whether she's made any headway in her quest for her rightful place in society.

So, if you're interested in a Gemini woman, you are in for some real challenges. The first is to try to keep up with her, literally, and the second, is to try to understand what's in that pretty little head of hers. Just because she was warm and friendly the first time the two of you met, don't assume that she's ready to ride off into the sunset and live happily ever after. It ain't happening here.

Geminis are fiercely independent. Although they are definitely attracted to the strong, silent type (I say silent because the brother probably won't be able to get a word in edgewise), they must have their own space. They must feel that they can do their own thing. Control freaks need not apply.

For example, a Gemini sister and her girlfriend decided to go out for drinks after work. Shortly, and by coincidence, two brothers joined them. The next person through the door was the Gemini's companion. She promptly announced to her girlfriend, "I was supposed to have dinner and drinks with him. It's his birthday." Ouch!

When love calls, the Gemini sister doesn't always answer—mainly because her standards are so high. There's always the possibility of overlooking that would-be prince for the more buffed and gorgeous studs who may turn out to be the frogs of life. For Ms. Gemini, image is everything! For Ms. Gemini, it's just as easy to fall in love with a rich man as a poor one, or a handsome hunk instead of the star of the geek show. In any case, a relationship with the Gemini sister (once she decides to pay attention to her admirer) will be far from boring. The companion of Lady Gemini will be thoroughly entertained. Geminis have a great sense of humor; they're intelligent and definitely have the gift of gab, along with a few other gifts: tabletop dances and a few under-the-table surprises or "uprisings" at dinner.

Some men feel that the Gemini woman is not approachable. Usually she's dressed to kill, from her hair salon "do" to her manicured toes, and the brothers are sometimes reluctant to approach. Don't be. Gemini is the sign of the twins, with the dual personality, and this may be your lucky day. Then again . . . you never know with the Gemini sister.

The Gemini woman is what the brothers consider "high maintenance." These sisters work hard to achieve their goals, and dressing in the latest style is something they do for themselves. Therefore, most Geminis have two jobs. Because of their dual personality, they may also have two hobbies, even two companions sometimes. But for crying out loud, get the names of the companions right!

This sister will expect you to know how to dress. The bell-bottom pants, polyester leisure suits, and Jheri curls must go! Say, brothers, don't forget the shoes. "When I see a man with turley-tappin' ass shoes (the sole is so thin the shoe turns up at the toe), I know what time it is. He won't be going anywhere with me looking like that," declared one Gemini woman.

Once the Gemini sister is in a relationship, there won't be any pressure to share nuptials. If marriage is to be discussed at all, it may be in the form of a prenuptial agreement. A discussion of this type will give the Gemini sister a good idea of where your head is and if you're supersensitive about the subject. Gemini women are very comfortable being single, and they simply must have their freedom. There's no mad dash to get married. That's because they're so busy enjoying themselves. Their attitude is, why screw up a good thing?

This air sign must be in control of the relationship, or any situation for that matter. If they're feeling vulnerable and too emotional about a situation, they'll disappear. Ms. Gemini may apply for a transfer to another city without telling you until moving day, or she may move into that new house that she never bothered to tell you about and then get an unlisted telephone number. You just never know with a Gemini.

Sometimes disappearing acts can backfire, however. A Gemini woman recalls an embarrassing situation. "I was dating this guy for six months and we were becoming serious, but I broke it off unexpectedly. Two months later in another town, I met this wonderful guy and we saw each other constantly for three months. He was so excited that his cousin, who's like a brother, was coming to visit and he wanted me to meet him. As it turned out, the cousin was the companion I dated for six months. I parted from both men."

Once you get this air sign's attention, the chase will be a wonderful experience. Geminis enjoy the chase more than the actual capture. The key here is to play hard to get—Geminis love a good challenge. To get the Gemini sister going, simply tell her that something can't be done or that she is incapable of doing it, and, more times than not, she will rise to the occasion. When the Gemini sister falls in love, the fun, adventure, and romance are all-consuming. Geminis are always on the go. So you better have your skates, in-line skates, or bicycle handy. They will expect much affection and much attention. As one Gemini woman explained, "Showing some form of affection in the A.M., such as a kiss, a hug, or words, is important. This also applies to the P.M., and not just when it's time to go to bed."

Gemini women don't do windows. Trying to force them into domesticity is like trying to break in a wild stallion—it's going to be tough. Whatever the Gemini sister attempts, her creative touch makes it one better, but she doesn't have the time or the inclination to bake cookies and try new recipes. Many Geminis can cook, but it's a matter of finding the time. Collecting cookbooks and recipes is not for her.

If you're going to make a relationship with a Gemini work, you need to have a life apart from her. Try not to interrogate this sister every time you see her; she values her privacy and independence. As one sister put it, "I hate when I meet a man and he loves my personality and free spirit. As soon as I'm in a relationship with him, the very thing he claims to be so in love with is the first thing he tries to change."

Guide to a Love Connection

Gemini and Aries

Both respect the other's intelligence. Most of all, the two won't bore each other to tears. Both are fun-loving, adventuresome, and spontaneous. Taking a trip at a moment's notice is definitely to their liking. Of course, Aries will want to dominate, and that's fine with Gemini, who is far too busy with a host of other projects to care. Aries will rant and rave about Gemini's lack of attention. Gemini will sit quietly, assessing the argument in his mind and not saying a word; this will steam Aries. But during the making-up time in the boudoir, it's full throttle all the way. These two take the bedroom aerobics to the far reaches of the stratosphere. Whew! This match could really work well.

Gemini and Taurus

Gemini, the air sign, and Taurus, the earth sign, are so far apart in outlook and demeanor that they make better friends than lovers. Gemini is an airhead who flies from one project or person to another without much rhyme or reason. Taurus, on the other hand, is grounded, sensible, and stubborn and won't put up with Gemini's devil-may-care attitude. Although Gemini loves the passion that Taurus exudes in the bedroom, she is put off by Taurus's demands of devotion and love. Gemini is out meeting and greeting people and thrives in the social setting. The social setting Taurus wants is at home with family and friends. Gemini will be turned off by Taurus's no-nonsense, my-way-or-the-highway attitude and may seek other outlets.

Gemini and Gemini

This relationship operates at fever pitch. These two are racing in all different directions, constantly on the move, while at the same time picking up suitors, friends, and supporters all along the way. They put the F in fun. The term "party animal" had to be coined for a Gemini. They're charming, aggressive, and versatile, and the conversation will be stimulating. Now with all of that you'd think this relationship is all that. Well, it'll be all that and more in the beginning. But as the twins move forward, boredom will set in and the relationship (by mutual agreement) will be left behind. Most Geminis are usually too busy losing keys, forgetting appointments, and overextending themselves to put any real quality time into a relationship. Even when they're around physically, their minds are somewhere else, in perpetual analysis of everything they do, contemplating a new job, trip, or relationship. There's just too much going on with these two. A long-term relationship is not an option, not for these two, anyway.

Gemini and Cancer

This union will definitely take work, work, and more work. Gemini's overly animated personality gets Cancer's attention. Cancer has a great sense of humor and loves to laugh. The conversations will be stimulating. Cancer, with all of her culinary delights, will create a haven for Gemini. Gemini, though impressed, remains unemotional and aloof about the union. Cancer's approach is simple. She simply wants Mr. Gemini to stay home so that she can take care of him. Gemini is simply too busy with all of his current and future projects and work to slow down. In bedroom matters, Cancer takes the lead and Gemini follows willingly. But all of Cancer's demands about hearth and home have Gemini running for cover. Skip this one, folks.

Gemini and Leo

Both will have to nurture and cultivate this union. Gemini, the air sign, and Leo, the fire sign, can create some seriously hot action here. Both love to travel and are adventuresome. Leo must be the center of attention in all of the social settings, and that's fine with Gemini. Gemini's busy in her sassiness wowing the crowd too. Both love intellectual stimulation and ideas and concepts with far-reaching effects. When it comes to money, Gemini is a bit more prudent. Leo will spend her last dime on the all-important killer outfit. But Gemini hoards a stash of cash as a precautionary measure. Sexually, they complement each other as well. Leo has a serious libido and Gemini will be hard-pressed to keep up. But Gemini does go willingly. This relationship could really work!

Gemini and Virgo

Mentally, the combination is in sync. These two can talk for hours on the telephone on a variety of subjects. The ruling planet of both is Mercury, which rules intelligence and the power to reason. But you would think that they would have thought out why such an unlikely pair would be trying to deal with each other in a relationship. Gemini, an air sign, moves endlessly in twenty different directions at the same time. Virgo's head is spinning from Gemini's perpetual motion. Virgo simply wants a nice companion to settle down with in a comfortable home. Gemini will not be controlled, and her attention span is short when it comes to being devoted to and focused on one person. Bedroom maneuvers are not any better. Gemini thinks Virgo is a geek in bed, while Virgo thinks Gemini is a freak. This union is better as a friendship.

Gemini and Libra

These two air signs complement each other as a couple. Both must have freedom to explore their many commitments and outlets. Both are flirtatious—Libra shamelessly so—but Gemini will be a little more subtle with his come-ons. Neither is threatened by the antics or personality of the other. Sexually, Libra will guide and create passion and romance in luxurious surroundings, to the delight of Gemini. These two have everything going for them. Both love to dress to the nines, because for both image is everything. And both have a tendency to shy away from a commitment. If these two can settle down and slow down, this dynamic duo could create a serious union.

Gemini and Scorpio

Yes, the sex is on! Gemini is definitely interested in reaching new sexual highs. The trouble is, after the morning after, it's business as usual with these two. Gemini is preoccupied with everything from matters in the workplace to the social calendar. Of course, Scorpio feels shunned and unappreciated. Scorpio's jealous rantings create problems for both since Gemini can't figure what the fuss is about. Gemini's taste for the unusual and variety has Scorpio wondering if a new companion is on the horizon. Scorpio's emotional outbursts and passion for the relationship have light-hearted Gemini feeling pressured for a more intense companionship. Gemini must be free to fly. Scorpio wants to clip Gemini's wings and mold and control. This union is better left alone.

Gemini and Sagittarius

These opposites of the zodiac will be totally enthralled with each other at first. The conversation will be stimulating, for both have an insatiable appetite for knowledge, spontaneity, and adventure. Gemini, the airhead, will be intrigued by Sag's intelligence and over-the-top sense of humor. Sag won't be put off by Gemini's matter-of-fact approach to romance. But because they're opposites, the great sex will not be enough to sustain a long-term union. Gemini's feelings will be hurt by Sag's tactless behavior. Sag will be annoyed at Gemini's lack of attention to the relationship and roving eye.

When these two decide to call it quits, there won't be any sad faces, songs, or reflections on what might have been. They're out!

Gemini and Capricorn

This relationship fizzles before it gets off the ground. Gemini's mental masturbation is constantly in the forefront of the relationship. Capricorn is a thinker, too, but not to the point of distraction. Gemini's lackadaisical attitude about the relationship has Capricorn frustrated and annoyed. Gemini perceives Capricorn as far too serious and a stuffed shirt. Capricorn is grounded, down to earth, and sensible in his approach to most things. Gemini is a free spirit who is prone to disappearing acts. There's a whole unexplored world out there, you know. Gemini, air sign, will not be harnessed to simply live a boring life by Capricorn's rules of order. Sexually, Gemini, who loves to experiment with toys and props, will show conventional Capricorn a thing or two. But don't mistake the sex for something more. It ain't happening!

Gemini and Aquarius

Well now, this pair could become the bomb! Both are creative types who must be in the mix, where they come alive. Gemini is analytical and Aquarius keeps him interested with her thought-provoking concepts. Both revere independence and guard their freedom. Both are spontaneous and will take a trip or try something new at a moment's notice. Gemini is restless and constantly seeks new challenges. But Aquarius has no problem keeping Gemini curious and being delighted by the unpredictability of Aquarius. The difficulty of the relationship will be during money matters: Gemini can be a miser and Aquarius can be a spendthrift. When these two find their way to the bedroom, they won't resurface for days. A sizzling affair or a long-term marriage is where it's at for these two.

Gemini and Pisces

These two probably got together at the urging of a mutual friend, because they wouldn't knowingly get themselves into this disaster-waiting-to-happen. Gemini is an air sign and simply can't commit to staying at home playing footsie for the rest of his life. Pisces is insecure about the relationship and wants a commitment.

Gemini is too busy with her many friends, projects, and social functions to give homebody Pisces the attention he seeks. Sexually,
Pisces makes Gemini stand up (no pun intended) and take notice.
Pisces can definitely be one of the stars of the freak show. Those antics will get Gemini's attention for a while, but Pisces's emotional
attachments and insecurities will get on Gemini's nerves. This
union is not in the cards.

Romance and the Gemini

The kiss of death of any relationship with a Gemini is to be boring.
You absolutely must be spontaneous, adventuresome, and exciting
with the Gemini, who expects to be entertained and amused on
dates and in general. And if you're planning a romantic outing, the
creativity of the date is what is significant to the Gemini. The key is
to get their attention first because they're usually so preoccupied,
they probably won't even notice you the first time around.

They are certainly not interested in staying at home with you
watching videos or sitting at grandmama's while she is going on
and on over what a cute baby you were. And please don't bring out
the photo albums, for Pete's sake! What you will find at the end of
the date is a sullen, annoyed Gemini who is ready to end the date
and go home early without you.

After you graduate past the first date, it's always a good idea to
call up and simply say, "Pack a bag and include a bathing suit and
clothing for a warm climate." Who knows, you might be making
love that night under the moon and stars on the beach. Gemini
loves surprises and trying new things and experiencing life to the
fullest. These air signs are in the fast lane. And if you plan to keep
up, you need to first get off the sidewalk and get moving.

There must be a variety of activities for the Gemini. He is restless and simply won't sit still for the routine or sleeper date. Geminis thrive on excitement. A Gemini sister from Texas explained
that although her companion sent cards and flowers, he really
didn't know much about her likes and how to cater to her. After he
consulted with her best friend, the subsequent dates included all of
her favorite things. Once they became intimate, her mate was so
grateful to the best friend that during the sexual encounter he acci-

dently called out the best friend's name. "The mood was truly broken," she said.

If you're dating a Gemini man, you'll get a clear sense that he's interested in your mind, not your behind (not right away, anyway). He will want to know your background, where your head is, and what your goals and aspirations are. When the serious stuff, like sex or a long-term relationship, gets under way, he will have already assessed whether a relationship is feasible, so don't get impatient and flustered because he hasn't made a move. Actually, he has. But the meeting of the minds comes first before any bodies start slappin'. A word of warning here: One of the things the Gemini lacks is staying power, and not necessarily in the bedroom. This is why there is this long mental masturbation over whether they're going to commit to a relationship or not. But one of the ways to keep them hangin' around is to create stimulating and spontaneous dates.

For example, a Gemini sister casually met a Leo man and the two decided to go on a picnic that day. They bought food and wine and went to a wild field, rolled around in the grass, and had loads of fun. Impulsively, the Leo proposed marriage right on the spot as they romped. The point is, spontaneity is high on a Gemini's wish list, along with being sensitive to the Gemini's needs: asking about her day, giving him an impromptu massage, making plans for an event unbeknownst to the companion. Geminis love surprises, especially when it's for the them.

How about this for a birthday surprise? One Gemini speech pathologist said her companion received major points after he arranged for her parents to take her to her favorite restaurant. The parents diverted her while he created the romantic setting. Then he arrived and the parents left shortly thereafter. The table was set with a dozen red roses by the window overlooking a pier with sailboats in the distance.

One Gemini sister described her most romantic date as a rainy day when she and her companion take the day off. The house is flowing with jazz, both clean house, bathe together, and place candles all over the house, order in Chinese food, and then . . .

The idea of fun for a Gemini doesn't include being taken to your mother's house to sit at her kitchen table and the two of you talk about family problems and your siblings. Borrrrr-ing!!! That's okay one time around. If you expect to keep the Gemini on your arm, the endless chatter about family matters should be saved for the church picnic or the family reunion.

An Aquarian sister from Atlanta met a potential Gemini companion at a party. She thought he was a very down-to-earth brother, talkative and sincere, but she soon realized that he couldn't kiss, and that was a red flag. On another date, he offered to rub her feet, and he couldn't do that task either. "First of all, he grabbed my left foot first instead of my right, and then he was squeezing it in a halfhearted manner instead of massaging it. It drove me crazy and made my flesh crawl!" She skipped this relationship.

A Gemini woman in Memphis remembers her date of a lifetime. "I met this man, who lived in Nashville, through a mutual friend. When he invited me up for the day, we had drinks, walked around the downtown area. We later saw this brand-new stretch limo and, curious, we asked the driver if we could look inside. After we looked inside, he thanked the driver and then introduced himself. The driver then said, 'Mr. Jones, I'm here to pick up you and your date.' Inside the limo was my favorite wine-and-pizza combo, which I talked about during earlier conversations. The date was all prearranged. It was fabulous!" Are you getting the picture?

In another example, a Gemini female had urged her companion to be more creative in planning their dates. The Virgo was the type who would go to dinner and then a movie; this was very boring to the Gemini, especially after the third time. But then the next time the Virgo picked Ms. Gemini up, he had Dom Pérignon champagne in the backseat, along with an overflowing basket of strawberries, cheeses, and other snacks. And this time, they went to the drive-in. Gemini was impressed!

Another Gemini sister said that a romantic turn-on for her is for a man to hold her in his arms all night without sex and to serve her breakfast in bed. For this sister, the brother scored major points because she felt that sex was ever-present on her companion's mind and it turned her on.

Geminis are usually morning people. Watching the sun rise after a night of fun, sex, more sex, and fun, is very much to the Gemini's liking. This way, she can start the play-by-play day that will soon follow.

Sex, Sex, and More Sex

Getting the Groove On . . .

Remember the song "Your body's here with me, but your mind is on the other side of town"? It was probably written with a Gemini in mind. The point being, Gemini is so preoccupied with all of the many analyses of every minute detail of her life that she scarcely has time to realize that she's supposed to be into the person she's with. And you simply cannot be boring if you expect to hold the Gemini's attention in or out of the bedroom. Asking a Gemini what he's thinking about would get a response like "Where do I begin? Or do you have a lifetime to listen?"

Getting this groove on is going to be a real challenge because you'll definitely have to create a memorable liaison to get this dual personality's attention. In other words, you've got to come on with it!

Geminis definitely know how to make love, including the right moves, the oral and manual stimulation. But once you find yourself in a bedroom situation with a Gemini, if you're an emotional and passionate person, you may feel like you're going to bed with a robot. The sexual encounter may include all of the right moves in some semblance of order, but high emotional drama and waves-washing-up-on-the-shore kind of passion may be lacking. Please don't take this as a personal affront; Geminis simply can't help their lack of emotion. Remember, the ruling planet of Gemini is Mercury, which is associated with intellect; therefore, the brain never rests even when there are intense matters like high-drama sex going on.

Even during the steamiest sex possible, his mind can wander off. Or he's probably analyzing your reactions and responses to what's happening. You may feel like you're in a study group with Gemini. Don't feel threatened or annoyed, keep your eyes closed, and enjoy the encounter.

Geminis must have visual stimulation that translates to mental and physical areas, so lavish surroundings are a good attention getter. Taking the Gemini to an out-of-town getaway is a sure bet. Being in a place where he can maintain his anonymity is always a winner. There, he can truly relax without having to worry about who's watching. Gemini people guard their privacy fiercely. On the other hand, the idea of getting caught during sex keeps them aroused and intrigued. For example, after the two of you leave a restaurant, the Gemini might suggest that you engage in sex not in the car but against the hood of the car right there in the restaurant's parking lot. It's called dessert! Just go with it. I know it's bizarre—but hey, you wanted the Gemini's attention, and now you have it. Hopefully for you, it's nighttime and the car isn't parked at the entrance!

To get his attention during intimate hours, you may have to resort to tabletop dancing or a striptease routine. Again, he's always preoccupied with all of his many projects and he's always distracted.

There aren't any single killer positions during sex that the Gemini prefers. If it's left up to them, they will want to experience every position possible before the night is over. They're into variety. Besides, you just never know with a Gemini.

Just as you plan the intimate lights-down-low, in-the-groove music and dancing-close-and-I-want-to-know-you-intimately-tonight encounter, the Gemini may not even show up. Remember, the dual personality of the Gemini will have you constantly wondering which way is up! Of course, when she loses track of time, she'll have a million and one excuses for not being in da house.

A Gemini sister was pleasantly surprised when her Leo companion gave her a sexy nightgown and matching shoes. Ms. Gemini had just entered the room after taking a bubble bath to find her presents attached to helium-filled balloons floating above the bed in her bedroom. Well, now.

Gemini people enjoy making the trip much more than arriving at the destination. That's why you have to keep making the relationship fresh and intriguing. You look up one day and he'll be gone, never to return again. It's the total package that he's looking for, where all of the pieces fit together to make the whole. Beauty and brains will attract the Gemini brother.

Making love in out-of-town locations is always a good idea. You'll definitely get more out of the sexual relationship when you're away in unfamiliar surroundings. Geminis come alive when they're certain that nobody from work is there or they know that one of her parents' friends won't suddenly appear. They're constantly concerned about the ol' image. It's hard for a Gemini to truly relax. And one of the ways that they can do so is when they're out of town or, better still, out of the country. But again, the dual nature of Geminis will also find them totally intrigued by the possibility of getting caught having sex.

Once you maneuver a quiet, out-of-the-way place, well, watch the sparks, romance, sex, conversation, food, and your dress fly. Gemini will definitely show her appreciation. You'll get some good head and a heavy dose of teasing, dancing, role playing, and plenty of loving!

A Gemini who dated an Aquarian commented that her companion was the best lover she had ever had. "I would put on a coat and nothing else, and go and pick him up. We'd pull up in the garage and make love right there in the car. I had a house and he had a house, but that didn't matter." Basically, it was the excitement of doing it somewhere other than familiar surroundings. The relationship also ended as spontaneously as it began. "I was working nights and I came home and he's got some other woman he was pleasing in my bed. He could have invited me, too," she said. "Needless to say, I put them both out!"

EROGENOUS ZONES . . . SOME PHYSICAL, SOME NOT

For the Gemini, erogenous zones may not necessarily be physical touching of the body. It's also mental stimulation and preparation before the physical contact begins. So it's noteworthy to come up with an attention-getting antic before, during, and after bedroom romps, to get the preoccupied Gemini focused on one thing—you! Of course, he will want to know all there is to know about you, including all of your secrets. But don't think for a minute that you'll know any of his.

A game of strip poker or strip chess may be to her liking. For strip chess, each time a player takes a chess piece, he gets to ask his opponent for an article of clothing, jewelry, etc. Once the king is in check, the player may decide what area of sex he wants to delve into first. While the opponent scrambles to protect the king, Gemini is bargaining about other aspects of the sex play that he prefers.

In terms of the body, stroking the Gemini's hands and arms gets her attention. Hand kissing and massages, along with feathery touches on the arms and shoulders, will make the Gemini come alive—for a while anyway. You must keep in mind the dual nature of the Gemini, the sign of the twins; your immediate responses to the two personalities will create an interesting and rewarding evening on the part of both.

Talking dirty and using sex toys pique the Gemini's interest; it's something else to do in the bedroom besides the routine tried and true. Geminis also like to take baths together, because they can covertly assess your body parts. Sex in the shower or the bathtub delights the Gemini.

They must be able to see the body. They plan to know your body intimately, and they want to be able to accomplish that goal without looking directly. Eye contact is also a major thing with them. If you're looking directly at them, the Gemini knows that you're paying attention.

Once all the rules of the game are established, the Gemini might emerge with a full costume and a totally different look. Wigs, costumes, and role playing are all to the Gemini's liking. For example, a Gemini man used to insist that his girlfriend (and later wife) wear a variety of different-colored wigs each time they went to bed. On Sundays, her wig would be jet black and she would have to dress like a prostitute with spike heels and a garter belt, along with his favorite flavor of edible underwear. He explained that these steps satisfied his need to be faithful to one person, which was hard for him to do, while allowing him to enjoy many different partners in his fantasy world.

A Gemini woman said she is definitely turned off by a man who talks too much in bed. "If he's talking too much, that just lets me know there isn't going to be too much going on," she commented. "I'll tell him, 'Here, put this [her breast] in your mouth, will you, please?' That's the way I shut him up for a while. Then, when he thinks he's finished, I say, 'Here—this one over here is jealous. Put this one in now, okay.'"

Another Gemini woman said she loved to have a man play in her hair. "I used to have a man who could make me come by playing in my hair. The foreplay was so intense that I used to have to tell him, 'Hold up, I can't take any more. I need to get up and walk around, I'm weak in the knees.' "

A big turn-on for a Gemini is to offer to hire a high-class prostitute for his or her birthday so they can live out all of the fantasies that the Gemini is obsessed with. Of course, you could save your money and dress up as the prostitute yourself!

PLAIN OL' SEX AND NOTHING MORE: WELCOME TO THE FREAK SHOW

Of the twelve signs of the zodiac, there are the participants of the freak show, those on the sidelines, and the stars of the freak show. Geminis are participants. They will try just about anything once, including orgies and sex with the same gender.

If you're interested in approaching a Gemini about freaky sexual matters, the prerequisite is for you to be sworn to secrecy. If the Gemini trusts you and determines that you have as much to lose as she does by divulging intimate details of the encounter, she will be your freaky secret lover indefinitely!

If you catch these air signs in a good, playful, freak-show kind of mood, their sexual appetite may become adventurous. Both the men and women of the sign love to experiment sexually; group sex, spouse swapping, and bisexuality are all possibilities. For example, a Gemini woman broke up with her Aquarian boyfriend after she caught him having sex with another woman. But her reason for the breakup was interesting. "I came home and found him with another woman. He didn't invite me [to join them], so I felt like he needed to find someone else."

So the next time you're looking for sex and nothing more, then you may have hit the jackpot. Geminis sometimes find themselves in perverted behavior that could include multiple sex partners. They can definitely be unpredictable and unconventional in their approach to sex. It's really hard to know because most of the time they don't know what they're going to do themselves. They are totally unpredictable. It depends on which personality you meet first.

The Gemini brother may even casually mention to a gay man in his presence that he is endowed with a 9½-inch penis. An announcement of that nature may seem weird to someone, especially if the Gemini's girlfriend is in the next room. It's just his way of testing the waters. Geminis will enjoy a homosexual experience out of sheer curiosity. But their twin nature does incline them to bisexuality.

MONEY MATTERS

The key to success in money management for Geminis is to have someone manage their money for them—a financial planner or a spouse who will contact a professional. Geminis are far too busy to take the time to do it themselves.

Most Geminis are highly successful people. Gemini, being the sign of the twins, often have two careers, two hobbies, two homes, etc. But because they are usually so busy with their many projects, traveling and with a bulging social calendar, they simply need a professional to organize their finances and get the investment portfolio going.

The key here is delegating the task. They know the value of money because unless they're buying something for themselves or a parent, they can be tightwads. Of course, they spare no expense on themselves because they work hard and feel that they deserve it—and they do! But their dual personality has them spending money that they do not have (meaning credit cards) or hoarding it yet always crying broke.

With Geminis, these air signs won't impulsively invest in any harebrained get-rich-quick schemes. Geminis are mentally agile types who will mull things over and over and over in their heads until all of the details are worked out to their satisfaction.

Geminis want to save because they plan to have the lavish lifestyle, including a chauffeur-driven limo whenever it strikes their mood. For the most part, it's the reason that they work. Image is very important to them, and they plan to have all of the trappings: the house, luxury cars, the boat, the summer and winter homes. . . .

And just because you may be a potential companion of the Gemini, don't think you've hit the jackpot, because the Gemini will expect you to bring something to the table as well. So don't start licking your chops too soon.

After the financial planner, accountant, or consultant is hired, it will be best if he or she simply makes the decisions for the Gemini. You can bet that the Gemini has done his research to determine if the planner is credible and has a good track record. After it has been determined that all systems are go, well, the Gemini will want the planner to just do it! And he will expect to see some tangible results immediately. If that isn't the case, the planner will need to explain this up front.

From as early as their teen years, Geminis knew that they were going to have money, in abundance. If you're dealing with a young Gemini, good luck: He will hoard his money and spend yours without a second thought. He will spend money as he gets it. This Gemini will buy a different pair of $100 tennis shoes for every day of the week unless some restraints are exercised. Then, of course, he'll cry broke when it's time to take his date to the movies, or when she has to pay for the extra set of fake nails for Friday night.

If the planner simply takes charge of Gemini's finances, it will be beneficial to all concerned. You can bet that the Gemini is going to have money and plenty of it someday.

PAMPERING TIPS FOR GEMINI

✧ The best approach to pampering a Gemini is through the element of surprise. Geminis love surprises and spontaneity.

✧ Plan a trip to a place neither of you has visited. Throw caution to the wind and explore the city and each other.

✧ Create a haven at your place for your Gemini. Plant love notes throughout the house, along with unexpected small gifts of perfume, candles, or chocolates.

✧ A makeover or a total new look would meet with Gemini's approval. Changing their image delights them.

✧ If you hire a masseuse, don't forget the manicurist, the hairstylist, and the personal trainer, too.

✧ A cruise with the option of going ashore is definitely doable for the Gemini. Try and make it a surprise!

✧ Send a manicurist to your Gemini's house for hand and toe

treatment. He will enjoy it.

✻ Arrange for a baby-sitter for the children, then plan an adventure like in-line skating, hang gliding, or hot-air ballooning. (The gondola may be an ideal place for getting your groove on!)

✻ If funds are low, a hotel room in town will serve the same purpose. But creativity is the key. Sing to each other, dance together, and make beautiful music together.

✻ Breakfast in bed works, too. But then there's washing the dishes, doing the laundry, and later having a picnic in the park or the backyard.

Gift Ideas for Gemini

✻ The uniqueness of the gift is more important to a Gemini. Skip the tie for the man or blouse for the woman. Borrr-ing!

✻ Try concert tickets for a favorite performer, followed by the after set, a late-night dinner and a midnight stroll.

✻ Surprise your Gemini with a daytime birthday party. Invite guests before work, during lunch, and after work. Gemini will be thoroughly entertained.

✻ Plan a scavenger hunt with titillating clues that lead to a sexy bikini and tickets to a place with sun, sand, and sea. Your Gemini won't stop showing her appreciation!

✻ Books on tape work best for the Gemini, who is in perpetual motion.

✻ Secondhand stores or antique shops yield unique gift ideas. If you're not sure what he wants, take him with you, let him point the item out, and buy it later.

✻ A framed print or original piece of artwork is always a winner. Geminis are intellectuals and love the arts, too.

✻ Season tickets to spectator sports make great gifts for Gemini. But you have to include the tailgate party, too.

✻ Create a grab bag of goodies with all her favorite stuff, like perfume, lotion, shampoo, body scrubs, candles, nail polish, hair combs, belts, and scarves. Then include these items in a travel bag with her initials on it!

* Any item that's made especially for the Geminis will have them geeked. Monogrammed towels, a watch with an inscription, a handmade purse, or a leather briefcase with his or her initials is the bomb!

Cancer

(June 21 to July 22)
SYMBOL: THE CRAB

Positive love traits: Emotional, considerate, passionate,
and sensitive lover.
Negative love traits: Hypersensitive lover, lackadaisical
and insecure.
Ruling planet: The moon is associated with emotions,
feelings, and intuitive powers.
Word to the wise: If you're thinking about a relationship
with this moon child, it's going to be for keeps.
Think it over carefully.

Cancer is the sign of the crab, which means he'll hold on for dear life and never let go, either in love relationships or friendships. Cancer people will be lifetime friends, reliable and there for you no matter what their present station in life is. Cancer people (the men included) are the mothers and nurturers of the zodiac. In short, these people are one big lump in the throat. They will cry and pray with you, and hold your hand through any crisis, offering support, tissues, and understanding.

Their ruling planet, the moon, is associated with emotions and feelings. If you've ever noticed the man in the moon, he has a somewhat jolly look about him, and so do Cancerians. Consider the moon and the various stages, new moon, full moon, crescent, etc. Such are the various changes or moods you'll find in this water sign. There will never be a dull moment with this chameleon of moods.

For example, one minute the Cancer sister will be trying to reach her girlfriend to tell her about the new beau, then later she'll be distraught over the story of a man whose best friend died of cancer. Of course, the man is a man she never laid eyes on until that moment. But for Cancer, it was perfectly natural for this man to confide in her.

You'll find these people in the church choir, hanging with the homeboys at a bar or a card party, playing sports, chillin' at home, or just kickin' it. Both the men and the women have full, round faces like the moon. Their arms are usually long and slim in proportion to the rest of the body. They usually have wide mouths with broad grins.

Cancer people are great storytellers and are usually the life of the party. Once they get going, it's hard to stop them because they're in overdrive. On the other hand, the moon child has a dark side and can be moody, selfish, sometimes even a straight-out liar. For example, a commercial underwriter tells the story of a Cancer who said he was a Vietnam veteran and lied about his age and his marital status. "Once I talked with his family, they revealed that he was in fact married and a minister working on a divinity degree. He'll have some explaining to do at the Pearly Gates" was her last comment.

They also have a zany, over-the-top sense of humor. And they are the first to laugh at themselves. For example, a Cancer woman and her girlfriend who had attended an all-day party found that they had no time to return home to get dressed for an affair that night. Her girlfriend was resigned to wearing what she had on, but the Cancer said, "If I've got to wear this, I'm not going." So the two women ended up changing clothes in the car. As passersby tried to figure out what was going on, the contortionist act began. "Stockings were put on inside out, makeup was less than perfect, a blouse was buttoned wrong, and clothes were somewhat rumpled—but we made it."

When you first meet them, they're charming, warm, and friendly, but just a tad guarded. If the vibes are right, then they'll open up a bit. But don't be too pushy or over the top. They are very stubborn when it comes to what they want in a companion. A lot of razzle-dazzle is not needed here. Cancer's needs are somewhat low-key: True friendship, consideration, and a little TLC every now and then will work for them.

Cancer people are water signs and their emotions run deep. They are also very intuitive and can sense the slightest nuance or overture, positive or negative. So if you're slightly interested, they will pick up the vibe immediately. Now, whether they respond will be another story because usually the person who made that little hint of interest has no idea that the Cancer picked up on it.

When you meet these down-to-earth, practical people, they won't play games. If you're interested in starting a friendship that might blossom into something more, act genuine. There won't be any cat-and-mouse shenanigans. You need to be straight up.

Sincerity, intelligence, and humor are all high on the list of a Cancer: You don't have to be the Playmate of the Month or Mr. Universe to get the attention of Cancer. Before any romance commences, they will get to know you first, so relax and take your time. Cancer people are not going to be rushed into a relationship. And they're not going anywhere. They are not apt to run off into the sunset with someone that they met earlier in the day. Once they decide this relationship is the real deal, they play for keeps.

A word of warning about these moon children: They're highly emotional and moody and very complex people. Many times you won't be able to figure out what's wrong with them. Save yourself some mental masturbation. Their mood swings are sometimes so drastic that by the time you figure what's wrong, they have moved on to another "crisis." But inside their tough shells crabs are soft; they need constant love, reassurance, and loyalty. This moon child gives back tenfold in appreciation.

The Cancer Man

This brother is the romantic of the zodiac. He's the one who will send flowers or a card just to say he's thinking of you. The Cancer brother will want to set the fanciful stage early.

Any initial moves from the Cancer will be subtle. They won't come on like gangbusters, so keep the aggressiveness harnessed. The Cancer man is more of a traditional guy from the old school. Even though he may be in his twenties, he has certain ideas and philosophies on how women should conduct themselves. He's a historian and likes to draw on events and cultures of the past.

When you first meet this brother, more than likely he'll be casually dressed. He doesn't go in for the clothing fanfare, the Armani and Brooks Brothers suits. Of course, he knows that clothing serves a useful purpose in covering the body, but he definitely won't spend his entire paycheck on the killer outfit—he's far too practical for that. But don't judge a book by its cover: This brother is intelligent, fun to be with, knows what he wants out of life, and is sensitive to boot.

Kissing is their thing, too. If you plan to get to know and eventually have a relationship with a Cancer man, then you need to visit your dentist to have your teeth cleaned. Then take a crash course in the art of kissing. If you fail the course, that's okay, because you'll be taught by the master himself. Kissing for Cancers is the highest form of intimate romance. And probably for the Cancer, more so than the actual sexual encounter, it's the prerequisite for any future relationship. If kissing was never your thing, it will be before any relationship with a Cancer is over.

For example, one Cancer brother from West Africa kissed his Sagittarian date for two and a half hours in public on the first night they met. How's that for romance? Oh, by the way, they're married now.

In another example, a Cancer man, leaving an outdoor Barry White concert, stopped in the middle of the parking lot to give his Aquarian date a deep, passionate kiss, still holding the picnic basket in one hand, his other arm around her in a desperate embrace. The two completely blocked traffic. After they were brought back to reality by the blare of car horns, he apologized and explained that he couldn't help himself. Don't get me wrong, the Cancer man definitely loves sex. But intercourse begins as outercourse with this water sign, who loves passionate foreplay, intimate talks, walking along the water's edge hand in hand. General thoughtfulness ranks high with these moon children.

The Cancer brother is going to take his time before getting knee-deep in a relationship. This brother doesn't take rejection well, so he must be slow in his approach to the courtship. He wants to be assured that you won't break his face with a resounding "No!" And trying to force the issue by constantly calling him and interrogating him about his whereabouts will only alienate the brother forever.

A Cancer brother commented that a pet peeve of his is a woman who calls constantly. "If a person is so jealous or sprung that they call me over and over all times of day and night for nothing, that's the quickest sign for me to never call her again." The brother's feeling was this woman didn't have a real life and her main priority in life was calling him. So if you're sprung on this brother before he makes a move on you, well, you need to head for recovery road because nine times out of ten he isn't planning a long liaison with you.

The Cancer brother is very complex. He'll have you laughing hysterically one minute and in a deep funk the next over something that a relative or coworker said that he can't put behind him. For example, a Cancer brother may call you with a lilt in his voice to tell you he is on his way to pick you up for dinner. But by the time he arrives, he's sullen, quiet, and angry. Why? Because someone called him on his cell phone to borrow money or ask a favor. Now the mood is spoiled. Let him work through it. Don't try to coax him out of it.

On the other hand, Cancer men can laugh at themselves. For example, a Cancer brother related the story of how he fell out of a boat while he, his son, and his brother were fishing. He panicked, started waving his arms and pleading for help. "I thought I was drowning, but then I realized my feet could touch the bottom and my head was above water and the killing part was that I was yelling louder than my son."

The Cancer man is very affectionate. He will shower you with love, affection, and gifts. He believes that nothing is too good for "his" woman. If pampering, devotion, and emotional passion are what you want, well, start your search and seizure now. But the Cancer brother has very definite ideas about love and what he expects from his companion—not the least of which is devotion. And as one Cancer brother put it, "I like attractive women who are not conceited gold diggers. Appearance attracts me, but what comes out of the mouth and actions keep me."

He's very intuitive. He knows innately when there are problems or emotional distress signals. He's the strong, sensitive type. This moon child will surface in a timely manner with a call or a visit, en-couraging you to discuss your problems. Let him help. He needs to be needed, especially by those he cares for deeply.

For the Cancer brother, infidelity rates right up there with homicide and rape. It destroys their well-being and self-confidence and makes them sullen and vengeful. So if you're dealing with a Cancer on the rebound, this relationship will be a hard nut to crack. Cancers have total recall of any wrongs done to them in their lives and will call up the scene of a former companion being unfaithful again and again. Of course, the past relationship doesn't have any-thing to do with what's happening currently, but they can't forgive and forget.

Cancer brothers are good fathers and husbands and revere home and family life. The Cancer man also has emotional ties to family, es-pecially his mother. You'll be seeing a lot of his mother, so get used to it. When he was a youngster, his mother was the first female he knew and adored, and he'll be looking for those same characteristics in you.

I know you're thinking, "That's all I need—a mama's boy!" But hey, you can tell how a man is going to treat you by observing how he treats his mother. You'll have lots of observation time!

The Cancer Woman

The Cancer sister is the mother and nurturer of the zodiac. This moon child is the one whom everyone comes to for comfort, advice, and friendship. Cancers are the great listeners, and their sense of humor runs the gamut from the ridiculous to the sublime. But the mood can shift very easily for them and they can also bellyache continuously about the wrongs that they feel have continued to plague their situations for decades. Cancer, your family and friends have heard these stories all of their lives. Get over it!!!

The Cancer woman doesn't like a lot of fanfare, but her goal is to know her partner intimately. That includes all of your inner work-ings, whys, wherefores, and whatevers. The point is, although she loves going out to dinner, picnics, and out-of-town trips, those ar-eas are secondary to understanding what you're about and working on an unmistakable closeness in the relationship.

If you're starting to get that claustrophobic feeling, don't over-react—not now anyway. Cancers want an intimacy with you that's not necessarily physical. This sister doesn't want to be left out of any part of your life. The Cancer woman will want you to confide in her and tell her all about your problems. This situation is kind of like the mother asking the child, "Tell me where it hurts" so that she can kiss it and make it better.

Just as it's hard to get out of a relationship with Cancer, it can be even harder getting into one. Cancer sisters, though very sensual once they're in a relationship, are not very aggressive when it comes to the dating game. They prefer subtle, understated approaches to romance. They prefer to meet a potential companion through a mutual friend, on the job, or at church. They're very careful when it comes to love because to a Cancer, falling in love is as essential as breathing. These sisters will definitely proceed with caution.

The Cancer female is a water sign, which means she's highly emotional, intuitive, and compassionate. Both men and women are drawn right to her. She's old-fashioned about love and romance, and plans early on to be married to only one man in her life. She has no trouble attracting men, who probably feel that she needs protecting. Don't let that fool you. This crab is stubborn and has specific ideas of what she wants in a man. And she's not settling for less than what she wants. Kindness, honesty, and integrity are right up at the top of the list with being sane and drug-free.

You know that you're in trouble when the Cancer woman says, "Tell me about yourself." She'll expect to sit for hours listening to scenes from your life, and there's no sense in trying to cram twenty years into twenty minutes because she'll ask you pointed question after pointed question, sending you off on another leg of your life. She'll want to know your parents' names, what they do for a living, whether you get along with your siblings, if you like your job—even if you can cook. And please, all those who perpetrate need to stay away. Cancers can spot a phony a mile away. If you don't mean it, don't say it!

If you're reading this section, you're apparently interested in or looking for a Cancer woman. You may find them on the Internet or through a personal ad. Cancer sisters are traditional types, but sometimes, after kissing many frogs, the moon child will break down and use an off-the-beaten-path means in search of a companion. A Cancer woman who had grown tired of meeting only men who wanted to get physical put this ad in a newspaper: "Conversationalist wanted: Is the artform dead or do you know its mysteries? Divorced Black female in search of single/divorced Black male 35 to 40. Let's talk." Well, it worked. These two talked for hours on everything—the good, the bad, and the ugly.

Cancer women love strong men. They want a man to take charge. With all of the counseling and advice she gives to others, at the end of the day she doesn't want to have to think anymore. That's when her strong man enters. Although she projects this tough-cookie image, the Cancer sister must feel a sense of protection from her companion, much like a child feels when she is wrapped in her mother's arms.

The Cancer sister also wants security and a classy man, not one whose idea of recreation involves sitting on the stoop in front of the liquor store. And don't think for one minute you're going to waltz out of her life as easily as you walked in. It ain't gonna happen. Cancers are like flypaper. If they fall in love with you, you're stuck. You'll be called, poked, prodded, and coaxed about coming back "home."

Female Cancers want security, both physical and financial. A Cancer psychiatrist was dating a mental health counselor, a Libra, but she later decided to marry a dentist because he could provide her with security and all the trappings: a big house with a three-car garage, a summer home, and the like. Nights with the Libra included swinging from the rafters and passion like she'd never had before, but she opted for the security. Go figure!

To your delight, this Cancer woman will sing to you! Not the current stuff, but the old tunes that bring back memories. If there's no music, she will sing or hum while taking the lead on the dance floor, which could be in your den, in her bedroom, in the grass near the lake under the stars. Don't worry—you'll be mesmerized.

But bro, slow it down. True love cannot be rushed. Don't think at this point in the game that you're going to score. In fact, just when you're at fever pitch, letting your erotic imagination run away with you, there won't be any of that, not right off the bat, anyway. What you need to do after the slow dances is chill.

During the home life stage of the relationship or marriage, you'll think you've died and gone to heaven. For Cancer, home is a haven, warm and inviting, and she'll worry you about eating properly, give you a pedicure, and even scratch your dandruff. It's called pampering.

The Cancer sisters love to cook. When they were small children, they would hang around the kitchen and watch Grandmama bake the rolls, cakes, and pies—and beg to help. So all of the wonderful recipes are still in the memory bank. Adding a few inches to the waist is inevitable.

Guide to a Love Connection

Cancer and Aries

Although this couple can't seem to stay away from each other, they have little in common. Aries will spend money. Cancer will hoard it. Cancer sees any companion as a prize possession to be spoiled, pampered, and rarely let out of his sight. Aries is unpredictable, flighty, hot-tempered, and impatient. The spoiling part is okay for a minute because the ram loves attention. But Aries simply won't stand for Cancer's overly jealous outbursts and power surges of emotion. The view from the bedroom is hugs and kisses all the way. They do a lot of kissing and making up because abrasive Aries constantly hurts the tender feelings of Cancer. This relationship is better as a short affair, but certainly not a marriage or live-in arrangement.

Cancer and Taurus

This relationship has great possibilities; these two may grow old together. Cancer is the homemaker and Taurus is the breadwinner. Both are loyal, committed, and accepting of the other's quirks. Cancer is moody, emotional, and insecure, but that's okay with Taurus, the strong, dependable one who thrives when Cancer comes a-calling. Taurus is very possessive, but Cancer is amused by it all. Jealousy is not a question here because they stick and stay with each other constantly. In the sex department, Cancer's passion and creative tricks in bed delight the conventional bull. Although both are sociable, all they really, really want is to enjoy a quiet evening at home with a Do Not Disturb sign on the door.

Cancer and Gemini

If Cancer can get the attention of Gemini, who is in constant mental debate over any move that's made, well, this association may be okay. But that's a big if. Cancer thrives on the domestic scene. Gemini is always on the go and comes home only to sleep and change clothes. Gemini's matter-of-fact approach to romance leaves clinging Cancer an emotional wreck. Cancer thinks Gemini is too flighty and uncommitted on matters of the heart. Gemini loses patience with Cancer's constant whining. Sexually, however, passionate Cancer maintains the attention of distracted Gemini, who loves to try new things in and out of the bedroom. Over the long haul, this relationship goes nowhere.

Cancer and Cancer

Skip the after-dinner brandy and go home early. But if you stay, you'll be looking at yourself in the mirror—probably a magnifying one at that. These two are emotional wrecks and very insecure about how they fit into life in general, not to mention a relationship. Besides, they both can be whiners: she's not appreciated in the workplace, he should've been the one to sing the solo during the pastor's special banquet, and so on. Feelings get hurt very easily with these two. And because they're so much alike with all of their emotional demands and courtship requirements, there's not enough balance for either. Sexually, this is where the relationship thrives. However, the two will have to resurface from the bedroom eventually. The complaints and the put-upon attitude go on and on. Relationships with Cancers can be rewarding, but two crybaby Cancers together can get to be a bit much even for them.

Cancer and Leo

If Cancer is looking for someone to take care of and dote on, Leo is it. Cancers need to feel needed, and this is not a problem with Leo. Leo must make an entrance even if it's a family reunion. This grandiose attitude annoys Cancer, who prefers the background to the spotlight. Leo's extravagant and Cancer is frugal. Cancer, do not

produce a coupon on a dinner date! Both are highly sexed. But Cancer will not appreciate Leo taking over the bedroom and running the
show. Cancer must lead in that area. At least they must think that
they're leading anyway. Cancer's mood swings will annoy Leo, who's
always upbeat and positive and getting ready for the next entrance.
An affair will fizzle like day-old champagne. And marriage? Puleeze!

Cancer and Virgo

Cancer's honest and open personality won't take crabby Virgo
seriously. These two admire the qualities of the other. Both are all
for building a nest egg. Virgo, the analytical one, will be a bit more
systematic and steadfast about financial planning. Virgo is far too
serious all of the time for fun-loving Cancer. Of course, Virgo constantly criticizes and Cancer couldn't care less. Virgo's practical approach to everything will offset the emotional roller coaster of the
crab. Cancer will be grateful for Virgo's conventional and sound
way of approaching most areas. Cancer needs a strong, stable relationship, and Virgo most assuredly fits the bill. Regarding bedroom
matters, Cancer can show slow, methodical Virgo a thing or two.
Let's get it on!

Cancer and Libra

This couple spends many nights together and vows to love each
other forever. But when boudoir antics are over, Cancer is too
moody, insecure, and possessive for free-spirited Libra. Libras are
social butterflies, and they must spread their wings and reach for
the stars. Cancer just wants a quiet evening with a video, wine, and
dinner. The domestic scene is fine as long as no one asks the Libra
to participate. They are far too busy with their social calendar, community projects, and admirers to settle for baking corn bread and
ironing shirts. None of that! A strong physical attraction is evident
between the two, but before you start checking each other out from
across the room, best find out what your astrological signs are!

Cancer and Scorpio

This union, although troubled, sometimes will have these two
going back to each other again and again. Cancer's passions and
emotions run deep, and so do Scorpio's. Although they offer emo-

tional support, tenderness, and sex, sex, and more sex, this union will still need prayer! These two are highly intuitive, and each knows what the other is thinking. Cancer is possessive while Scorpio is jealous, but they are devoted to each other. If Scorpio can stay focused and abandon some of the many projects on his plate to spend more time with Cancer, then it's on! If Cancer discontinues the constant interrogations of Scorpio's whereabouts, then round two is won. If neither can compromise, enjoy the passionate liaison and then throw in the towel.

Cancer and Sagittarius

Cancer's down-home sense of humor and Sagittarius's quick wit will have this pair constantly entertained. They will need a few laughs after they recover from the relationship. At first the relationship will be the bomb because Sag loves the chase. But Cancer's possessiveness and insecurities about the relationship will send optimistic and curious Sag looking for a new playmate. Sexually, though, these two can definitely make sparks fly. Always curious, Sag will appreciate the passion and creativity of the crab in the boudoir. Cancer's sweet potato pie and peach cobbler will have Sag in a quandary, weighing the pros and cons of leaving. Although Sagittarius is a gambler and has more good luck than most, it ain't in the cards, folks.

Cancer and Capricorn

These two are opposites of the zodiac, and you know what that means. They cannot, I repeat, cannot resist each other. If you're a Cancer, you've probably run into lots of Capricorns, and vice versa. The conversation is stimulating, the sex is out of this world, and the two of you laugh a lot together. But calm, controlled Capricorn simply cannot deal with all of Cancer's emotional surges. Both are money-conscious. Capricorn's rigid, no-nonsense personality won't sit well with Cancer's zany outlook on life. So just have the hot-to-trot affair and move on.

Cancer and Aquarius

This relationship will be a real challenge for both parties. Although these two are not opposites on the horoscope, personality clashes and differences make cohabitating impossible. Cancer clings frantically to aloof Aquarius. Aquarius is touched, but must have space in any relationship. Watch out or Aquarius will ride off into the sunset for spiritual rejuvenation. Cancer wants total commit-ment and faithfulness, and that's fine for Aquarius, except that their definitions of love and happiness differ. Moody Cancer wants security, emotional support, and constant companionship. Aquar-ius is basically a loner who needs mental stimulation and support for all her humanitarian projects. The only time these can come to-gether is in the bedroom, and that alone is not enough for either.

Cancer and Pisces

This pairing stays, most of the time, in the throes of passion. They're both water signs, which means emotions and feelings run high. That's okay, though, because these two are on the same level. Cancer takes the lead in money matters and the home. Insecure Pisces loves a strong person like Cancer to make the hard decisions. Both are particularly sensitive to what each needs emotionally, and they provide mental stimulation to each other. Both are homebod-ies. Pisces' key word is confinement, and Cancer's domestic leanings make for a comfortable and cozy home life for these two. Cancer's moodiness is offset by Pisces' creative streak and ability to produce the romantic settings that they both seek. This relationship will thrive, and perhaps even blossom from a blissful affair into a long-lasting marriage.

ROMANCE AND THE CANCER

Whenever you consider romancing the Cancerian, you must con-sider the full treatment. Cancers want the total scenario—full moon, waves washing up on the shore, long walks, and intimate talks without the pressure of sexual matters forever looming. The topic of sex will forever come up. That's a given. But for Cancer, the aforementioned is exclusive of the sex itself. Foreplay for Cancer is a true form of romance. Lovemaking begins long before these water signs reach the boudoir. Cancers want foreplay, foreplay, and more foreplay. These crabs are the true romantics of the zodiac.

They definitely have a photographic memory about everything, especially romance. Both men and women have total recall of every scene of true love and ecstacy that they've experienced. The Cancer sister gets off on a true love story. She will sit alone at a movie, watching undying declarations of love as she runs out of her tear-soaked tissues. In other words, Cancers wrote the book on romance.

And you, Ms. Cancer, are not going to settle for less than the full treatment: moonlight, music, dancing cheek to cheek, walks by the lake as you soak up his every word. If any of the details are overlooked, the crab will sulk and retreat to her shell. You'll have to coax her out again, and that may take a while.

One thing the Cancer sister will never allow is the bim-bam, thank you, ma'am treatment. But once she finds the love of her life, her companion will definitely get the royal treatment, including the all-day-in-the-kitchen meals of chicken, dressing, greens, peach cobbler, and sweet potato pie and after-dinner treats like a full back rub, bubble bath, and serenade. What's not to like here? The brother will love it. But the insecure nature of Cancers won't allow them to believe that they have the power to reel in that all-important catch. A Cancer woman needs constant reassurance; this can be a bit wearing and get on her companion's nerves.

The Cancer brother, on the other hand, provides that constant reassurance readily to his mate, even if she doesn't require it. He also needs support and reassurance, but he isn't as vocal about it as the Cancer sister. This brother will cook for you, clean up the kitchen, and feed you grapes all in one night.

One of the things that turns off a Cancer woman is when you ask to borrow money. Don't even try it. Unlike Taureans, Cancers are not obsessed by money, but they do like to know where their next meal is coming from. They don't want to have to worry if the utility bill is going to be paid or the eviction notice is in the mailbox.

As one Cancer woman said, in addition to trust and love, which are the most important things in any relationship, a good financial portfolio is also significant. "I want to live my fairy tale in a comfortable fashion, and good financials make it so much easier."

On a date with a Cancer brother, leave those nose rings at home, because the Cancer man won't be able to take his eyes off them. Hair weaves are okay as long as they're not past your waistline and somewhat believable. But if the weave is so long you look like you're going to a Halloween party, well, need I say more? Hair colored blond or light brown is acceptable, but the Dennis Rodman look with matching fingernail polish is out. As for light-colored contacts, moderation is the key just so long as you don't look like you're starring in *Children of the Damned*.

Both the men and the women love to be outdoors during a full moon, their ruling planet. In fact, Cancers have a hard time taking their eyes off of it. Walking along a lake, listening to golden oldies, drinking a little wine, and engaging in stimulating conversation is all that they need. It's called a cheap date.

For Cancers, intimate talks, remembering a birthday, and calling just to say he's thinking of you or he loves you will substitute just as well if money is low. It doesn't take a lavish outlay of material things or expensive trips to get the attention of the crab.

One Cancer brother, a machine operator, said his idea of a romantic date is a quiet place with soft lights, fruit and wine, and mellow music like Maxwell or Kenny G. Feeding each other the fruit and taking the time to seriously get into each other. No sex. Ladies, are you impressed?

Spending quality time with a Cancer is 75 percent of the courtship. They want you there, in da house, present and accounted for. So leave the excuses—"I lost my keys, I had to work late, the dog died"—to yourself.

Their idea of romance is outings that take time to plan and execute. One of the biggest turnoffs for crabs is if *they* have to tell *you* to send flowers or call. And don't dare put money in a birthday card that you picked up in a rush at the store while looking at prime cuts of beef. The Cancer woman will know that no thought was put into the purchasing of the card. She will definitely ask about where you purchased it. And once you say, "The grocery store," the conversation will go like this: "You only think of me when you're around food because I'm always cookin' for your ass!" You'll be in the doghouse for weeks and all you'll get to eat will be Gaines Burgers. Don't try to defend yourself. Simply take your medicine and do better next time!

In order to redeem yourself with the Cancer, you must apologize profusely. The Cancer sister may even require you to write one hundred times, "I will be more romantic and I will put more thought into the relationship." Just kidding! But the Cancer will take pride in making you feel miserable. She knows how to push all of the "How could you do this to me?" buttons.

If you're married to a Cancerian woman, you can start by calling her at work, arranging for a baby-sitter, and taking her out to dinner. She's usually the one who has to arrange for all of the household details. And begin by doing something different every week or so. A Cancer loves surprises, especially those coming from his honey.

The Cancer man, like most men, loves sexual encounters. With him, sexual encounters away from the usual places, like his pad or yours, will get his fire burning, but good. Cancer men also love frilly nighties and sexy underwear. For once, don't wear the flannel nightgown and leave off the pink curlers and satin cap. If sexy lingerie isn't your usual getup, he'll probably be more than suspicious and question your motives. But he'll definitely appreciate your efforts.

SEX, SEX, AND MORE SEX

GETTING THE GROOVE ON . . .

Guys, you must learn how to kiss. I cannot stress this enough. I don't mean mouth open like you're a shark with accompanying saliva. That's definitely a turnoff. But if you don't know, you better ask somebody! Seriously, there is nothing more devastating to Cancers than for their potential or current mate not to have ever mastered the fine art of kissing. I'm talking about deep soul kissing. This doesn't mean the feeling you get from a dog licking your face, or sucking your face for that matter. Kissing for Cancers is a lot like having sexual intercourse. There's got to be a groove to it. Consequently, if the setting is perfect, with mellow music, candles, champagne, a fire, and all that jazz, but you don't know the proper maneuvers when it comes to kissing, you need to turn in early. Intimate talks, thoughtfulness, and consideration are important to Cancers, but kissing is the most important for getting the groove on. Knowing how to dance and groove a little without stepping on toes or stumbling over shoes also wins cool points. This is all a part of what was described earlier as foreplay. And to the Cancer woman or man, it's so important to learn the art of kissing that you must invest the time and energy. Otherwise, let me tell you, you will be talked about—bad!!! At every happy hour, every bachelorette party, and every casual gathering. And I know you don't want that scenario, right?

With a man of the sign, it's a little less intimidating if he's offering instructions on the art of kissing to his female companion. This is why there's a plea from Cancer women for you males to be schooled or get a book on the subject. Whatever it takes.

First of all, for Cancer, entertaining the thought of heading toward the bedroom means several things. The foreplay begins long before you lie down on the Sealy Posturepedic. For a Cancer, everything has to be right with the goings-on all day. She's got to be in the right mood. And she's got her own quirks about bedroom etiquette. First and foremost, the manuevers must be moves that she approves of, and you must have the green light. As one Cancer woman commented, "I don't like to be pawed. I hate for someone to touch my body before I give them permission. The chemistry must be right."

Hopefully, you won't have pissed off the Cancer brother before the big doing begins. And hopefully, some outside influences haven't caused him any undue stress and strain. If you observe a mood shift, it's best not to talk and ask a lot of questions. Silence is golden, you know.

For Cancers, this erotic exercise means acting on the situation, not analyzing it. You need to be involved in the moment with a Cancer. The moment involves compliments, light kisses, deep sexual kisses, slow dancing, and a titillating air of what's to come.

The Cancer man doesn't want to have to think about what's in store for him. He doesn't want to be told. He simply wants to experience what is happening. He's got enough neurotic leanings, insecurities, and the like. Of course, this brother is kick-ass when it comes to his abilities, both mental and physical. Actually, it's pretty awesome—but try to convince him of that!

For Cancer women, disrobing is the last and final approach to the erotic and sensual night you're hoping for. Although a Cancer woman is somewhat shy when it comes to making the first move or initiating new ones, her performance in bed will depend a lot on her partner. Basically, this sister will mirror whatever her partner is doing. If the partner is a considerate, artful lover, she will be, too. If he's quick and abrupt, he will be met with the same behavior. So if you expect to get the full monty, you've got be willing to give.

Okay, guys, when it's time to snuggle and get up close and personal, make sure you have lotion, Vaseline, or Keri deep-moisturizing lotion on your hands, feet, and elbows. Even though you may feel that this approach is not masculine, Cancers love to snuggle, and they don't want abrasions and scratches on their bodies. Posing in sexy underwear or thong bikini panties (hopefully, the thong is not swallowed up by the enormity of the booty) is a turn-on for the Cancer brother, along with high heels, not to be used for spikes to the back of the body, of course.

Just as the physical appearance of Cancer people runs the gamut, so do their sexual preferences. Cancers enjoy oral sex, a little role playing, masturbation, and watching porno movies, too. But many stick to the tried and true. As one Cancer woman commented about all this sex stuff: "I prefer man-on-top, penis-in-vagina sex, the traditional way. I'm not interested in eating or beating or anyone eating me, thank you."

With the women of the sign, avoid the 69 position. These women don't relish the thought of having their butts in the air so their companions can get a faceful. They are much too inhibited for that. Instead of getting involved in the pleasure of it all, this Cancer sister will be preoccupied with the fact that her companion cannot see around her butt and how big he thinks it is. You know that the burden of the big butt is ever-looming for the black woman. Doggy style is acceptable. Any position where the Cancer woman does not have a lot of eye contact is best for her because penetrating eyes and probing looks can sometimes unnerve her. Cancer women are somewhat shy. They definitely enjoy sex and are some of the most creative creatures in bed. They can hang in there with the best of them. But the initial sexual encounter may be a bit shaky and embarrassing for this moon child.

As for the Cancer man, anywhere, anytime, anyplace is usually his motto. He loves to have spontaneous sex. Sex outside the bedroom delights him. But his only requirement in the boudoir is to allow him to lead. At least allow him to *think* he's leading. He's the traditional brother, who will not be accepting of surprises in the bedroom, especially confessions like "I'm really a man dressed as a woman" or "I'm gay."

Cancer women are strong but sensitive about the feelings and the emotions in a relationship. In their heart of hearts, these moon children simply want to be left alone to explore, savor their own erotic experience, and not be intruded upon by the partner.

One Cancer woman created an island inside her home during a groove that wouldn't quit. "A rainy, cloudy Saturday morning, between 4 A.M. and 6 A.M., where my mate awakens me with kisses and teasing. No sex, just kissing all day long. The bed acts as our island all day, and we leave it only to go to the bathroom or to replenish drinks and food."

EROGENOUS ZONES . . . SOME PHYSICAL, SOME NOT

While you're enjoying the emotional and passionate night of your life, here are a few tips for enhancements. Once Cancerians feel completely safe in the relationship, they will throw caution to the wind and anything goes in the boudoir. They will trust you completely, and surrender completely, too.

Cancers love to have their nipples, breasts, and chest caressed and kissed all during the sex act. Any light touches to the chest area, along with those bona fide Cancerian-trained kisses, will drive the cool, calm crab wild. The stroke should be tender but deliberate. "Don't touch me like you're waxing your car," one Cancer woman said.

Soft whispering in the ear is also a serious turn-on. It doesn't have to be an all-out confession of love, but a sigh, a moan, a few words about the wonderfulness of the body are titillating for these crabs.

Standing together nude without penetration is also a favorite position with Cancers. Cuddling, touching, and tender caresses get high marks too. Long bubble baths, candles, and mellow music set the stage for the performance of a lifetime, along with intimate talks. If the full moon is suspended in the air that night, watch out! There will definitely be some barking at the moon, and I don't mean Rover, either.

They will not want you to do a lot of talking—just "Baby, does it feel good?" and "Where do you want it?" A lot of fanfare and drama is not needed or appreciated. The unspoken word is much more erotic to them. A bunch of noise, or "jaw jacking," as one Cancer said, is simply not needed. The mindless, emotional outercourse encounter intrigues the crab. For Cancerians, sometimes the actual sexual encounter is anticlimatic. They are definitely more interested in the buildup and the anticipation of the encounter . . . and acknowledgment of how special the night is going to be. Cancers want to go for it. These moon children don't want a narration about what's to come. Don't say it, just do it!

Cancerians will want to stare into your eyes for hours, searching your soul and all that they can find in your inner workings. But when the love connection kicks off in the bedroom, the all-important eye contact early on will be forgotten. When the intimacy or intercourse begins, that's when Cancerians retreat into their most intimate selves.

PLAIN OL' SEX AND NOTHING MORE: WELCOME TO THE FREAK SHOW

Getting the Cancer involved in a freak-show performance is going to be akin to pulling teeth. Cancers are traditional lovers from the old school.

Now, they will definitely have sex for sex's sake. They may be looking for someone for a more serious relationship. Although shy, Cancers have their needs, too. If the situation is presented as just that, sex and only sex, well, the Cancer may take you up on it. It will depend entirely on their mood. Although Cancers are not prone to accept the bim-bam experience, they may consent to the kind of encounter that renders satisfaction only between the sheets. A warning here, though: Although all of the ground rules may have been laid earlier, Cancers may decide that they want more. That's when you have a problem.

One way to keep them coming back again and again is to make it memorable—not scary, but memorable. The scary stuff can come later, after you gain her trust. To gain her trust, don't kiss and tell. When the sex is so good, you feel like you must run and tell someone, but be prudent. If you want a command performance, take heed of these words. If the Cancerian finds himself or herself in the throes of passion, there's no telling what may happen.

One approach is to be straightforward: "One of my fantasies is to have you as a sexual partner, but I never thought I'd have the nerve to ask. No strings attached, will you consider it?"

MONEY MATTERS

"Hold on to a dollar until it hollers" is a familiar saying, especially with Cancers.

Cancers are insecure regarding many areas of their lives. When the money equation is also calculated in the mix, then they've got problems that they don't need and try to avoid. Consequently, saving money, working hard, and investing wisely are areas that the crab is all too familiar with. Not having enough money is one of the most unsettling concerns that Cancers can face.

If the Cancerian sister is a housewife, she will buy products wholesale and visit the produce market regularly. Eating out for her family may include the church banquet once a year or the annual meal at a restaurant to celebrate a birthday—but certainly nothing on a regular basis.

The Cancer man is similar in that he loves to spend money on his lady love, but he has a photographic memory about most things. And he can readily recall what money is available. So if he's looking at fine jewelry and the money is low, he'll decide that a nice ring or bangle from the pawnshop and a jar of jewelry cleaner will do nicely.

Family is important to Cancers. And when any areas in the lives of family and friends are in question, then you've got an emotional roller coaster for the Cancer that won't stop unless the whole problem is derailed and shut down. What affects their family and friends affects Cancers as well. Although Cancers will definitely save for a rainy day, many times they will put the needs of others ahead of their own. And underneath it all, they really don't feel that they deserve all the lavish trappings that others feel are their right.

So the rainy-day fund becomes partial payment for Uncle John's funeral; or a wedding dress for a cousin who *had* to get married; or tuition for a nephew when his sister ran short.

One problem with Cancers is that they have no problem saving or investing for the children's education, but they will let the world know, and friends and family will take advantage of the situation. Anyone who has a sob story will have a sympathetic ear from the moon child and a generous purse or wallet to tap into.

When the nest egg is running low after the crab has helped all those in need, his own security is threatened. Cancers can become moody when they need help and don't get it. But they constantly feel that they have to come to the aid of everyone else. Actually, Cancers are much more comfortable giving than receiving. That's the problem: family and friends come to expect it.

Cancers won't have any problems wearing clothing from Walmart, Kmart, or any other mart. With intuitive powers that draw them to the sales and the bargains, they know how to stretch a dollar. But no matter how desperate the situation gets, Cancer usually has a stash somewhere.

Pampering Tips for Cancer

- ❋ Picking up the children and allowing your moon child to hang out will take some needed stress off her shoulders and have you gentle on her mind.
- ❋ Plan a simple but romantic meal at your place and include his favorite drink, music, and pastime. You may not get through the entire meal!
- ❋ Start with a love note in her car, followed by an invitation to join you in the Jacuzzi at a hotel, and, of course, room service. And don't take no for an answer!
- ❋ A full body massage, along with hot oils, candles, and good music, and you are in business.
- ❋ Have his pager, cell phone, and telephone service temporarily turned off. Of course, notify family members as to your

plans. Then take him prisoner. Dancing close, whispering sweet nothings, and enjoying an uninterrupted two or three hours will work wonders.

✤ A complete makeover would definitely work if you can convince your moon child that you like his original look as well, but that this is your way of giving some well-deserved pampering.

✤ Have a manicurist and a hairstylist make a home visit to your Cancerian. Your moon child will be eternally grateful.

✤ A long, unplanned drive up the highway to enjoy the countryside will help your Cancer relax. Then stop at a roadside inn and get busy!

✤ The practical Cancer looks for pampering in practical ways such as cutting the grass, taking out the trash, or going grocery shopping.

✤ Breakfast in bed on a not-so-special Saturday or Sunday is always a winner for both the men and the women. The two of you will play for the rest of the day.

Gift Ideas for Cancer

✤ Cancers revere the home. Gifts like framed pictures, lamps, or cookware are ideal gifts for these homebodies.

✤ Expensive gifts are not required, but putting time into buying them is. Write her a poem and have it framed; an engraved flask or bracelet will delight your moon child.

✤ Try sending your Cancer companion a birthday card every day for a week leading up to his birthday. Then personally deliver a card on the birth date, along with any other surprises. Your Cancer will appreciate your thoughtfulness.

✤ A framed collage of pictures chronicling the courtship will have your Cancer giddy, grateful, nostalgic, and ready for love!

✤ Both the men and women love to receive flowers, especially roses.

✤ Singing telegrams are great for a laugh. Cancers have a great sense of humor. But don't send a stripper to the workplace.

✳ Books, including cookbooks or books on tape, are a welcome gift for your Cancer, who likes nothing better than curling up with a good story.

✳ A Bible with your Cancer's name on it will be appreciated.

✳ Try giving your Cancer a gift he would never buy for himself—like an expensive pair of engraved cuff links or a silver chalice.

✳ Regarding gifts, the main point is, if you have no money, you need to show up and acknowledge the special day. If you don't, you'll live to regret it.

Leo

(July 23 to August 22)
SYMBOL: THE LION

Positive love traits: Conventional, traditional lover; dramatic and overly enthusiastic about love.

Negative love traits: Selfish in bed, not prone to much foreplay; an aggressive, domineering lover whose ego requires constant stroking.

Ruling planet: The sun is associated with vitality and authority.

Word to the wise: Don't bring a two-for-one coupon on the first date. A date with a Leo is no time to cut corners.

Leos have a definite presence, partly because of their overall demeanor of self-assurance and partly because they plan it that way. Leos have an innate addiction to the spotlight, being out front, running the show, or being the show. When you first meet the Leo, you'll be impressed. But what you're witnessing is a representation of contradictions. Although the Leo brother may wink and come over and ask for a dance, don't assume that there's a budding relationship: He simply must have some attention. Plus, he'll expect you to compliment his dance techniques and his duds. A Leo woman will rant and rave but is a tenderhearted person. Leos love to be around hordes of people, but they are self-centered. In short, the signals that these folks dole out will be a mixed bag, but you will continue to be intrigued.

Leos will definitely be in the mix, surrounded by people and would-be suitors. And you'll no doubt conclude that they're not only the life of the party, but the party itself. Actually, they feel like there's no party unless they are in da house. They will have to make some sort of grand entrance, even if it's at a bowling alley.

Leos enjoy outdoor events, movies, picnics, plays, or nightclubs. The bomb for them is to enter a room dressed to kill and have all eyes on them. For just such a moment they will spend weeks searching for that killer outfit, the shoes, the hairstyle, and all of the accessories. In short, Leos live for that adoring attention, for accolades real and imagined.

For the most part, these fire signs are more interested in the idea of being in love than love for love's sake. Both the men and the women have a tendency to fall head over heels in love at the drop of a hat—with you, with your cousin, or even with the next-door neighbor. When a Leo falls in love, the whole world knows.

But they can fall out of love just as quickly or dramatically. Their idealistic concept of a relationship sometimes overshadows the realities. When his companion shows behavior such as burping or, heaven forbid, passing gas in public, the flames can die just as quickly as the fire was ignited.

The ruling planet of Leo is the sun, which is associated with vitality and authority. The sun is essential for the earth's survival. Very few life-forms can survive without its illumination. This is the attitude of the Leo. Yes, they believe, without question, that they are all that and a bag of chips. And believing it is more than half the battle. Leos strive to reign supreme, and if you're interested in a Leo, hopefully, you'll be one of their favorite subjects.

The symbol of Leo is the lion, which is brave and dominating, possessing a regal air. And yes, with Leos, you'll become one of their subjects. Leos are fire signs. Like the element of fire, Leos are unpredictable, feisty, aggressive, impulsive, and hard to control. Basically, the Leo will feel that most things should be the way that he sees them. And because these lions are so headstrong, it's going to be their way or the highway. Make no mistake about it, Leos will definitely run your life if you let them. They will give you unsolicited advice because they believe that they can run your life better than you can.

Most Leos have thick hair. Even if it's thin, it's usually long. Their eyes are very direct and intense. Their mouths are usually wide, with big, full lips. Their bodies are well proportioned, neither top-heavy nor bottom-heavy. And they're usually slim.

As a rule, a little "jungle fever" will always be part of the itinerary with Leos. Skin color is not a big issue because they are also pretty open to relationships with other ethnic groups—Latinos, Iranians, Indians, or any other race, for that matter.

They definitely know how to create the image of class with very little money. By the way, melodrama is their middle name. Leos will have a different kind of soap for the face, the body, the hair, and the feet. Retailers love to see the Leo coming. Both the men and women of the sign love to jump sharp in all of their finery. And if you're dealing with a Leo companion, you need to pour on the compliments. They soak them up like a sponge. Even lie if you must! But keep your fingers crossed.

The attention getters of the zodiac truly believe that your life would be completely boring if there were no Leo in it. You see, the sun comes out to shine on them.

The Leo Man

Getting to know the Leo brother will be a snap. He's upbeat, optimistic, and always full of fun. He thrives on attention, and you'll find him wherever the action is or wherever he can be the center of attention: on the dance floor, surrounded by people discussing current events, or giving orders as the supervisor or head of a company.

Many women feel that a Leo man can't be faithful to one woman. He can, but somewhere in the back of his mind he feels that his "wonderfulness" should be spread around to other females who are lonely and could benefit from his expertise in love and romance.

Even if you're not interested in a Leo (you'll be hard-pressed to convince him of that), his friendly and outgoing personality is just what you need when you're crying the blues over some dude. Leo's upbeat mood and over-the-top humor will coax you right out of your blue funk in a matter of minutes.

Once you're designated "his" woman, you'll be expected to conduct yourself accordingly. Your role as his companion will be to wait on him, cajole him, flatter him, and give him the attention he craves. I know this directive may sound a little one-sided, but he's a very generous, caring, and loving person and you'll be rewarded handsomely for your efforts.

For example, a Capricorn woman began a long-distance relationship with a Leo brother from Arkansas, a dental student in the military. The Leo was very supportive when she was experiencing trouble on her job. He'd call frequently from Asia, where he was stationed. But when talk of possibly living together and marriage came up, Mr. Leo started laying down the law. "Since I will be making most of the money, I should have the most say-so," he declared. He later mentioned that his friends would be coming over frequently to play cards and women would be among them. After Ms. Cap announced she would participate, too, Leo seemed surprised. "I didn't know you liked to play cards" was his comment. Duh?!

Leo brothers are very jealous. When you're with this brother, it's best that you not look around, period. They expect and want your undivided attention. If you're caught looking, there had better be a good explanation. An Aries woman in a relationship with a Leo brother relates this story. "My man is quiet and keeps his feelings inside, but when he makes a comment, I listen. This guy, whom I worked with, made me a card to show that he was interested in me. I told my boyfriend about it. But when I started wearing more upscale clothes to work instead of blue jeans, he thought that it was because of my male coworker." It just so happened that the Leo didn't know that the company had instituted a dress code policy. The Leo brother commented, "Do I have to come to the job and make my presence known?"

If you're in a relationship with a Leo man and you're getting compliments from other men, he will definitely ask, "Do I compliment you enough?" The Leo man never wants to be outdone, even if it's something as minor as a compliment. One Leo recounts one of the most embarrassing situations he could recall: "My mother walked in on my girlfriend and me wrestling and I was losing. I told my mother that I was letting her win," he said.

Although a Leo man is very conscious of his image and of not appearing weak, he's vulnerable and needs his companion's support and reassurance. Of course, he'll never admit this in a million years.

If you're thinking about becoming involved with a Leo brother, it's going to be first-class all the way—well, in theory, anyway. He's definitely not the type to be stingy or cut corners on a date. But as a Leo computer specialist put it, "Assuming I will pay simply because you are a woman is a big turnoff." The Leo brother loves creating glitz and glamour in his life. He loves to show off. Therefore, any relationship with a Leo is going to be fun, frolic, and definitely high drama.

These lions love the element of surprise and hate being bored, so you might be whisked off after work or during spring break to a secluded, out-of-the-way cabin, served breakfast in bed, pampered and catered to until your head is spinning. A Leo plans for his companion to have fond memories of him before, during, and after the affair is over. Wait a minute, you're thinking—"after the affair is over"? Well, while the relationship is in full swing, Mr. Leo is all-attentive, and he wants that same attention and then some from you. But sometimes for Leo, the *idea* of the passion-laden affair is more appealing than what's going on in the real world. His imagination far exceeds the realities of the relationship. When annoyances occur, like snoring, slurping your drink, talking too loudly, or other behavior that he perceives as unbecoming, then the liaison can fizzle like the champagne the two of you shared the night before.

The Leo brother will have his own gallery of adoring females, laughing at his jokes and enterprising spirit and noting this cutie pie's overall good looks. Everybody loves a Leo. A Leo brother from Tennessee regularly visits older women who are widowed, single, or divorced to help with handyman-type chores like shoveling snow, to play chauffeur, or simply to talk. Of course, the women love it and he could have his pick of the ladies, but that's not his motivation. It's his generous spirit that drives him to do these things.

This brother prides himself on looking good at all times. Even if he's simply dashing out to the store, he makes sure that he's well groomed. And if you're planning to get with a Leo brother, you need to make sure you're well groomed, too.

Leo men want to be seen with a beautiful woman on their arm. But this is not an absolute requirement. What a woman has to work with, what physical features she possesses, is also noteworthy for the Leo. Enhancements like hair weaves or extensions don't turn him off. Actually, he's impressed that you have gone that extra step to look good. "Five percent of people are beautiful, five percent are unattractive," says one Leo. "The rest of us use our intellect to project what we've got in the best possible light." And with Leo, he definitely knows how to accentuate the positive.

Leo men love smart, enterprising women. Yes, looking good is one thing, but having something to say, having ambition and goals, are also essential. Being Leo's woman as a profession might work for a minute, but you need to have a life apart from what's going on with this lion. Besides, your demeanor, attitude, savvy, and intelligence are a reflection on him, so he wants someone who's all that and then some.

The Leo Woman

When you first meet this woman, you notice that all eyes are on her because of her dazzling outfit and accessories, right down to her toe ring. She will smile and may even flirt a bit, but don't be misled by what's going on. Actually, this is a test, and if you fail to notice the painstakingly meticulous preparations she's made for her public, she won't have any time for you.

She's overly dignified and sedate—what some of you might call "sedidy." But in all honesty, this sister is a genuinely warm and generous person to all who can hang around long enough to get past the facade.

The Leo sister is a fire sign, which means she's feisty, aggressive, unpredictable, impulsive, and hard to control. There won't be any control freaks hanging around this opinionated and strong-willed sister. She ain't having it! Besides, her opinions and philosophies about how she is going to live her life and what is going to happen in it were set as early as junior high school. So there aren't going to be any drastic changes now.

For example, a Leo woman fooled her companion into believing that she had gotten a strawberry tattoo on her ankle. Actually, the tattoo was a temporary one. Previously, her boyfriend, who had accepted his calling to the ministry, had expressed his disdain for tattoos. After he saw the tattoo on his girlfriend's ankle, he got so upset that his brother called to find out from Ms. Leo what had happened. The point is, Ms. Leo makes her own decisions.

Her emotions and passions run hot and cold. Her demeanor will keep you guessing and wondering what this lioness is up to next. She may scold you about bringing her to a less than fancy restaurant and then turn around and pay for the meal, and order wine to boot. Her personality and movements are motivated by how she can garner support and attention from her admirers.

Before you attempt to talk to Ms. Leo, I advise you to shine your shoes. If you don't, you may get a nice pair of Italian shoes for your Christmas present.

Self-love is the refrain for Leo's expectations and how you as a mate are supposed to function. Public displays of affection and calling to say I love you rate high with the Leo woman. There's that attention thing again!

Leo women love to be spoiled and pampered, but catering to her every whim won't work either. Wussies need not apply because she will only be bored to tears and you definitely won't be respected in the morning. Take the Libra husband who catered to his Leo wife's every need. He cooked and cleaned the entire six years that they were married. She cooked one meal. Where is he now? He's history. Leo women are too independent to be spoon-fed; they must get out and meet and greet and enjoy life.

Fidelity is also a major concern with the Leo. Leo sisters want your undivided attention. If the roving eye is too obvious and the rendezvous too open, Leo will be in the wind as quick as she entered your life. As a 43-year-old Leo sister commented, "I'm at a time in my life when I am too old for games and diseases."

If you're playing the Mr. Slick or the Mr. All That role, you can save your act for some other lucky person. The Leo woman is not interested. She also doesn't want the pretty-boy type because the Leo sister is the only person who will be taking over or staying in the mirror.

Although the idea of love sometimes overshadows any real notions of a long-lasting relationship, the Leo woman is loyal. That loyalty will only go so far after a while, however. For example, a Leo library assistant had been trying to get her Libra man to commit. They had been dating for about two years. He was quiet, but would never make a positive commitment toward a long-lasting relationship. Although it hurt, she ended the relationship. "I broke up with my Libra love. It has been really hard without him, but I'm working on my happiness and self-love," she said.

If you're invited to her house, you're in like Flynn. The Leo sister loves to entertain. She knows how to lay out the table settings with the fine china and crystal. Leos learn very early about the finer things of life, even if they can't afford them, initially.

All attention should be on your Leo woman; she demands and expects it because all of her attention is on you. Recounts one Leo: "When my boyfriend and I were in Paris, the most romantic city in the world, he asked me what souvenir he should get his ex-girlfriend. Although it didn't ruin Paris for me, it put a damper on the day!"

If you happen to be married to a Leo, you must demonstrate leadership ability and a strong sense of who you are and what you're about. And most important, stand your ground. If not, the Leo will run right over you and you'll be left carrying her bags or drawing her bath—the menial jobs of life.

Children are also very important to Leos. Even if they don't have children of their own, kids from the neighborhood will gravitate to them. Lionesses love to play the big-sister role. If the Leo woman has children, she'll be the neighborhood mom, and the kids will all come to her house for social gatherings.

If you have a Leo wife, everything will have to be just so in household furnishings, clothing, and most material things. I would also suggest separate bank accounts. That way, you'll be able to separate the household budget account from her expense account. And she will have one whether you like it or not, so get over it.

What the Leo woman seeks is a strong take-charge kind of guy who knows where he is going and will shoot for the stars. She wants to be the copilot in a role to enhance her life and his simultaneously. She definitely won't take a backseat to a man's career and life.

The Leo sister is intelligent, witty, strong, and aggressive, but at the same time ultrafeminine. Trying to harness and control this free spirit would be a disaster. A Leo college student was given an engagement ring by her Scorpio boyfriend during her sophomore year. At first Ms. Leo was elated over the ring and the idea of being engaged, but over time, she was turned off by the controlling and possessive nature of the Scorpio. She simply bided her time, and when she moved to another city to attend law school, she ended the engagement. "I barely got out alive," she said.

GUIDE TO A LOVE CONNECTION

Leo and Aries

These two infernos know how to get it on, whether it's a fight, the sex thing, or simply facing life head-on. Look out, world, here they come! And that's fine as long as they don't turn on each other. Both are born leaders and feel that they must rule. We know, but someone has to be a little bit more compromising in the relationship. Both are energetic and feisty. Leo must have the required attention, and that's fine with Aries, but this Ram may not be the one to give it. Aries people won't hang around long enough. Leos want lavish surroundings and killer outfits every day of the year. Aries has no interest in image. The ram may put on anything that fits. This annoys Leo, whose social calendar continues to bulge. But if the minor details can be tolerated, this is a good match all around.

Leo and Taurus

Yes, these two are definitely sexually drawn to each other. But what's working here is two blockheads who want things their way. Leo will take the leadership role and expect Taurus to bow down and be grateful. Taurus ain't having it. Both are strong-willed and stubborn. Leo loves a lavish lifestyle. Frugal Taurus cannot understand why a suit for Leo costs $300. For Taurus, that's enough for three suits. Leo is in the mix and Taurus is in the home. For these two, the sexual encounter creates a false sense that this relationship is going somewhere. The two of you need to understand that, over the long term, it ain't happening, not in this millennium!

Leo and Gemini

We've got air and fire going here. Airy Gemini will fan the flames of fiery Leo. These two will get along very well. Leo has to be dressed to kill and so does Gemini. Even when they go to the store, the all-important image thing is present. Both create the social scene that neither can beat. It's on!! Of course, Leo should be worshiped and Gemini's attitude is, what for?!! These two can really get it on without even thinking about it for the spontaneity and the pleasure. Sexually, Leo orchestrates the program to a lackluster attitude by Gemini. Gemini simply wants to be in the mix. The attitude is who cares. But Leo will create drama and intrigue, which is okay with Gemini.

Leo and Cancer

This union will require a little overtime if it's expected to work. Leo tries to be patient with the Cancer's insecurities. But patience wears thin. Cancer's moodiness and put-upon attitude send attention-loving Leo into orbit. Once Leos set their sights on a person and declare their love, that's it. They simply expect the companion to rise to the occasion—to be attentive, forthright, and a step-right-up kind of person. Instead, Cancer dwells in the depths of despair, not believing Leo could love the crab, constantly questioning the other's devotion and putting a strain on the relationship. Fun-loving Leo does not have time to be depressed or in despair. See ya!

Leo and Leo

If these two cohabitate, who's going to balance the checkbook and save for a rainy day? Maybe they can hire someone. To survive financially, they'll have to. Leos love a lavish lifestyle. Each will try to outdo the other by buying expensive gifts. And two Leos together spells double trouble. They'll have to be prudent because both revere and enjoy the good life. Two Leos together make for a royal family, but someone has to rule and someone has to be the subject—and you can bet neither plans to be left in the background. As for romance, Leos sometimes love the idea of being in love more than the actual relationship. So in the beginning, love will reign supreme and so will the Leos. The sex will be awesome, but don't let bedroom matters cloud your vision in this relationship. These two headstrong lions will have problems in the long term.

Leo and Virgo

There definitely won't be any love lost between this pair: They are opposites in every way. Leo is the bomb, but Virgo is unimpressed by Leo's pretentiousness and melodramatic attitude. Virgo is too cautious, reserved, and hypercritical for Leo, who wants to sit on the throne being fed grapes by his subjects. Virgo's stay-at-home attitude and lack of compliments to gregarious Leo leave both frustrated. Virgo will create a little eroticism in the boudoir, but has to be coaxed into what she perceives as over-the-top behavior. Leo is simply amazed by prudent Virgo's reluctance. The straw that breaks the camel's back for Virgo is the ease with which Leo runs through a bank account. Virgo finds this wasteful and intolerable. Leo thinks Virgo is a tightwad. That's when it's time for both to go in opposite directions!

Leo and Libra

These two headstrong and aggressive types will occasionally have to give in to the other. Libra is the diplomatic one and Leo is the bossy one. Leo's hot temper can hurt Libra's feelings. But this union can be pretty harmonious. When these two get physical, Leo takes charge and shows why he's the king of the jungle, much to Libra's delight. Both love to travel in all of their finery and regalia, to discuss a wide range of issues and mingle with the in crowd. Both are extravagant and must have the very best. The only problem is, who's going to manage the money? Maybe they can hire someone, provided they listen. This intense affair has serious potential for a good marriage.

Leo and Scorpio

There is a strong physical attraction between these two that's hard to ignore. This relationship is what dreams are made of—at first. Both love stimulating conversation and adventure. But Scorpio wants to totally possess and control, and Leo simply has too many other fish to fry. Not that there's going to be unfaithfulness, but Leo is not going to be controlled by passionate and jealous Scorpio. Leos feel that they are *the one*, with all that that implies—so

Scorpio, get over it because it ain't changing. The sexual harmony between these two has them thinking that the relationship will work. Think again. Scorpio feels rejected because of Leo's insatiable need for the spotlight. And Scorpio's insatiable need for sex will not offset Leo's needs.

Leo and Sagittarius

These two fire signs are made for each other because neither is intimidated by the other. Both are intelligent and love to explore new ideas. Leo is the action person, while Sag is the cheerleader and interpreter of ideas. Leo will try to tell Sag what to do and how to do it. Sag ain't having it, and that's that. Once Leo stops sulking and feeling like Sag's comments are personal insults, these two can really have a kick-ass relationship. When these two bodies meet, the relationship solidifies. Leo will take the lead, of course, but Sag is never the intimidated one. Leo will complain about Sag's lack of style in dressing and Sag will lament over the price the lion is paying for the sake of glamour. This pair could really work.

Leo and Capricorn

This couple keeps each other frustrated, annoyed, and unfulfilled. Leo's enthusiastic passion for life gets on sensible, practical Capricorn's nerves. Leo needs boatloads of adoring fans and lots of attention. The few drops the lion gets from the reserved goat are never enough. Leo loves a lavish lifestyle even if there is no money. Capricorn wants the finer things of life, too, but Capricorn's carefully invested nest egg will not be spent on Leo's frivolities. This will infuriate Leo, who believes he deserves it. To add insult to injury, Leos want melodrama, enhancements, and adoration during sex. Capricorn doesn't understand what the big fuss is about. That does it—Leo is out!

Leo and Aquarius

These opposites of the zodiac can't seem to stay away from each other. But physical attraction alone won't sustain this relationship. Leo must rule, and Aquarius won't stick around long enough to be ruled. Both are intelligent, outgoing types, but Leo absolutely must be the centerpiece of all of the goings-on. That's okay with Aquarius, who's secure enough, but Leo, don't expect this air sign to bow down to you, too. It ain't happening. With bedroom concerns, Leo is more traditional in lovemaking, while Aquarius wants to push the envelope. Leo must be in control, but in the boudoir Aquarius takes the lead and won't give it up. Despite the good conversation and good rapport, Leo broods about Aquarius's indifference; this will drive a big wedge between the two.

Leo and Pisces

Both love a lavish lifestyle and travel. Leo is the domineering one, and Pisces doesn't mind being led or controlled. Leo's outgoing nature means the lion is always in the mix. Pisces is a loner and prefers a quiet, romantic setting at home, complete with candles, incense, and soft music. That's fine with Leo, who loves the attention. The sex is the most noteworthy area of the relationship. Pisces can definitely show Leo a thing or two or three behind closed doors. But Leo is put off by Pisces' nonaggressive behavior and sees Pisces as a wimp or wimpette. Pisces' lack of drive and motivation frustrates Leo, who is less about talking and more about doing. These two need to move on, and quick. This is not going to work, no matter how you look at it.

ROMANCE AND THE LEO

The romantic end of a relationship with a Leo is a no-brainer. Here's how it works. Simply consider all of the elegant, lavish, and romantic things that you'd only think of in your wildest dreams, and romance with the Leo is made in the shade. If you're planning a romantic evening, day, or night with any Leo, you need to put time and creativity into the planning.

Once the plan is executed, make sure all of the details are in place. The Leo pays attention to every minor detail. What you might consider as minor, like your lack of a haircut or hairdo, the Leo will consider a major faux pas. Romance for the Leo includes the full treatment. If you're going out on a date with a Leo, bring a small gift, such as perfume, a fresh rose, or even Godiva chocolates; she'll be impressed. As for Leo men, a book, video game, or trinket involving mental agility ranks high on the chart. Leo men love roses, too. The point is, plan ahead and be creative.

A Leo author recalled one romantic date. "I met this guy at the hotel. When I arrived he had champagne chilled and bubble bath waiting. The deal was sealed. But later in the relationship, he showed his other side, which was frugal, insecure, and kinda lazy when it came to personal ambitions."

The Leo sister wants to be taken to fancy restaurants, symphony concerts, banquets, and other black-tie affairs where she can flex her regal muscles and show off her latest sequined, strapless dress.

The Leo brother has a similar outlook, but he will take the lead and create a date that's fun, memorable, and reeking of class. He knows how to dress appropriately for all occasions, and he'll expect the same from you. If you're going to be the Leo brother's armpiece, I would suggest you go shopping. Don't show up in baggy jeans, a jockey suit, or overalls. He wants his date to look ultrafeminine when he's with her. And by the way, he's definitely not allergic to compliments.

Both the male and female of the sign love elegant, candlelit dinners at restaurants. But if money is low, never fear; they will create a similar ambiance at your place or theirs. Instead of Moët you might be drinking Cook's champagne, but the high drama, music, and low lights will all be a part of the mix. In short, don't plan a cheap date; it's better to wait until you can afford to order a good bottle of wine than to show up with a two-for-one coupon.

On the other hand, one Leo guy, a computer specialist, said that a big turnoff for him is "assuming that I will pay simply because you are a woman." Sisters, are you listening?

Many times Leos will have champagne taste and a beer budget; nevertheless, they will forever reach for the stars. And they will expect you as their companion not be the spoilsport, squelching their dreams with all that practicality. For Leos, there's enough practicality in the world without a mate getting into the act. A Leo law student rented a tiny apartment in Paris for a week for himself and his companion. Of course this was on a strict budget, but leave it to a Leo to make it work. After they arrived, his companion was so excited that she kept dashing from room to room, crying, "I'm in the bathroom in Paris, I'm in the living room in Paris, I'm in the kitchen in Paris!"

Sometimes the simplicity of the evening can be permeated with romantic overtones without even trying. A Leo brother from San Francisco remembers a memorable romantic evening walking across the Golden Gate Bridge. "An evening where we communicate on a soul level and time disappears. It could be walking, talking, exercising, whatever," he said.

A Leo woman explained that one Valentine's Day her Scorpio boyfriend prepared dinner for her in his college dorm room. "He had drawn hearts on the wall and made place mats out of red construction paper. It was the sweetest thing he'd ever done for me."

Another Leo described the best date she ever had. It was at a nightclub that included a swing built for two suspended from the ceiling. "We sat in the club, swinging and talking about everything without any accusations or judgments. I thought that was such a great concept. The swing was like a therapeutic couch," the customer service employee said.

If you plan to run a game on the Leo brother or sister, what you will find is someone you don't know: a raving lunatic. Lying and deceit rate right up there with stealing. If you don't have any money, simply say so, but at least show up for the day or a visit.

Leos love to dance and perform, either singing, writing, reciting poetry, or performing the spoken word. They love being in the mix, but going dancing and enjoying slow drag music are also a turn-on for them. So check on two things: Practice your dance steps; you don't want to be designated Dr. Scholl's, forcing your date to wear footpads after you step on her feet all evening. And check your teeth for leftover broccoli and make that all-important visit to the dentist to have your teeth cleaned!

Another example of a perfect date with overtones of simplicity but charged with romance is a picnic. Taking a Leo on a picnic in a deserted area with champagne, romps in the grass, and intimacy is always a winner. "The most memorable approach to romance was a picnic at the park, under a blue sky," said one Florida woman. "I swear I could hear angels singing!"

Another Leo commented that her idea of a romantic day is a

picnic by a waterfall, with flowers, champagne, and a simple meal prepared by her loved one. "My mate has a beautiful, rich voice, and I love it when he reads me poetry."

Calling to say I love you, public displays of affection, taking trips together, and remembering birthdays all get high marks when you're dealing with a Leo. A Leo brother from Atlanta who traveled frequently for his job couldn't be with his wife on her birthday but created a romantic setting, anyway. "My husband was out of town the week of my birthday, so every day he called to tell me what room to go in, what closet or drawer to look in for a romantic or humorous birthday gift." He was gone for five days, and she received five gifts. Are you listening out there, traveling salesmen?

SEX, SEX, AND MORE SEX

GETTING THE GROOVE ON . . .

With Leos, you had better come prepared for total submission, or at least be willing to settle for less than an equal relationship. Leos are pleasure seekers. If you're getting the feeling that it is indeed about them, well, you're right—partially, anyway.

Now that you know a little bit about Leos, it's off to the races! The race for the bedroom, in the case of both males and females, will be a matter of control and sheer will. They are the kings and queens of the jungle, born leaders, and the boudoir is no exception. And by taking the lead, these lions know that they can't pussyfoot around. Most of the time the lioness will do what is necessary to make her partner feel special, but sometimes there are stumbling blocks. A Leo sister complained, "The fact that my man is so ticklish limits my sexual desires. I can't explore his body and touch him the way I want to. It's frustrating!"

But atmosphere, music, and intimacy are all-important for both the male and female of the sign. For example, a Leo accountant commented on a night to remember. "I came home from a very hard day at work and my Leo husband knew I was in a bad mood, so when I opened the front door a trail of pink rose pedals, my favorite, led to our bathroom. There I found a bottle of my favorite wine and my husband chillin' just for me."

As for the Leo woman, melodrama is the key word here. If you're taking the Leo woman to bed, settle back and enjoy the show. For once you enter into the lavish spectacle of this woman perched on her throne—that is, her massive headboard, queen- or king-size bed, silk sheets, goose-down comforter, lots and lots of pillows—you must be properly impressed. She probably prefers any sexual encounter to be at her place because it would include her trappings: music, semilavish furnishings, and sexual enhancements such as dildos or vibrators. Usually she'll be wearing some exotic or erotic getup that you should notice and compliment. What she's wearing or not wearing is all a part of the erotic experience. She simply must create the total package. That package will also include sexy underwear, crotchless panties, and G-strings. And as her partner, all you have to do is show up on time and bring fresh flowers or expensive perfume.

The Leo woman prefers the woman-on-top position for two reasons. First, her partner can look up and admire her body, and, second, his sucking her breasts creates a surge of passion for this fire sign. "Deep penetration and all-night-long lovemaking is what drives me crazy in the bedroom," said a Leo woman. Guys, brace yourselves.

As for the Leo man, he will definitely want to run the show in his own lair because this fire sign expects to be in charge in every area of his life. He prefers the man-on-top position, symbolically as well as for his own pleasure. The added benefit is that you can admire his good looks and his six-pack abs and broad chest. If by chance his hair has been texturized, don't call him out. If he wants you to think that he's got naturally curly hair, well . . . it's obviously important to him. The Leo brother doesn't really mind complying with what his partner wants sexually. He's not intimidated, but he can't read minds either. Just tell him what you want and he'll do it. You won't hurt his feelings and you'll be glad you did. A Leo brother will show up in his French-cut bikini underwear for your eyes only, and then surprise you with some edible underwear or a sexy teddy to wear for the evening, maybe even a red wig. You can never fully predict what the Leo brother will do. "I like a woman to feel comfortable enough with me to let her hair down. Even if she's wearing a wig, she can take it off. The night for me is about pleasing her. I please myself because she's pleased," a Leo draftsman said. Well, all righty then.

One Leo woman airline employee wants a different approach to lovemaking instead of climbing aboard with a two-minute man and listening to him snore afterward. "Anything that's different or out of the ordinary is what turns me on. Somebody to come and draw a bath for me and who has sense enough to get a couple of candles and light them. I don't ask for much." She added that she has the candles and bubble bath at her home. "I just want him to do it for me. He doesn't have to bring anything but the willingness to do it."

Foreplay is a great appetizer for most Leos, but usually they are preoccupied with getting to the main course. It's fine if you want to tantalize them with maneuvers during intercourse. Playing with the clitoris or massaging the testicles during sex is a great avenue to heightened sexual pleasure for Leos—but the intercourse is what they most often seek. For the men, learning to hang in there is pertinent. And for the women, take your vitamins and practice the art of sustaining an erection.

When you enter the Leo's bed, the time for talking will be over. It's time to rock 'n' roll. Of course, there will be talk between banging sessions. Hopefully, for the Leo, it will be a discussion on how great the whole experience was or pillow talk on the next phase of the program.

To avoid pouring water on otherwise hot and intense sex play, avoid discussing personal or business matters, which are best reserved for the kitchen table. "You're going to learn about that person, if you stick around, anyway. So why go through all that bull in case you don't stick around? If there's any talking to be done, I would rather talk about current affairs—outside the bedroom, of course," a Leo woman said.

Leos love spontaneity. They cannot bear to be bored, even for a minute. Calling him up and suggesting a date mountain climbing, camping out, or at a hideaway resort will always please the Leo. The spontaneity of the outing creates spontaneity elsewhere—on the mountainside, in the woods, or in the shower at the resort. "If the time, place, and mood are right, I tend to be an exhibitionist. You know—like grabbing his ass or stroking his penis in a grocery store somewhere in another part of the city, where nobody knows my mama," said a Leo librarian.

EROGENOUS ZONES . . . SOME PHYSICAL, SOME NOT

The sign of Leo rules the spine and back. Any back rubs, massages, kisses, and simple touches in this area make the lion roar and provide a stimulating beginning to what has been reported by most Leos to be a very long night. "Kisses along the small of my back and making love while my man sucks my nipples drive me crazy in the bedroom," a Leo attorney said.

In addition to the back area, attention, attention, attention, and more attention set the mood and create an erogenous zone for the Leo that you won't ever want to leave. A Leo woman from Maryland lives by this philosophy, which pretty much sums up important elements of a relationship with a Leo: "Affection and other expressions of love are free and motivated by sincerity. I need affection, I recognize it and embrace it as a need. I am much happier and productive in a relationship if my partner is attentive and affectionate." Potential companions, are you listening?

Whatever you give a Leo, he will give back tenfold. So the more attention you give—through talking dirty, writing poetry or a song just for your special lion, sending flowers, or buying expensive chocolates—will be rewarded.

After you give your Leo man a full body massage, he might be inclined to pour honey or chocolate syrup on strategic areas of your body and eat to his heart's content—or until you can't take it anymore. Or if you're near water, he might perform oral sex under water as you're sipping champagne.

Bubble baths, scented candles around the Jacuzzi, strawberries, and champagne are another turn-on for the Leo. They simply must have all of the i's dotted and the t's crossed when it's time to fly by the seat of their pants, swing from the shower head, or spin around on the ceiling fan.

Leos can also be exhibitionists, so if they request that you leave the light on during sex, honor the request. They want to see and be seen. And if this is a first-time encounter, well, they definitely want to see the total package and what's in store for them. Leos are voyeurs. In anticipation of an impending sexual encounter, the Leo will mentally get herself ready by watching the passing parade or flirting, a move she's very skillful at. "I'm voyeuristic in everyday matters—not sexual acts. Watching men in the mall is fun," says one Leo. For her, watching men, speculating about their sexual abilities and physical features, and watching their movements helps to prepare for the sexual encounter. "Seeing other men creates fantasies and excitement that put me at an arousal level, which creates great anticipation for what's in store for me later that night."

In short, Leos won't have any trouble with the arousal process. They enjoy the total experience—the initial smile, the flirtation, the dates, the dance, and the doing it. All of this is a part of the erotic experience—from bed to breakfast. A Leo plans to savor every touch, taste, and tantalizing tidbit.

PLAIN OL' SEX AND NOTHING MORE: WELCOME TO THE FREAK SHOW

Of the twelve signs of the zodiac, there are those who watch from the sidelines, those who participate, and those who are the stars of the freak show. Leos are among the participants.

If by chance the Leo does decide to freak with you, you better come prepared for total submission or a less-than-equal relationship. As long as the Leo's needs are met, this lion will definitely want to please and participate in whatever strikes your fancy.

For the most part, however, Leos tend to want to receive rather than give. They can definitely get to the over-the-top sex, including a little S & M. The Leo woman would love to don a corset, garterbelt, and knee-high leather boots for the occasion.

The Leo man absolutely thrives on the sexual experience in all its drama and glory. If by chance he's approached about having a secret affair, peppered with a secret out-of-town rendezvous, he'll agree without hesitation. For this brother, it's the drama of it all, the latent possibilities that count. If you're willing to experiment with no strings attached, the Leo brother will definitely be willing to consider it.

Leo men also definitely enjoy threesomes—two women, of course—while the Leo woman may enjoy two male partners. They love the thought of having two admirers please them at once.

The freak show has possibilities, but the rules and the participants would be Leo's choice.

MONEY MATTERS

Luxury is what the Leo wants and thrives on. Nothing is too good for this fire sign, who expects to live large even before it's feasible. They will spare no expense in getting what they want. Consequently, saving, investing, and generating money are not their forte, but spending money is.

Leos are the big spenders of the zodiac. But they are very generous too. And they will give you the silk shirt off their backs. They will spend money—yours, theirs, or anyone else's. They don't discriminate. Leo people don't see the need to put off today for tomorrow. Their motto is definitely, Eat, drink and be merry, for tomorrow we die.

If you're in a relationship with a Leo, don't give him control of the credit cards or bank account. The only statement you'll see on a regular basis is a notice that the account is overdrawn or the credit cards are maxed out. Word to the wise: You need to keep a credit card stashed that the Leo doesn't know about for emergencies. Of course, an emergency for a Leo would be a pair of Donna Karan pumps that she simply must have for an affair this week.

Leos have no interest in saving for a rainy day. They are more interested in the here and now. They love to entertain, and they will spend on a grand scale, hiring expensive caterers, decorating with fresh flowers, and even arranging for a live band. Nothing is too good for a Leo, you know. Don't give a thought to the cost. Besides, they will worry about all that business when the time comes. But for now, it's about the event, the outfit, and setting the stage for the party of parties.

If you're married to a Leo, then you know through trial and error about the do's and don'ts of maintaining your financial sanity with a Leo. These strong-willed, opinionated people will have you second-guessing yourself as they explain why the checking account is overdrawn for the fourth time in one month, and both of you are working. For example, if the Leo brother is getting a promotion that may be effective in six months, he will take his homies out to celebrate, buying several rounds of drinks. When he calls with the good news and you're less than thrilled, he might go out and buy an expensive Armani suit. When the credit card bill arrives, of course, he will have what he feels is a good explanation: "If you had been more enthusiastic about my good news, I wouldn't have gone out and bought anything. This was my way of celebrating!" Huh?

The best approach for a Leo regarding investing and saving money is to hire a financial adviser. The next thing is to have the money deducted before it gets in the hands of this spendthrift lion, preferably as payroll deductions.

The only investing that the Leo will agree to or listen to reason on is the educational fund for the children. Children are important to Leos, and they will put the needs of their children ahead of their own. But don't push your luck in any other area, buddy. The clothing accounts stay put!

PAMPERING TIPS FOR LEO

   ❄ Pampering is a Leo's middle name. And the key is lots of it.

   ❄ A gift basket of the bath stuff, including a gift certificate for a massage, facial, and manicure, will do nicely.

   ❄ Leaving love notes or hints about a surprise trip for your Leo will pamper her with anticipation until the real deal comes.

   ❄ Giving your Leo the full treatment, including a bath, a back rub, some champagne or herbal tea, will create some peace and excitement for this fire sign.

   ❄ If you're married to a Leo, suggest renewing your wedding vows and taking a second honeymoon in the Caribbean. You'll see a side of your Leo you'd thought was long gone!

   ❄ Arrange to have your Leo visit a spa that includes all the trimmings for a week. Upon her return home, have the flowers and Moët waiting. That way it's a double treat.

   ❄ Leos want all of their needs met. Arranging for a lawn service for him or a cleaning service for her will allow much more time to stroke each other!

❋ Feeding your Leo man strawberries or your Leo woman chocolates while declaring your undying love is a good start in the pampering department.

❋ Volunteer to take the children for the weekend while your Leo pampers herself. If the children are with a responsible person, your Leo can relax and enjoy the weekend.

❋ Pick your Leo up and have the picnic, long drive to the country, or day at the beach all arranged. And don't forget to buy that sexy bikini or those French-cut bikini briefs to top off the day.

Gift Ideas for Leo

❋ If you can't afford a quality gift for Leo, then I suggest that you stick to writing a song or a poem. But a sexy garterbelt or nightgown will hold your Leo temporarily until you can do better.

❋ Fine jewelry, like diamond earrings or gold cuff links, set the tone for the relationship with Leo.

❋ Celebrating a one-month anniversary in anticipation of the one-year-old relationship will have your Leo delirious with anticipation.

❋ Leos love extravagant presents. Fine porcelain, crystal, and china are all great gifts for both men and women.

❋ A heavily ornate hand or wall mirror is a fine gift for Leos. They love to admire themselves.

❋ Books on tape might work for Ms. Leo because she certainly doesn't have time to sit at home and read. Her public awaits, you know.

❋ Leos love to travel. Any kind of getaway for the weekend, or for a week or two, will suit Leo just right. He'll need time to rearrange his bulging calendar, however.

❋ Season tickets to the theater and other cultural events are always to the Leo's liking.

❋ Original artwork, signed and numbered prints, or modern sculpture are all sure winners for Leos. They love the arts.

✳ Don't forget the flowers, including the single rose, a congratulatory bouquet for a promotion, Easter lilies, or poinsettias
for Christmas.

Virgo

(August 23 to September 22)
SYMBOL: THE VIRGIN

Positive love traits: Methodical, arduous lover; traditional and conventional.

Negative love traits: Unimaginative, even apathetic lover; prudish in bed; aesthetics count more than the sensuality of the act.

Ruling planet: Mercury is associated with intelligence, reason, and a high-strung temperament.

Word to the wise: Virgos are going to take their own sweet time about getting knee-deep in an uptight, out-of-sight love affair.

The symbol of Virgo is the virgin, which represents purity, perfection, and chastity. In other words, Virgo people, for the most part, are as close to perfection as anyone can get. That's a very admirable trait unless you are on the receiving end of all their requirements and critical analyses in their quest for perfection. They criticize everything from how the toilet paper is placed on the dispenser to how the dry cleaners hang and press their shirts.

Intellect rates high with Virgo people, both men and women. And they're not easily misled. For example, a Virgo who worked part time as an overnight package delivery employee challenged a coworker who claimed she worked full time as a teacher. In actuality, the coworker was a teacher's aide. Mr. Virgo pointed out that every sentence she spoke began with "uh." He went on to say that if she didn't know what the word "matriculated" meant, she couldn't be a teacher. The woman stopped speaking to the Virgo. It didn't matter, because he had made his point.

Virgos are devoted and faithful to a fault. They simply do not have time to worry if they are on the telephone talking to companion number one or number two. Besides, remember their symbol, the virgin, representing purity? They are the Goody Two-shoes of the zodiac. Of course, they expect their partner to have integrity, devotion, loyalty, and all of the other wonderful traits that Virgos feel most people should aspire to.

Like Gemini, their ruling planet is Mercury, which is associated with a high-strung temperament, intelligence, and reason. The brain of Virgos never completely shuts down. If you're involved with a Virgo, watch how he sleeps. Virgos toss, turn, talk, and make spontaneous jerks when they're asleep—almost like they're fighting the world. If by chance you decide to waken them, they will gratefully thank you.

You'll find these virgins at sports events, church, choir rehearsal, the neighborhood watch meeting, a movie, a play, or a community action meeting. They are a little more at ease with and receptive to events in controlled settings, where they don't have to strike out on their own socially.

If you have your sights set on a Virgo, proceed with caution. They're not at all impressed with a winning personality, fine clothes, fine cars, or any other material trinkets. You have to present yourself in a ladylike or gentlemanly fashion before they will so much as give you a second look.

These earth signs are also neat freaks. You won't have any trouble spotting a Virgo. They are usually starched, ironed, and creased. Both the women and the men love linen, cotton, and silk clothing, preferably in beige or white. The women will be outfitted from head to toe in stylish, tasteful clothes, whether for work or play. The men love heavily starched white dress shirts that subtly outline their muscles. Virgos are also conscious of good health and fitness and will expect a companion to exercise and eat healthily. These virgins stand out in a crowd because of their attractive faces, removed and guarded demeanor, and squeaky-clean appearance.

Don't come on like gangbusters. The Virgo will want to get to know you first; if the Virgo cannot tolerate you as a friend, nothing else is likely to happen. And although you feel that your conversation is the bomb, that does not mean you'll get a warm response. They have to weigh and analyze everything before they respond or react. Don't take it as a personal affront; it is just the muted response of the ever-cautious Virgo. Virgo definitely won't react based on emotion. Any decision made by the Virgo, especially in the romance arena, will be from a practical standpoint and based on factual information. In other words, "Just the facts, ma'am." By now, you're probably getting the picture that Virgos are pretty stuffy. The key, though, is for them to get comfortable with you. Once they reach the comfort zone, they can be quite entertaining. They will keep you laughing with their dry sense of humor and critical insights. In the area of comedy, they can step toe-to-toe with the best of them. Move over, Chris Rock!

THE VIRGO MAN

The dating game for the Virgo brother is serious business; none of the one-night-stand stuff for him. Virgo men are the no-nonsense types of the zodiac. Women love Virgo men because they are consummate gentlemen: intelligent, kind, considerate, with a high moral character unmatched by most. Of course, they expect their companions to be all that and a bag of chips on the side.

Ironically, women are constantly coming on to them, but most of these women don't realize that it's an exercise in futility. This brother feels more comfortable when he's doing the pursuing. Of course, he's not made of stone, and he definitely appreciates the female species. With the new millennium fast approaching, many courtship rituals have gone the way of the dinosaur. Subconsciously, however, the Virgo brother wants to do things in the proper order. For example, the way this brother sees it, a first date should be in a structured setting.

When it comes to women, the turtlelike pace of his moves is due in part to his low confidence level. And in part because he's busy analyzing the situation. By the time he makes his move, the woman may be going through menopause. Just kidding!

The Virgo will pick up his date, take her to dinner at the most elegant restaurant his wallet can stand, ask for the wine list, expect stimulating conversation, take her home, tip his hat, and leave. He won't be the brother finagling an invitation into your apartment, and if you do invite him in, he may accept. It will depend on the day of the week. He may have to conduct an early-morning meeting. He detests tardiness and inefficiency. He will want to be up early, go over his notes, and arrive thirty minutes before the meeting. If it's the weekend, he may have to record the statistics for the boys' basketball team at the community center or cut his mother's grass or drive the church bus. You get the picture.

They are critics by nature, but they are most critical of themselves. "How is that possible?" you may ask if you're dating a Virgo. Believe me, I know it's rough! But you need to understand that even if they weren't busy criticizing you, they would be criticizing a signpost, the condition of someone's toenails, whatever. You name it—it must be analyzed and criticized.

Virgos are good providers, sometimes working two jobs to provide a more-than-comfortable living for their mates. Work is their key word and that's where they feel most at home. They're also faithful and devoted. They simply don't see the necessity of having more than one companion. Their practical approach to everything won't entertain the possibility. Their attitude about such is, for what?!

When Virgo men finally fall in love, after what may seem like an eternity, they are at your beck and call constantly. These smitten creatures hang on your every word. They declare that they will give you the world. It may be on a shoestring budget since they're not prone to spend money needlessly.

If you're a smoker, then this little habit is going to be a problem. That's not to say that Virgos don't smoke. But Virgos cannot tolerate a companion who smokes. I suppose if you're already in a relationship and you begin this habit, well, that's another story. And you may need to smoke before the relationship is over because he will beat a point to death. Of course, he can't take what he dishes out, but that's okay. In any initial relationship with a Virgo, he will scrutinize you closely with his eagle eye, making mental notes about your demeanor, assessing from every angle whether you're kind, considerate, and what he considers sane.

A Virgo gay man from Cleveland out on a date thought that things were going pretty smoothly until his companion's pager went off (very loudly) in the movie theater. Not only did his date *not* turn off the pager, he proceeded to return the call on his cell phone, talking for several minutes until the usher gave him a warning.

Virgo brothers, gay or straight, won't be around for any of the bedroom stuff with partners who are loud and boisterous or who cuss and try to order the Virgo around. Although you may see this well-dressed tight-bodied bonanza, don't think for a minute that your constricting clothing, pretty face, and material wealth will get you in bed with Mr. Dudley Do-Right. Mental stimulation, discussions about current events, far-reaching projects, money matters, or personal goals will turn on the Virgo man much quicker than any visual stimulation or aids.

The Virgo brother would just as soon skip the club scene. Although he can be sociable and very entertaining, the nightclub and bar scene are not his cup of tea. He may be ordering just that—tea.

The Virgo man doesn't have any aversion to color contacts if the colors are in good taste. But light gray and light blue—and the unrealistic colors—are a turnoff to him. As for the nose rings, pierced navels (not to mention rings in eyebrows, lips, and tongues), Virgos won't understand the need for such nonsense. "I don't like to see piercing on the body," a Virgo salesman said. "It looks bad and it makes me think that they're a bunch of loose folks who don't have good judgment." A hair weave is acceptable to Virgos as long as it's a believable length and done well. With Virgos, less is more. But if your hair is colored blue or burgundy to match your outfit, the Virgo will probably develop some kind of problem, like a headache or indigestion, so the two of you won't have to be seen in public together.

Virgos don't like surprises. One Virgo computer analyst got the shock of his life when he was introduced to a blind date who was six months pregnant. Did his date think the man wouldn't be able to see?

By now, you're probably getting some idea of the quirky, fastidious nature of Virgos. They know very early in life what they want in a mate. And they will take great pains to ensure that the relationship is going as planned. Once they find who they want, it's usually for keeps.

The Virgo Woman

If you are considering a relationship with a Virgo sister, you will need plenty of patience: This relationship is going to take work. Don't think for a minute that just because you're interested in her it's a foregone conclusion that she's interested in you. This sister is so preoccupied with all of her many projects, concerns, and worries, she probably hasn't even noticed you. The Virgo woman is very complex, a neat freak with a good heart. Her ruling planet is Mercury, which is associated with intelligence and a high-strung temperament. Need I say more?

On first glance, you will notice her ultraneat, squeaky-clean appearance. Her hair doesn't have a strand out of place. Image is everything to Ms. Virgo, so if you're thinking about approaching her and you've just come from work painting a house, you need to go home and bathe and change clothes first. Saying "I just got off from work" won't do in this case because she won't be able to ignore your appearance. Virgos will sometimes concentrate on a person's appearance and lose sight of the inner beauty and sterling qualities of a potential companion. One Virgo sister refused to talk to a man whose shoes were run down. What she didn't know was that he was businessman from out of town who had been running to a meeting; in his haste, he tripped and almost fell, and the buckle came off his shoe. The shoe repairman simply gave him a pair of shoes to wear until he could pick up his own later.

If you're meeting by chance at a restaurant, a subway stop, or in the park, it's going to be a hard sell. Virgo people generally prefer meeting new people in controlled settings—at church, on the job, or through a mutual friend. You won't pick up a Virgo sister in a bar. Of course, she'll meet her girlfriends there for happy hour or to celebrate a friend's birthday, but she doesn't do the bar scene very well, and she would rarely go on a date with someone she had met at a bar. She's far too cautious for that. The Virgo sister is picky about everything, from the food she eats to the men she meets.

By the time she actually considers accepting a date with you, you will have passed her test. This woman has a checklist for any potential mate, and she doesn't make too many concessions on appearance, rude behavior, public drunkenness, or being too loud. Her practical approach to love and romance overshadows any leanings to emotional or lovesick behavior in a relationship. If she is lovesick, you'll never know it. She won't wait for hours, crying, sulking, and telling her girlfriend how she wishes you would call. She's got too much pride for that.

Mr. All That or Mr. Look-So-Good will get the same treatment as Mr. Average Joe Blow. Actually, her treatment for the cutie pies may be a little more harsh. Virgo women are very practical when it comes to most things, including hooking up with Mr. Fine.

And don't lie! It's simply not necessary. That's one of the biggest turnoffs for Virgo people. Lying and deception rate right up there with failure to bathe regularly.

Loud, lewd, or violent behavior is a total no-no. I know you may be accustomed to hanging out with the homies, but if you're planning a successful date with Ms. Virgo, pace yourself on the drinking. She was probably one of the founding members of MADD (Mothers Against Drunk Driving). A Virgo paralegal who was trying to break off a relationship with her man-turned-drug-addict announced that she was leaving. "If I can't have you, no one can," he declared and proceeded to try to detain her. When he threatened to kill her, that was it! She ran for cover. Although the man later commented that he was only kidding, he would never hurt her, the threat was enough for her—it was over!

Listen up, brothers: If you're wondering why this no-nonsense Virgo is not returning your calls or is never home when you call, this may be the reason. As one Virgo woman explained, "Thank God for caller ID." She doesn't like scenes or confrontations, so she simply looks at her caller ID box to determine who's on the other end of the line.

A Virgo sister is committed to any endeavor she undertakes. She will definitely work outside the home as well as inside to provide a comfortable nest for her family. She'll be the den mother for her son's Boy Scout troop, volunteer to carpool twice a week, and even make the costumes for the play or the pies for the church picnic.

If the undertaking happens to be a business venture with the one she loves, you couldn't have picked a better business partner. A Virgo sister longs for a strong man who is intelligent and has integrity. She wants nothing more than a man she can rely on totally, without question, without worry, and with total trust. Although she's independent and conscientious, she would like nothing better than to turn over all of the responsibility and hassle of her life to her man. She's independent and always on, but she wants her man to take charge once in a while. On the other hand, the Virgo's independence can give way to total dependence when her insecurity overtakes aspects of her life. For example, a Virgo office manager from Chicago, who worried so much about minor details in her young life, for the most part missed coming into her sense of herself until she was 35. "I didn't know who I was. I was reactive to things that happened instead of setting out to control my own destiny because it was more comfortable to go along with others, including bad relationships."

Because of their high-strung temperaments, Virgo women keep a lot of serious matters bottled up inside. Before long, the pressure gets to be too much and the Virgo goes off. For example, a Virgo sister from Chicago started having panic attacks en route to O'Hare Airport to the point where she had to pull over and allow someone else to drive her car. Until she sought counseling, she never realized that her two near misses on the expressway, one with a tractor trailer and the other with a car spinning out of control, were the reason for the attacks. She never showed any emotion or acknowledgment of either incident, until they finally took their toll.

GUIDE TO A LOVE CONNECTION

Virgo and Aries

Virgos are not happy unless they are in control of a situation. Aries have to run the show as well. But Aries' lack of organization and preparation drives the methodical Virgo nuts. Virgo is cautious, down to earth, and practical. Aries is impulsive, free-spirited, ready to meet life head-on. Virgo wants to spend quiet evenings at home. Aries is a crowd pleaser and thrives on being in the mix. If these two make it to the bedroom, it'll be a miracle. Virgo approaches bedroom matters like life: planning, discussing, and moving with reserve. Aries, who will probably already be swinging from the rafters by the time the virgin enters the room, will find such behavior strange. When Virgo becomes hypercritical about Aries' approach to living, Aries will take his ball and find another play-ground.

Virgo and Taurus

These two have the potential for a match made in heaven. These soul mates have more in common than most other combinations. Both are highly motivated by money and security. Both work hard and are goal-oriented. Virgo's nervous energy and worrier behavior will be calmed by Taurus's steady, sensible, and reassuring attitude. You'll find these two at home if they are not at work. Their sex life is like the rest of life, boring to some but definitely satisfying to them. Taurus's libido is greater than Virgo's, but Virgo appreciates the passion of the bull. Both can be very stubborn, however. As long as Virgo doesn't become too hypercritical or and nagging, there will be no need for Taurus to brood or leave. All systems are go!

Virgo and Gemini

Although these two are intelligent and very mental people, meaning they must analyze everything, the romance part of the li-aison quickly fizzles as soon as it begins. Virgo is a homebody, happy to read a book or watch a movie. That's fine for Gemini some-times, but the social calendar constantly beckons: She must get into the real world and hang out. Virgo sees this as a personal insult and complains that Gemini is not attentive enough. Gemini becomes annoyed and feels that Virgo should hang with him, ease up, and enjoy life. If the relationship gets as far as the bedroom, Gemini will show very little patience with Virgo's conventional behavior. This combination will be short-lived.

Virgo and Cancer

These two can get along famously. Virgo's no-nonsense, practi-cal nature has Cancer curious and amused. Cancer's moodiness and insecurities are eased by conscientious, down-to-earth Virgo. Virgo's grouchy behavior is offset by Cancer's wacky sense of hu-mor, which keeps conservative Virgo in stitches. Cancer takes the lead in the bedroom, but that doesn't bother Virgo. Cancer's fever-pitched emotions and passionate lovemaking awaken some unrealized sexual intensity in Virgo. Cancer creates a cozy cottage for workaholic Virgo to come home to. Both are security- and money-conscious. The crab will hold on to a dollar until it hollers. Virgo will too, but not until he buys Cancer the niceties the crab would not think of buying. There are wedding bells in this couple's future.

Virgo and Leo

Virgo's practical and conservative personality is not going to stand for Leo's extravagant and lavish lifestyle. Virgo sees this approach as wasteful. Leo feels that Virgo is putting a damper on life. Both are conscientious about work habits, but after work, Virgo wants to retreat to his safe abode and Leo wants to paint the town red. If by chance this couple ends up in bed (which I doubt), Virgo's prudish and judgmental behavior will leave lustful Leo feeling unappreciated and unloved. Leo must have lots and lots of adulation. The lion deserves it, you know—it's simply difficult for Virgo to pour on the compliments when he doesn't mean it. These two are too different to ever come together as one. No matter how you slice it, this coupling is history!

Virgo and Virgo

Well, with these two, all you need is some popcorn, a few rented videos, quiet surroundings, and they're all set. This is where you'll find this pair, not only once in a while, but every weekend! I know—you're thinking, How boring! To you, yes, but for the two of them it's perfectly natural. This is probably one of the few same-Sun-sign couples that could survive in a long-term relationship. They love peace and quiet. They are perfectionists and require just as much from themselves as they would from you. They also are very meticulous when it comes to assessing a potential mate. If you decide to hook up with a Virgo and think during the process that you're being interviewed for a job, you're probably right! The thought of being interviewed would be an insult to most. But for the Virgo, it's what they want and expect—their standards are exceedingly high. So who else would put up with another Virgo but a Virgo? Both Virgos could relate story upon story about how many frogs they had to encounter before meeting that prince or princess.

So why wouldn't another Virgo fit the bill? It's better to be safe than sorry! Let the wedding bells ring.

Virgo and Libra

Both are well-dressed people who definitely have class. But Virgo's down-to-earth, guarded, and practical approach to romance turns Libra off. Librans want moonlight and music, starlight and melody. That's fine for Virgos as long as it's in a song. Mr. Serious No-nonsense cannot muster the fanfare it takes to keep flamboyant Libra occupied. These air signs thrive on independence and not being controlled. Virgo, who on the other hand wants stability, predictability and loyalty in a relationship, perceives Libra's attitude as frivolous. Sexually, sparks fly initially, but the fireworks soon fizzle. These two are too different in outlook and philosophy to be compatible. They're better suited for other companions, not each other.

Virgo and Scorpio

Virgo views everything with a skeptical and critical eye. Therefore the relationship with Scorpio is no different. Scorpio knows long before Virgo can come in out of the rain that this relationship can work, mainly because Virgo is faithful, dependable, down to earth, and financially sound. All these traits are a turn-on for Scorpio, who values faithfulness and devotion as the top priorities on the list. Of course, Virgo, being the conscientious person that she is, won't mind Scorpio calling three times a day. An enchanted evening for these two is some wine, popcorn, rented videos, soft music, and each other. They definitely can make their own good time without benefit of props or amenities. Virgo, the earth sign, and Scorpio, the water sign, can definitely make this hookup work!

Virgo and Sagittarius

Virgo is initially intrigued by Sagittarius's intelligence and gift of the gab on a variety of subjects. Sagittarius admires the work ethic of Virgo, but Sag is the "wild child" with very little protocol and structure to her life. Virgo is appalled by Sag's lack of polish, procedure, and judgment. Sag shrugs and is off and running in many directions in pursuit of happiness and doesn't need Virgo's analytical approval to do so. Virgo is a homebody. Sag is everywhere but at home. Virgo wants a solid, predictable, and conservative rela-tionship. Sag is too busy meetin' and greetin' to sit still for Virgo's boring approach to relationships. As for bedroom matters, Sag wants to experiment and try most things, and prudish Virgo won't try much of anything. By the time the fat lady sings, these two are long gone.

Virgo and Capricorn

This matchup is in sync from the very beginning. Virgo is sen-sible and grounded and has a very practical approach to life. Virgo's needs are simple: a stable mate who is not dysfunctional or crazy and is definitely drug-free. Enter Capricorn. Capricorn's cut-to-the-chase attitude supports Virgo's disdain for smoke and mirrors and frivolous behavior. Both work hard to achieve goals. Capricorn is an action person, setting career goals in motion, using Virgo's ex-pert analysis for the blueprint. These two work hand in hand in every aspect of their lives. Regarding bedroom matters, their ap-proach to sex—traditional and conventional—works for them. But these two strong signs are both bossy and headstrong and must be careful not to turn on each other.

Virgo and Aquarius

When these two meet, they immediately think that they have the potential for a long life together. *Warning:* They don't! Virgo is conventional, practical, and grounded and simply marvels at the out-in-the-stratosphere attitude of Aquarius. Both are very mental people. Virgo's analysis of the world is more down to earth than Aquarius's, which is far-reaching and enlightened. Sexually, they are drawn to each other, but Aquarius's tendency to push the enve-lope has prudent Virgo wondering if there's a freak in the house. Virgo is devoted, dependable, and faithful in the relationship. Aquarius, though faithful, is not as attentive as Virgo would like. Virgo and Aquarius are both reserved and guarded in their ap-proach to each other. The disharmony in the relationship and their dissimilar approaches to life only strengthen their belief that this is not meant to be.

Virgo and Pisces

These two opposites are probably the only opposite combination that could really work out. But this union may require more than each is willing to give. This pair is an easygoing combination. Virgo is the sensible, conservative, loyal person who is devoted to Pisces. Pisces is insecure, tentative, and mysterious, relying on intuition for decision making. Passionate Pisces fans some smoldering embers in Virgo, but Virgo finds Pisces' anything-goes behavior in the bedroom unsettling. Virgo's perfectionist attitude and work ethic counter Pisces' need to dream dreams and create a romantic setting in which both can indulge. Virgo is the realist and Pisces is the dreamer. A sizzling affair, yes, but a long-lasting marriage . . . well, that's another story.

ROMANCE AND THE VIRGO

Now that you've finally wrangled this date, there is another checklist that needs to be addressed. For starters, a nice long walk hand in hand through the park, stopping awhile to feed the ducks and squirrels—this is most relaxing to the Virgo. Virgos love peace and quiet. The peaceful surroundings will give him the opportunity to "interview" you and find out what you're all about. If there's a lake or pond nearby, all the better.

If you're trying to score cool points, by all means avoid controversial topics on the first date. Virgos hate to be wrong. They pride themselves on being well read and doing jobs or tasks in an efficient manner. Most of the time, they do their homework and can readily give you all of the whys and wherefores without so much as a stammer.

It's okay to be short on cash occasionally, but not again and again. Excuses like "I need to go to the ATM machine" or "I haven't cashed my check yet" get old real quick with a Virgo. These earth signs made a mental note the first time it happened, so by the fourth or fifth time, your luck has run out. A Virgo who was a registered nurse had a lovely dinner with her escort at a very romantic restaurant. But when the check came, he realized that he didn't have enough money. When the Virgo sister offered to help, he accepted, but the evening was ruined because he was too embarrassed and she was too miffed to continue.

Drinking Ensure on the porch is not the Virgo's idea of romance. Although Virgos are not all that responsive to unusual, daring, or spontaneous dates, they do move a tad quicker than some. A Virgo related this wow scene for her most memorable date. "We were driving along in the rain. Luther Vandross was jamming, Lutherizing one of the old slow drag standards. My man stopped the car, we got out, and we danced in the rain."

In order for Ms. Virgo to get involved, not to mention get involved sexually, she must trust you completely. So gaining her trust is the essential first step in a rewarding relationship. With Virgos, the response always depends on how they're approached. If you come on like gangbusters, they will look at you with suspicion. Their critical eye doesn't see what others see. Being self-effacing is one thing, but Virgos are often totally preoccupied with and insecure about their attractiveness. So if you're the brother who's salivating over this lovely creature and she doesn't know you exist or she shrugs off any overture you make, take heart. She simply doesn't believe your conversation laced with compliments because she is so hypercritical of herself. Virgos, especially the women, have a tendency to downplay their best qualities or good looks.

If you're looking for just plain ol' sex and nothing more with Virgo, you're kinda barking up the wrong tree. They want the romance, the wining and the dining. Sex usually comes much later, and with a lot of strings attached.

Virgos are under constant stress, from imaginary and real causes. Relieving tension is what they seek constantly. But they also want the total package. They want a partner, companionship, the whole nine yards. Timing is everything with Virgos: At the right moment, you may get much more than you bargained for. She might even sit on your face without being prodded.

They're also eager to please, and in the spirit of cooperation, they tend to consent to things that are contrary to their nature or better judgment. For example, a Virgo woman reports that her first sexual encounter was a disaster. A classmate who had a serious crush on her tracked her down after she had gone to college. He visited the city where she had settled, professed love, and proposed marriage, all in one fell swoop. She was visibly moved by the proposal and finally agreed to have sex for the first time with him. The experience was painful and traumatic because neither had any experience. After the encounter, the Virgo refused the marriage proposal, and he never called again. No problem. Ms. Virgo was more than relieved.

A Virgo artist from Memphis described her most romantic date: a limousine ride, complete with champagne and snacks. Her companion read poetry and caressed her body during the ride. The evening was complete with what she termed "dessert"—her date performing oral sex as the driver drove on. Well, all righty then!

Virgo people are definitely turned on by thoughtfulness and the time spent planning a date. They constantly make mental notes regarding what's working and what's not. For example, a Virgo woman said that after thirty years of an on-again, off-again relationship with a Pisces, her opposite, the quality time they spend working on respect and romantic areas, including dancing and musical interests, sustains the union. "Part of my appeal is that I know as much as he does, and he doesn't talk over my head." Ms. Virgo is still smitten after three decades. "The first indication that he was not interested in controlling me endeared him to me."

The bottom line, and a must for both men and women, is that they won't be controlled by anyone. As one Virgo put it, "I need my own space. I've got to have an area where I can retreat to when stressed or annoyed by my mate. There won't be any romance if I don't have the space and time I need."

A Virgo sister was especially impressed with one romantic vacation, a Caribbean cruise, but the added amenities, like the private bath and huge bedroom, impressed her so much that she just wanted to retreat to her luxurious quarters for the trip.

"If you want a romantic date with a Virgo," said one Virgo nurse from Chicago, "start the date by bringing the woman flowers—or a single red rose for the Virgo man. A quiet, romantic, and lavish dinner, a moonlight stroll by the lake, a bath together, and great sex, followed by breakfast the next day and stimulating conversation."

"Sharing intimate talks is a big turn-on for me," said a single Virgo woman. "Waking up when neither one of us can sleep, lying there in the dark and talking until dawn without thoughts of sex or playing games is a big turn-on."

SEX, SEX, AND MORE SEX

GETTING THE GROOVE ON . . .

Before any romance, sexual leanings, and getting cozy with each other will commence, you must stimulate the Virgo mentally. Dummies need not apply. When you first meet these neat freaks, they will talk for hours on a variety of subjects. You need to know about current events, books, places, and philosophies. "I don't know" won't work here.

Having a good sense of humor also helps. Lord knows, some Virgos are so uptight that a good joke or a laugh will always help to break the ice. If you're thinking about a long-term relationship, the first date will give you a very good idea of what you can expect. Virgos are very forthright and open-minded. They don't pull any punches, and they are never at a loss for words on any subject, person, or thing known to humanity.

To get this party started, a shower together is always a good idea and will get Virgo's attention. Whether you're clean enough is always a preoccupation with Virgos. To put her mind at ease, take a shower together so that she can see for herself. Allow him to bathe you if he must. Don't freak out; he won't use lye soap or a scrub brush—I hope! And don't get offended; it's simply one of the quirks of the Virgo. If you haven't bathed during the day prior to the actual sexual encounter, there won't be any recovering by saying your deodorant has failed and the like. You'll be the "unforgiven."

"I don't want a man with bad breath getting in the bed with me," declared one Virgo woman. "You can tell if he's got bad breath if he takes off his shoes and his feet smell. Then the breath is probably bad, too." So listen up: While you're bathing together, it's a good idea to have brought your toothbrush along—and some mouthwash. For both men and women who are involved with Virgos, don't forget the trip to the dentist.

A pet peeve for one Virgo woman is a man with less-than-smooth feet. "I've got a thing about feet. If a man takes his socks off and he's hiding scratching [jagged] toenails and husky feet, I'll give him a pedicure. Vaseline petroleum jelly is the only thing that you can use in the winter."

After you've jumped that hurdle, the relaxation factor has to be addressed. Soft music (a seven-disc CD player of uninterrupted music), clean or new sheets, disconnected telephone, scented candles, or even a game of chess—all this will relax the Virgo brother.

Virgos function at their best when they're in familiar surroundings. To get the groove on, on the real tip, you need to be at the Virgo's home or apartment. The next best place is a neutral place. But if the Virgo is at the companion's place, he may not be able to relax. If the telephone rings, the Virgo brother will spend the balance of the night wondering who was on the other end, what the phone call meant, and on and on and on. In short, the Virgo brother is easily distracted.

Now that the arousal process is working, cut the chatter. Granted, Virgos are usually chatterboxes, but this is not the time to be constantly asking, "Is it good?" "How is this?" If all systems are go, trust me, you won't have to ask. The other stupid question for a female Virgo during sex is, "Whose stuff is this?" That is such a lame question because she only has a relationship with one person at a time, so if she is having sex with you, she won't be having sex with anyone else. The question is pointless and an ego-stroking maneuver that she simply has no time for. In short, you won't get a response.

After the Virgo trusts you completely, then some off-the-beaten-path stuff can commence. Virgo men are constantly running from all the women who are drawn to their nonthreatening, gentlemanly qualities. But again, trust is the key word here. Yes, Virgos can definitely participate in unusual behavior, but they won't be tied up or handcuffed during sex just so you can fulfill all of your fantasies. They simply must be in control of any situation in which they find themselves.

Generally, they're not quick to generate hotter-than-July sex, but if you come on to them at the right place (their own place or on an out-of-town trip), it's a sure bet. The wild and kinky stuff usually comes much later in the relationship, say, after the prenuptial agreement is signed, along with a sealed affidavit swearing never to disclose to anyone what went on in the bedroom. If she is in the right mood, hey, she might surprise you delightfully.

Although at first the Virgo sister may appear to be cold, she will go beyond the call of duty to make any date, escort, or potential companion feel comfortable. For example, a Virgo pharmaceutical sales rep was told by a potential companion that he didn't believe in oral sex. Well, of course, Ms. Virgo was mortified because she never thought that she would encounter someone who was *more* conservative than she. It wasn't what he said but the manner in which he said it that was hurtful and embarrassing. Of course, homeboy is history.

Okay, boys and girls, remember the phrase "It's not the size of the ship, but the motion of the ocean." A Virgo insurance benefits assistant explained it best: "When a man can't work the middle, I'm totally turned off." Well, the motion of the ocean should be rehearsed. Virgos won't tolerate not knowing how to work the middle. So you need to practice, or should I say target practice.

Now that the groove is on, you'll probably be in for a long night. How about from dusk to dawn? Back rubs are always in order. Virgos are always tense. For the most part, the sexual arena for Virgos includes oral sex, masturbation, watching porno movies, scents, full body massages, and some biting. Some may even have sex with the same gender, but S & M accompanied by whips, chains, and leather skin-diving costumes is a bit much for the Virgo. You're going to have to take them slow.

A Virgo from California explained that she prides herself on being a considerate lover, but she has her pet peeves. "I'm turned off by men who want you to perform. They think by encouraging me to perform, I won't guess he has no technique. In other words, all he has is the equipment." Some would say, that's not a bad thing!

Virgos are traditionalists as well. During sexual intercourse, the missionary position is the standard deal for them, and doggy style is fine too. But hanging upside down or bizarre rituals complete with smoke, dust, and flickering black light will have the Virgo disappearing before your eyes, never to be seen or heard from again.

EROGENOUS ZONES . . . SOME PHYSICAL,
  SOME NOT

If you want these virgins to throw away their chastity belts, stroke their stomach and lower chest area in a light, feathery manner to jump-start the arousal process. You may also get a rise out of this earth sign by massaging and stroking the upper groin area. Virgo people don't initiate wild, saucy, hot sex. But if you catch them at the right moment and create a passion-laden experience, you just never know.

Virgos also enjoy watching the undressing process. They may pretend that they're not looking, but believe me, they are—they don't miss much unless they're asleep. For example, a flight attendant from San Francisco commented about disrobing, "I like having my clothes taken off passionately with lots of eye contact and a small light on."

Seeing a companion nude is a big turn-on for them. After the clothes are off, a little flexing of the muscles and a dance or two are a great turn-on as well.

Mental stimulation is as important as physical stimulation. And it doesn't always have to be a game of chess or scrabble. Talking dirty to them in the privacy of your home or his is a good move. They can do a lot of fantasizing, which helps the arousal process. Fantasies are a great way to get a Virgo going, because whatever the Virgo can create in his head is safe and the sanctity of his image isn't threatened. If she is considering the initial sexual encounter, she has definitely considered all the angles of the impending rendezvous. So fantasizing about whatever is to come is a great first step without others knowing what's going on. These people guard their privacy fiercely.

One Virgo sister complained that when she reluctantly expresses "Right there, right there" during sexual intercourse and you, her bedmate, alter course, don't expect to be called back for round two. First of all, it takes a lot for a Virgo to give sexual direction. To have her requests dissed or disregarded means you're not in tune with the Virgo sister's needs—or sensitive to what it took to make the request in the first place!

One Virgo took issue with my comments about Virgos' reluctance to give direction in the boudoir. "I ask for what I want," he said. "For example, forget the bed, let's go to the backyard and let me look at the stars while you perform oral sex." Any questions?

Atmosphere is just as important as the sex act itself. If you want to get Virgo's attention in the bedroom, remember these mental creatures are detail-oriented. They are paying close attention to all of the goings-on. Scented candles, incense, potpourri, or the smell of a freshly bathed body is an instant turn-on for Virgos.

Also, minutemen need not apply—you'll be met with a "Don't call us, we'll call you" response. Remember that caller ID box? Most Virgos find such contraptions essential. They definitely screen the unwanted callers and avoid any confrontational behavior.

PLAIN OL' SEX AND NOTHING MORE:
WELCOME TO THE FREAK SHOW

Do you want the Virgo to freak with you? Well now, you have to be sworn to secrecy. Swear on your mother's grave. As Samuel Jackson said in *Jungle Fever*, swear before four white people to never in your wildest dreams discuss any sexual escapades that any Virgo enjoyed, performed, or even thought about having. Is that clear?! Let me put it this way: Of the twelve signs of the zodiac, the Virgos are the most likely to watch the freak show from the sidelines.

If you find a Virgo who is inclined to become a member of the freak show, well, congratulations! That's great! Like anything else that they undertake, they'll pursue it with gusto. It may take years to get them into the frame of mind to participate in over-the-top sex for sex's sake. If they have in the past, they may not fess up to having participated in wild and crazy sex before. "Some men think you're a whore or slut or that you've been with lots of men when you want to be creative in bed," said one Virgo sister. "Little do they know that all it takes is one man, the right man."

If by chance she consents to this sex play, she's gotta know about all of the details. Virgos don't like surprises. He will want to know if another woman will be joining the party. Having a résumé or health card from the participant is not a bad idea. Just kidding! One Sagittarian brother from Florida said it best: "I am totally intrigued by Virgos and Scorpios because they are undercover freaks and they hide it well."

MONEY MATTERS

The conservative personality of Virgos also carries over into the money side of their lives. They don't like to waste money or spend it needlessly. Virgos love to be well dressed and will spend money for quality merchandise. But these practical people are not prone to a lot of impulsive spending while overloading the credit cards and credit line. Like Donna Summer says in her song, "She works hard for the money." And so do Virgos.

If you're invited to the home of a Virgo and it feels like you stepped into a lavish layout of finery, don't jump to conclusions. And don't think you've hit the big time. You won't be mowing through Virgo's carefully saved and guarded nest egg. Virgos take their time to plan, save, and invest, and what you are feasting your eyes on is years of hard work, sometimes from two jobs or the return on carefully invested stocks, bonds, and the like.

Being frugal is a main point with them. Along with the frugal philosophy will be the point-by-point analysis. For example, a Virgo physician changed a patient's surgical dressing in the hospital, then left the remaining bandages and gauzes, telling the woman that she should keep the packages because she'd been charged $30 for them on her bill.

One Virgo brother invested the money he saved annually when he stopped smoking. When the dust, or should I say smoke, cleared, his return was $50,000, which he put in an education fund for his nieces and nephews. He is not married and has no children. Everything must be in the proper order with the Virgo. You know—meet, marry, then have children.

If you plan to visit the casinos regularly, you're going to have a problem with this brother. An occasional visit here and there or to accommodate out-of-town guests is okay. But going to these places and camping out is not going to work.

Like the Capricorn, when the Virgo brother first learns that his wife is pregnant, he calls his financial planner to talk about the portfolio he wants to initiate, including an education fund for the unborn child. Virgos definitely plan ahead, taking their own sweet time to accumulate all the details of the undertaking.

Your Virgo mate won't ever be in the "just do it" mood. Everything about money, assets, and insurance has to be examined from all angles. So while you're pulling your hair out, just chill. During the later years, when you're relaxing at your summer home, drinking lemonade, and canning peaches while enjoying early retirement, you'll be glad you listened to your frugal Virgo.

PAMPERING TIPS FOR VIRGO

❋ Having sex as often as humanly possible is a great stress reliever for Virgos, who are constantly under stress, whether real or imagined.

❋ Giving your Virgo a bath is a big turn-on. For Virgos, cleanliness is next to sexiness.

❋ A head-to-toe massage by a masseuse, preferably you, is always good because their lives are oh, so stressful.

❋ A Virgo would feel that he's got the inside track if you gave him a sex coupon that entitles the holder to decide the dates, times, and locations of the encounters.

❋ Virgo women love to receive sexy lingerie and see their men in those ever-so-brief briefs. It makes them feel special and pampered.

❋ Get him his favorite cologne (hopefully, not Clorox for Men). Virgos usually have a squeaky-clean appearance. You'd better ask because guesswork won't work here.

❋ A meal (no potted meat on toast or fried chicken) with candles and fine china will delight and impress your Virgo.

❋ Write your Virgo a poem, and either have it framed or read it aloud in a romantic setting. Pamper with class.

❋ Leave a thoughtful note by the phone that reads, "I like the way you talk." Or in a pair of shoes: "I like the way you walk." This will create a day-long pampering process.

❋ Take the children for a day and allow your Virgo time to pamper herself and at the same time feel pampered by you.

❋ Create a quiet getaway where every detail is planned, from the initial hello to the long good-bye. This is a great start to a month of pampering.

Gift Ideas for Virgo

❋ Books are always a winner. Virgos are intelligent people and books provide a great stimulus for their brain, which never shuts down. Even when they're asleep, they're probably having nightmares.

❋ Buying quality clothing is an absolute must! Being impeccably dressed is essential. El cheapo clothing is a big turnoff!

❋ To be on the safe side, get a gift certificate. Virgos are highly critical and have discriminating taste.

❋ Season tickets to his favorite sport are a sure bet.

❋ Season tickets to the community theater also score big points.

❋ Any subscription to a magazine promoting good health or business is a plus. But of course, you'd be expected to talk the talk and walk the walk.

❋ Any electronic gadget such as a calendar, phone book, or portable CD player. No matter how intricate, it's no problem to the Virgo.

❋ An upscaled pager that includes daily stock market updates and national and world news reports. She simply must keep up with the latest stock reports and what's going on in the world!

❋ A Bible with her name engraved on it. A personalized gift reinforces the notion of her commitment to her religion and at the same time allows a toe in the door.

❋ Any work-related item such as a new nameplate, clock radio, or lamp for the desk is always in order. Virgos are always working. In fact, that's where Virgos spend most of their time.

Libra

(September 23 to October 22)
SYMBOL: THE SCALES

Positive love traits: Exotic lover, confident partner, sensual and passionate; one of the participants in the freak show.

Negative love traits: Prone to infidelity; enjoys multiple partners; can be moody, distracted, and very kinky.

Ruling planet: Venus is associated with love and beauty.

Word to the wise: The scales tip up and down for Libras. Trying to figure them out will be a challenge you may not be up for.

When you meet the Libra, you'll be totally intrigued by the female or enjoy the cutup antics of the male. Libras love to be in the mix, and they're extremely popular with the opposite sex. They're charming, engaging conversationalists, and of course, they'll be tastefully dressed for any occasion.

The downside is that this air sign is a calm, easygoing, warm, and engaging person who can become, in the blink of an eye, an argumentative, stubborn, mean, tactless person you don't even know. You'll be dumbfounded by the change and convinced that this Libra must have an identical twin.

Libra's symbol is the scales, typifying a lifelong quest for balance in life. Libras swing from one extreme to the other, and only during the intervals are they able to reach that perfect place where peace and harmony reside.

If you're dealing with a Libra, good luck—there will never be a dull moment! And don't ask them why they have such a contradictory personality because they don't know any more than you do. Being around the Libran when the scales are out of balance is a headache you definitely don't need. So heed these words of warning: Stay away until they contact you, which will mean they're ready to be civil human beings. It's a Libra thang!

Librans are air signs: independent, aloof, analytical, intriguing, and very hard to keep up with. They simply must have their freedom. So if you're a control freak, your approach to the relationship should be about compromise, give-and-take, and enjoying each other for who you are.

One reason for Libra's indecisiveness is that these people are able to examine both sides of a problem with great clarity—making it easy to straddle the fence. For example, when asked if he was indecisive, a Libran brother couldn't decide if he was or wasn't. I rest my case!

If a Libran wins you over to his side of an argument and you concede that he's right and you're wrong, well, the discussion ain't over yet! By the time you throw your hands up and give in, he's coming around to *your* side, saying, "Wait a minute, you've got a point there." Just give it up—there's no hope at that point.

One of the things that's hard for Libras to accept is that not everyone can live up to their expectations. Libras feel that everyone should be like them: kind, generous, and diplomatic. Until, of course, the scales are tipped in the other direction; then you've got problems with Libra's dark side: mean, resentful, frivolous, and indecisive.

Physically, the only discernible feature of black Libras is their big butts. This is the case no matter how skinny or tiny the Libra. In both men and women, the booties are substantial and well rounded. The women are neither top- nor bottom-heavy and usually have neat waistlines with rounded hips—not too big and not too small, but just right. Usually, both the men and women are average size.

The key word for Libra is marriage. Libra is the sign of partnership, and Librans are generally happier when they're married, in a live-in relationship, or going with a long-term steady. They make very considerate mates, but remember, the scales of a Libra's life must be balanced. Marital bliss will come in spurts. Even if the marriage does not work out, the Libra will forever search for that all-important mate. A Libra sister from Chicago, who had divorced early and had no children, continued her quest for the perfect mate and family well into her forties. However, when her two nephews came to visit for an entire summer, she was constantly irritated; it finally hit her that having a child was not what she needed to do.

A relationship with a Libran needs to be slow-going. If you're pursuing a Libran, you will have to be the voice of reason. This air sign will act on impulse, and many times, both men and women will rush into a relationship prematurely without thinking things through.

Libra's ruling planet is Venus, which is associated with love and beauty. Need I say more? They love beautiful surroundings, clothing, art, and all of the amenities of life, including the BMW, the Benz, or the Lexus. And they will order the very best, regardless of cost. They may know that check will bounce later, but before "later" arrives, the Libra will have figured out how to float a check here and borrow money over there just in the nick of time. Both men and women of the sign have a natural, irresistible charm, and with their keen intelligence, they can use these traits very effectively to get what they want.

THE LIBRA MAN

Ladies, a word of warning: The Libra brother is very popular with the women. He prides himself on knowing just what a woman wants in a relationship. And he delivers! Falling in love with a Libran man will be easy. Trouble is, after you fall hopelessly in love with this honey, he may move in another direction. Sometimes the brother can be more in love with love than with you. He loves the chase and the whole romantic process.

He's charismatic and charming and has a style all his own. And he won't be caught dead in polyester, tattered clothing, or looking unkempt, ever. Anything you require will be executed by the Libra with his own creative spin to top it off. One Gemini woman who commented that her best relationship was with a Libra man said, "My man would take me shopping and I wouldn't say a word. We'd go into a store and he would select at least three outfits and have me try them on. . . . Afterward, he would decide to buy all three. He would then take me to get the accessories, including the shoes."

Librans make good partners but take forever deciding which
woman is for them. Their indecision will drive those impatient,
take-charge decision-making types nuts. Remember, their symbol
is the scales. They must weigh the pros and cons of any relationship
with you. They must have a perfect balance with the perfect mate,
meaning someone who can just about walk on water to sustain his
attention. Just kidding! If all of the aforementioned sounds contradictory and confusing, well, so are the life and personality of the Libra. He's confused, too! The areas of his personality that you are
aware of are all you have to go on in figuring him out. What about
the other area that you have no knowledge of? Trying to sort out all
of the pros and cons and ups and downs of his life keeps the Libra
in a state of confusion. There's the straddling-the-fence syndrome
again.

Sometimes he never makes a decision and strikes a balance between two women instead. "I've been in a relationship with two
women for almost two years," one Libra man commented. "It works
because it fulfills the needs that both women have, although they
don't know about each other."

But most of the time, he deals in extremes. The Libra will jump
headlong into a relationship without thinking things through—or
take forever deciding what to do. The woman may realize that she's
nearing menopause soon and bow out, to Libra's great relief.

Libra brothers are tender lovers who like imagination and fantasy. Libra men are good at foreplay. They hate confusion and chaos
in a relationship. Librans can participate in slam-bam sex, but prefer romance and atmosphere.

These air signs won't be controlled, contained, manipulated, or
told what to do. Like the element of air, they'll disappear. If you're
prone to jealous outbursts, accusing the Libra brother of screwing a
hole in the ground, he will be out the door. They must have balance
in their lives: a pleasant work environment, nice surroundings, and
a rewarding relationship with very few arguments. When any of
these areas is out of kilter, then you've got a miserable Libra who is
sullen, silent, and distant.

In many ways, a Libra brother's take on women may be somewhat chauvinistic. He wants a woman who is ultrafeminine and

who gets her nails done, a woman with style and grace, the damsel-in-distress type who is looking for a knight in shining armor. "What turns me on is femininity," said one Libra brother. "I don't want a woman who almost seems masculine. I like the southern belles and Georgia peaches because I want to open doors, send flowers, pull out a lady's chair, and all those things."

Being organized and having a clean house are also priorities for the Libra man. A Libra printing company worker admitted that he cannot stand a house to be junky or unclean, his or anyone else's. "It really irks me when people who have been laying up all day have not cleaned up the house," he said. Another Libra said he cannot abide a nasty, disorganized, clothes-all-over-the-floor house, calling it a "clothes carpet."

Like Scorpio, the Libra brother sets the stage to continue a relationship long after the spark has gone out. "I haven't had a reason not to call any of the women I've been involved with," a Libra insurance agent said. "I've always carried myself in a manner that required respect for the woman whose company I'm in," he said. "Even those that I meet in the passing parade, I can call, if the number hasn't changed, and we can talk about anything."

Being self-centered and talking about yourself constantly are a real turnoff for Libra. They are communicators and if you're only talking about yourself, then there's no real dialogue and under-standing of the other.

Once this brother *finally* falls in love, it's usually for keeps, as long as you provide a loving home with peace, harmony, and beau-tiful surroundings. They like beautiful surroundings, and they love beautiful companions. But good looks will only get you so far. You must know about current events and what's going on in the world, a Libran brother said. "I've had relationships with women who didn't have the looks, but had the appeal. The appeal is the turn-on for me: the smile, the walk, the talk, the overall appeal."

Libras love to spoil their companions, but asking for money is a big turnoff for them. "I get really pissed when my lady asks me for money more often than once a week," said a Libra. "She can look in my face and tell that I don't like it."

All it takes is a little stroking and they will give in readily. He loves to have his ego stroked, and in the case of the Libra, flattery will get you everywhere. The balance act with the Libra will often have you weary, but this brother is fair-minded, easygoing, and a genuine nice guy. Yes, he will send you over the edge with his nit-pickin' and indecisiveness. But if you're going over the edge with a Libra, at least it will be an adventure.

THE LIBRA WOMAN

The Libra woman will be a challenging, intriguing sister who will expect your undivided attention. Fortunately, she's an air sign and she has her own life and will not expect you to be at her beck and call 24 hours a day, 7 days a week. But when the two of you come to-gether, romance, intimacy, consideration, and communication will be key areas with this energetic, high-maintenance female. A Libra writer from L.A. commented on the most important thing in a rela-tionship: "With God as the center, people are humbled; if couples can laugh, they can love, and communication is the key to under-standing."

The Libra woman specializes in looking good at all times. Some-one may be watching, you know. She's got to have her nails, toes, and hair done on a weekly basis, if she can afford it. And what with maintaining the "look," working, and social commitments, when the two of you finally get together, every moment counts. The Libra woman must create melodrama and intrigue so that the interest will move on to the next phase—the courtship and romance, the best part for her.

This air sign loves to shop, and she will expect you to go along with the status quo. Don't rush her or get impatient. She must have that kick-ass outfit for when that special occasion rolls around. She simply must be the center of attention.

Say, brother, if you're wearing outdated clothing from two decades previous, then while she's shopping for herself, she will pick up a little somethin', somethin' for you! Don't be a slob when it comes to dressing. Even if you don't wear designer clothing, which she prefers, you must be neatly dressed. And if you don't get the hint to clean up your act or your image, you may be whistling all alone because she'll be gone like the wind.

Although she may sound self-centered (and she is sometimes), she's a very attentive partner. She believes that a lavish lifestyle and personal pampering are what she deserves. And if you happen to be along for the ride, you'll be pampered, too. A Libra from Chicago agreed. "I am a giver. If I love someone, I enjoy providing gifts for them. I've always been told that I love too hard, and sometimes I need the same in return. But it's important. . . . It's just me."

Being in love with the idea of love, a Libra can blindly fall head over heels—but it's an infatuation, not necessarily love. Such was the case with a Libra who found her herself in the most embarrassing situation: "My first husband caught me cheating on him with his best friend. Hey, I was young and very dumb. I paid the price, the marriage ended in divorce," the Libra woman said.

Loud, aggressive, and boisterous brothers need not apply. It's almost as though Libras have to have chamber music playing in the background to function. They must maintain peace, harmony, and that all-important balance. And even if you've got a six-figure salary and no home training, you're history, buddy. (Well, maybe she can live with the six figures.) As one Libra writer commented, "The worst turnoff for me is rude, crude, and insensitive behavior. This guy can't get me to give him my correct name, no less the time of day." Lady Libra is a woman of principles. She wants her companion to have class, money, the right friends, and a decent job. She's usually the social butterfly. She just has to be in the mix, to see and to be seen.

However, if she spots a fine Lord-have-mercy motor scooter with the six-pack abs across the room, and he happens to be looking in her direction, then all of the breeding, principles, and the pretense will be history. She'll flirt shamelessly. This meeting could very well be a one-night stand. She has a weakness for the fine specimens of the world!

A Libra woman loves beautiful surroundings and lavish furnishings, clothing, and people. In fact, she considers herself one of the "beautiful" people. Even if she's average-looking, she can accentuate the positive and create an image that can and will turn heads.

If you're invited to Lady Libra's house, all of the trappings will definitely be in place—the best champagne, the most seductive music, the candles, and you. The food will be delicious and so will she. She knows how to create an enchanting evening that you won't forget. Her approach is to delight, amaze, and tantalize. And don't forget the compliments. She'll soak them up and have you for dessert!

Lady Libra will also expect you to be attentive and have an enchanting evening exchanging ideas, philosophies, and observations. But take heed: A person who suffers from "I" strain is going to have problems with Lady Libra. Librans can't bear would-be suitors who talk about themselves in the I, me, my mode. Ms. Libra has plenty to say as well. And she will let you know readily that it ain't all about you! Do you hear me, chile?

Intelligence is a big plus with Libras. They won't tolerate a companion who is not well versed on a variety of subjects. Intellectual stimulation is second only to sex for this air sign. So don't gloss over areas of importance, because they *are* paying attention. "I am very, very smart. I am an excellent listener, and I'm not afraid to remind a guy of what he said in a previous conversation," a Libra public relations person said.

The Libra sister is a lesson in contradictions. She's attracted to intelligent men, but at the same time she likes the strong, silent types. She admires a man who has the guts to boss her around, yet she's really her own person and more than likely won't be controlled.

This back-and-forth approach, going from one extreme to the other, is also a part of the Libra makeup. For example, Libras are either high-spirited or sullen and quiet. They can have tons of energy or retreat like a hibernating bear only to resurface during the next season. "I have great energy spurts and times of great idleness where I appear to be doing nothing. (I'm thinking and meditating.) I can go for hours without talking. All three of my ex-husbands have told me that I don't wake up like normal people; I jump out of bed like a Pop-Tart," a Libra woman commented.

Straddling the fence is the Libra's forte. For example, you may think the relationship is moving along at a progressive pace and you suggest that the two of you take a weekend trip together. What you might find is a sullen, quiet Libra, who will interrogate you about why she should go with you, saying it's too soon. The next thing you know, the relationship is all but a passing fancy. This happened to an Aquarius brother. "I couldn't understand this woman. . . . Whenever we went out on a date, it was fun and romantic. And the sex was great! As soon as I told her that I wanted her to take a weekend trip to meet my folks, she started trippin', asking me why I wanted her to go and what did it mean!" The Aquarius brother realized, by the time he got out of the discussion, that he was confused about the trip, too. Don't bother to figure this one out. She can't explain what the problem is any more than you—she's just as confused!

And the next day, of course, she'll be apologetic, but she still won't be able to determine in a definite way what went wrong. It's baffling. The Libra woman can be very lazy when it comes to nurturing a relationship, but she'll demand a lot from you and expect you to know what she wants even before she realizes it herself. Go figure!

Her expectations of a potential companion are high. If you don't put in the E for effort, you'll notice a change in what you thought was a budding relationship. The other problem is, whether you put up the effort or not, there may be some microscopic problem—blowing or picking your nose in public or getting too smashed at her high school class reunion—that tilts her scales and threatens the perfect balance. Of course, neither you nor the rest of the world knows what happened. With a Libra, you simply can't predict which way the relationship will go.

Guide to a Love Connection

Libra and Aries

These two are opposites of the zodiac, but they are so sexually drawn to each other that they're mistaking sex for a viable long-term union. While Libra is trying to leave, Aries spends a lot of time in that "wait a minute, baby" mode, which means give the ram a chance to explain. Give it up, Aries, you're opposites! Libra loves peace and harmony. Aries rants and raves constantly. Libra loves a lavish and elegant lifestyle. Aries is interested in roughing it and eating food on the run. Libra must be dressed to kill. You'll be lucky if Aries has on clothing, and if Aries is wearing clothes, they will probably be from the 1970s. Libra requires an attentive partner. Aries is off and running in a hundred different directions. Need I go on?

Libra and Taurus

This couple will need a lot of prayer, patience, and perseverance to make this work. Taurus is patient and will persevere through most stresses of life, so maybe Libra can pray a little. Libra is the so-cialite and must be in the middle of all of the goings-on. Taurus is bored by this behavior and simply wants a quiet evening at home. Libra must be the star of the show and will spend money shame-lessly over the objections of frugal Taurus. Libra will soon get bored by Taurus's slow, cautious nature because Libra wants adventure, spontaneity, and fun. That's okay for Taurus occasionally, but Taurus will look at Libra's flighty behavior as weird. The sex is great, but it's put on hold too often to deal with other problem areas.

Libra and Gemini

When these two meet, the chatter is nonstop. This pair is fun-loving and enjoys life to the fullest, together or apart. Libra shops for days for those must-have outfits and Gemini wants all of the de-signer labels, too. Both are party animals and must make the social scene. These two air signs are self-assured and won't make the other feel guilty when one of them is not around. Both have sepa-rate lives. Sex between these two is an adventure. Libra loves to ex-periment and Gemini will be a curious participant. Gemini loves being free and single, and so does Libra—to a point. But there won't be any applied pressure. This companionable arrangement is more than satisfying for them both.

Libra and Cancer

The physical areas of this relationship are made in the shade, provided that hurt feelings can be kept to a minimum. Libra is in-dependent, while Cancer is more dependent emotionally and phys-ically. Libra will play the sitting-at-home role, enjoying Cancer's company, for a while—but that soon gets old for this sociable air sign. Libra loves the glitz and glamour of the parties, the people and the places. And Libra must have the outfits to accompany all the sets that he must make. Cancer, although friendly and sociable, wants Libra all to herself. Once the dust clears, Cancer will retreat to lick her wounds and Libra will be off and running to the next adventure. These two need to be friends.

Libra and Leo

Libra's love of luxury, romance, and pleasure works well with Leo's affinity for intrigue and adventure. These two are soul mates. Libra keeps the peace at all costs and provides Leo with support and the voice of reason. Leo's aggressive nature and desire to be the center of attention get on Libra's nerves. Libra has it going on, too. Compromises are definitely in order. Both have career goals, love the arts, and must be involved in the community. Libra, the air sign, is more independent and freedom-loving, but Leo is not intimidated when Libra needs space. Whenever they come back together, a good time is had by both. Libra thrives when there is a companion in the mix and Leos love children. Wedding bells could definitely be around the corner.

Libra and Virgo

This relationship is doomed from the start. Libra wants fun, frivolity, and the finer things of life. Virgo wants home, hearth, and stability. Libra, the charmer of the zodiac, will be turned off by Virgo's reserved and highly critical nature. Libra's outgoing and flirtatious nature will drive prudent, no-nonsense Virgo to drink. Sexually, however, Libra will ignite some of Virgo's smoldering sensual tendencies. It may take Virgo a while to get crankin' in the bedroom, to the dismay of Libra, who has very little patience with Virgo's judgmental position on Libra's outlandish behavior. Each frustrates the other. Libra wants excitement and drama and will see Virgo's cautious, guarded behavior as a personal insult. These two are too ill matched to even playact at a relationship.

Libra and Libra

Just as long as there are no earth-shattering decisions to be made, everything will be fine. Well, temporarily anyway. These two need to chill and get over whatever ails them, including the what if . . . , I think . . . , but if . . . , and we won't be able to . . . ! Both love the lavish life of beautiful surroundings, beautiful possessions, and beautiful people. They *are* the beautiful people. The end result of this pairing is lots of big beautiful credit card bills and constant bickering over who's at fault. Good luck! You're gonna need it.

Libra and Scorpio

Libra is the center of attention in any social setting. Scorpio waits in the wings, observing every move Libra makes. Once these two get together, they're totally taken with each other. Enter complications. Libra loves to be wined, dined, and doted on. And that's fine with Scorpio until it's time for Libra to reciprocate. Scorpio's possessiveness and jealousy find Libra frustrated and annoyed. Freedom-loving Libra needs peace and harmony. Scorpio wants a total commitment, now! Libra can't decide what needs to happen in the relationship at a moment's notice. Libra wants the lavish lifestyle. Scorpio is prudent and careful about spending money. In the end, this matchup brings both to a blood-boiling level that won't simmer down until it's over.

Libra and Sagittarius

These two are definitely intrigued by each other. Libra's charm and grace get rough-and-ready Sagittarius's attention. Both love the party scene, meeting new friends, and discussing far-reaching ideas. Both are intelligent, with clear career goals. Libra is happier with a partner and Sag is content as the bachelor or bachelorette, but if these two do get together, there will definitely be a meeting of the minds first. Libra wants Sag's undivided attention and Sag is the flirt of the zodiac. Sag spends money wisely and is not going to let Libra squander money. Both are creative lovers, but Libra is a little more out there. All things considered, this could be the start of something big!

Libra and Capricorn

Contact will be very intense and curious. Libra is always impeccably dressed and so is Capricorn. No problem there. Libra loves beautiful surroundings and people. Although Capricorn loves a lavish lifestyle, he's cautious and conservative about spending. Librans spend because they feel they deserve it. Logical, practical Capricorn is skeptical of this thinking. Between the sheets is another talk show entirely. Conservative Capricorn is embarrassed by Libra's freaky, over-the-top sexual demos. Libra feels stodgy Capricorn should move into the twenty-first century and live a little because Librans have enjoying life down to a science. Philosophical and physical differences are enough to keep them permanently separated. There won't be any love lost between these two.

Libra and Aquarius

Libra is the peacemaker and can settle Aquarius's affinity for confrontation if pushed. Both are air signs and must have freedom and adventure away from the other. Libra loves the romantic scene with the candlelit dinner, the French wine, and the expensive tab. Aquarius could eat Spam. After-dinner love play creates more harmony between these two. Both can run through a bank account like there's no tomorrow. Aquarius's off-the-beaten-path demeanor and unique approach to living turn a curious streak in Libra on. Aquarius's decision-making skills help indecisive Libra. Aquarius drifts off into her many contemplations of the next millennium, but practical Libra keeps Aquarius grounded. This pairing definitely has potential.

Libra and Pisces

These two have many similar interests, and this helps the relationship initially. Both love fine dining, lavish surroundings, intellectual conversation, and the arts. Both are creative and will try most things in the boudoir, Pisces more so than Libra. Both are clotheshorses and must maintain their images. But the similarities end there. Libra simply cannot give Pisces all of the emotional support he needs. Pisces perceives Libra's need for freedom and independence as a personal insult. Libra is outgoing, loves people and being in the mix. Pisces loves being in the mix at home with Libra. Libra feels Pisces is too needy. Pisces feels Libra is too aloof. Skip this one.

ROMANCE AND THE LIBRA

Romance is the central most important area of the relationship to Libras. They love the chase, the romantic interludes, the warm and fuzzy feeling they get from the initial stages of the relationship. For them, the romance is the icing on the cake; it's what makes the whole experience worthwhile.

There are several reasons why this is so. Since Libras have this critical eye and nitpicking approach with most areas of their lives, including potential or current companions, the initial stage, before reality and the human element enter the picture, is very exciting for them. "I love the beginning of any relationship and the first few dates—that's when we're into each other and on our best behavior," a Libra woman from Seattle said.

Basically, what that means is the Libra's discriminating eye hasn't noticed any flaws yet, flaws that can turn him off as quickly as he is turned on. It's the *idea* of love that is so exciting to this air sign. Libra definitely enjoys taking the trip more than arriving at the destination. And the trip will be a trip!

For the Libra, intimate talks, taking excursions together, taking time with children, and attending family functions also get high marks during a relationship and can translate into romance as well. Libra is the sign of partnerships. Marriage, children, and family are high-priority areas in Libras' lives.

Although Libras are prone to be indecisive when it comes to making a commitment, they will expect your undivided attention. Their symbol is the scales, which means they will want the perfect companion and relationship. Of course, you won't know what constitutes a perfect companion because she won't either. The point is, she can't make up her mind about you, but she's not sure of what she wants either. Huh?

And just when you think you're on the mark with the courtship, things may take a turn for the worse. In an effort to keep the romance alive, the Libra may shy away from a long-term commitment. So retreat when questions about the stability and the feasibility of a long-term relationship surface. Remember, the Libra's quandary has very little to do with you. The indecisiveness is ever-present with these free spirits of the zodiac. When this happens, let the fun and games begin and skip all of the rules and regulations.

When Libras are into a date, they expect the romance to be an all-day or all-night encounter. They don't just want the dinner;

they want the walk along the lake, the midnight drive, and the intimate talks, too. "A romantic evening is dinner at a really fine restaurant with lots of red wine, a room in a wonderful hotel with fresh flowers and more wine, and a massage with exotic oils," says a Libra woman from Minnesota.

In short, they expect, and most of the time demand, the total package because that's what you get from them. They want you to drink in the total experience that they create from start to finish, with every minute detail in place. Here's how a Libra man described a romantic date: "I will cook a candlelight gourmet dinner with homemade bread. Then soft music or no music, depending on the mood, candles around the hot tub, some light, depending on the mood, and then we'll go with the flow."

Another Libra commented, "My idea of a romantic date is anything that requires imagination." Libras expect creativity and spontaneity, with serious overtones of intimacy. Having money when planning a date with a Libra always helps because she expects and wants the best. But using your imagination when there are few resources will work as well. A Libra resource specialist remembers one romantic encounter fondly. "I was seduced by his romantic side, poetry, thoughtfulness, and unexpected encounters. He pursued me. We met through friends."

Jumping in the car with a picnic basket and hittin' the highway, stopping at an out-of-the-way inn, will do just as well. "I like dates that start in the morning with breakfast and go throughout the day," commented one Libra from Philadelphia. "In general, I like day-long hangout dates, not fufu planned, structured occasions."

Although you may each have your own house, checking into a hotel will pique his interest. That way you can totally concentrate on each other: no ringing telephones, no answering machines, no unexpected visitors dropping by. Libras are social people and there's always some unexpected event to attend or friend, family member, or colleague calling. She simply must be right in the center of where the action is. So you need to get rid of those distractions for a while.

A Libra brother declared that dinner at an exclusive restaurant and getting a hotel room are always a good idea. Another Libra brother from Mississippi said, "I like an evening in a nice café." I hope by now you're getting the picture. Libras are fun-loving, spunky types with a great sense of humor. They will laugh with you, at you, or even at themselves. A Libra man was sitting at a table in a nightclub with his back to the dance floor when he was approached by another man, who asked him to dance. The brother clearly didn't realize that he was asking a man to dance since the Libra had a large Afro and he was the only male at a table full of women. Of course all of the females at the table laughed uproariously, and so did the Libra.

For the Libra, if the romance gets too hot and heavy, the two of you may not make it to the bedroom or the hotel, but that's fine with these air signs. This Libra recalls one night: "I got a call to request we rendezvous at a quiet bar, followed by a romantic and lustful dinner at a Brazilian restaurant, where I was spoon-fed deliciously. Then a lot of sexual healing—in the parking lot, on the stairs, and in the window." How's that for romance?

Or consider this: "My companion and I took a train to Montreal. We stayed in a youth hostel, but spent every evening in nice restaurants. We walked along the prettiest streets and held hands a lot. It was wonderful," an author from New York said. Warning: Libras are very analytical, and they have a knack for figuring out convoluted situations. If you're a liar or a perpetrator, your hole card will eventually be exposed. If you claim to own a Lamborghini, your Libran date may ask you to spell the word.

"I've had two disastrous romantic encounters, both married men who lied about their status," says a Libra from California. "Fortunately, since I am not sexually active, I was spared much embarrassment."

Sex, Sex, and More Sex

Getting the Groove On . . .

The key word for any bedroom scene with a Libra is open-mindedness. As one Libra brother put it, "All I ask during a sexual relationship is that you come with openness and a willingness to engage in something different." And if you're a prude, well, you can move on to another section of this book and save yourself some trauma. Libras definitely don't have time for your platitudes and condemnation of over-the-top sexual high jinks.

Actually, Libras are creative types and some of their mental musings are in the far reaches of the stratosphere. And these air signs can create a sexual experience to end all experiences in their minds before you ever enter their boudoir. They have keen imaginations and go for all the props: whipped cream, sexy underwear, scented candles, porno videos, seductive music, and, if you're receptive, even an additional partner. For them it's all about the pleasure principle.

A Libran brother had this to say about sexual behavior: "I'm very open and giving. And it turns me off when a woman is a selfish lover." But the sexual inclination for Libras, the sign of the scales, can also tip in the other direction, meaning ultraconservative Holy Roller types. Then again, depending on what kind of a mood they're in, they can be conservative with one partner and flying by the seat of their pants with another. With Libras, you just never know, and you can't predict.

If you're about to have a sexual experience—excuse me, sexual *explosion*—with the Libra, pace yourself and don't freak out. Freak, yes, but running out of the bedroom wearing only your shoes and a trench coat will cause you mental stress and strain later. I would suggest a nice talk with your Libra beforehand so that you can find out what's to come and determine if you can handle it. You'll be glad you did.

For the most part, this sign is one of the kinkiest of the kinky, especially the Libran woman. A pushing-the-envelope approach to sex will become apparent very quickly. "I've been called a freak, but I just like good lovin'. I know what I enjoy and everyone can't handle it in the beginning. I give it some time and then I begin to experiment with my man. What drives me crazy in the bedroom is aggressive oral and physical sex, with smells, sounds, and tenderness afterward," a Libra from East St. Louis, Illinois, said.

The Libra man has the fine art of making love down to a science, but will sip champagne from your navel or insert objects into your vagina and release them at the point of orgasm. As one insurance salesman put it, "It's all in the mouth and no woman can control herself. I love it. Every woman that I've been involved with has been intrigued by me. In a word, they describe me as charming." Another word the Libra needs to learn is modesty.

Both male and female Librans love to play in bed all day and all night. The Libra man prides himself on creating the atmosphere, along with effective, passionate foreplay. He knows what a woman wants and needs and he will leave no stone unturned in this regard.

The Libra woman is definitely in the advanced level of the sex classes. She's always open to being taught a thing or two or three in the area of sex. But if you're the partner and cannot "bring home the bacon," she's willing and able to do what is needed. She will masturbate or use a sex toy right in front of you if your efforts fizzle out. And she will try anything once.

Regarding maneuvers initiated by women, a Libran brother commented, "Show me all that you know; after all, a woman should know how to please." Another Libra brother had this to say: "If my woman shows me a maneuver I haven't seen in the bedroom and we have been seeing each other for, say, three years, then yes, I want to know where she got that from." But, he added, he delights in a woman being creative in bed.

As Freddie Jackson says in his song, "let's take it nice and slow." This is the philosophy and anthem for Libras because they want to enjoy every inch of the body, every moment and every hour, and will make full use of all five senses—taste, touch, sight, smell, and feel. A Libra sister from Jamaica commented, "It turns me off when my partner is not connected to what he's doing. It's as though I am experiencing his routine repertoire."

For Libra, melodrama and the setting are as important as the sex act itself—or maybe even more so. For example, a Libra brother sometimes invited his companion over and purposely did not play music or even have conversation during the visit. "Silence is erotic to me, too. When my lady comes over, sometimes I'll tell her, we are just here for one thing, to experience each other's bodies and not to talk at all."

One Libra brother's pet peeve is this: "I don't like it when there is not an equal sharing of the relationship, in the bedroom and out. I will not call again if there is not an equal showing of affection."

These air signs are turned on in their mind first. Phone sex can work well. The Libra will call up and declare all of the goings-on for the evening, giving you a play-by-play with Luther playing in the background or heavy breathing by the Libra as she works herself into a frenzy. Like the Aquarian, Libra is the foreplay guru. He simply wants to cover all of the bases when it comes to sexual matters. Sex to the Libra is as important as eating and breathing.

One Libra subscribed to the Eastern sexology philosophy of the more sex and the more heightened and intense your orgasm, the longer you'll live. Well, call this brother Methuselah, because he's definitely jumpin' the bones of many, and the line forms to the left. The brother has books on the subject with numbered diagrams of the vagina. A number denotes how an area responds to certain stimuli. Before you run out and buy a sexology book, don't forget the passion, genuine caring, and mental stimulation that must be present and that Libras pride themselves on.

Although urination on the body was not a particular turn-on for one Libran brother, the sexual encounters he experienced with his companion, including sex toys and porno movies, found his companion urinating on him during orgasm. "At first, she was totally embarrassed by not having control, but I made her feel okay and was accepting of it."

EROGENOUS ZONES . . . SOME PHYSICAL, SOME NOT

If you want the sparks to fly immediately with the goddess or god of love, stroke Librans on the small of their back or butt, erogenous zones for them. Any touches, kisses, or massages to those areas will put this sign in overdrive.

Actually, the foreplay and the anticipation of the day and evening are another erotic turn-on for Libras. These air signs have a vivid imagination. The brain is working overtime when it comes to the mental foreplay in which they're involved before the two of you come together in the grand splendor of the moment.

Librans can have a fixation on what most would consider minor details, not very erotic; for example, the thought or smell of her mate's cologne can create instant arousal, along with any subtleties and reminders of a companion's dress or demeanor. If Libras are preoccupied with thoughts of their companion, it doesn't take much to get them going.

A Libra brother who has a foot fetish must have a peek at his woman's feet during the arousal process. "I like nice, manicured feet. That's very erotic to me. If we're out at a restaurant and she takes off her shoes and her feet are pretty and manicured, I can't eat. I'm thinking about sucking her toes or something," the Libra brother from Atlanta said.

The many thoughts that a Libra might have about the erotic process can run the gamut. She might call and talk dirty on the telephone to her companion. He might show up unexpectedly in Speedo biker shorts and a fitted muscle T-shirt, just to titillate your desires. A Libra woman told her companion that she wanted to give him a full body massage—nude, of course. Her mate readily complied, showing up at her house in just a pair of shorts, which he quickly, willingly removed.

Any sexual position is fine for Libras. Their philosophy is, whatever works. The 69 position is okay. However, since the erogenous zone is the buttocks, doggy style drives this sign wild, creating erotic quivers that most aspire to. A Libra commented on what turns her on between the sheets: "I love for him to be unselfish, yet totally lost in his own passion. When my partner is working to bring me to climax, it shouldn't be work."

Any additional enhancements, like a dance, striptease, or massage, will always titillate the Libra and make for an excitable evening that the two of you can really get into. Sometimes Libra can be so wrapped in the foreplay, the "play" can get lost in the intimacy. "I like the lead-in to sex more than the intercourse itself," a Libra woman said. Hey, whatever works!

PLAIN OL' SEX AND NOTHING MORE: WELCOME TO THE FREAK SHOW

Librans definitely will participate in the freak show. They can also be one of the stars of the show. But Librans, in all of their indecisiveness, will find that others will take the starring role.

Yes, the Libra does have an image to uphold. Librans thrive on kinky sexual antics and erotic high jinks. Their approach to sex is similar to what they seek as a part of life—spontaneity, adventure, and fun. And this sign will try anything once. Their only requests are that the sex not be too violent, risking life and limb. Otherwise, the sky is the limit with these free spirits of the sexual arena.

The very nature of this air sign signifies that they want life to be light and breezy, without a lot of issues, arguments, and problems. Therefore approaching them about engaging in some sensual satis- faction, for the most part, will be just fine with them.

However, here's the rub. If you decide to make the approach, you better be able to deliver. If not, the Libra, who doesn't like to waste a lot of time, will talk about you bad! If your technique leaves a lot be desired, you need to be on with smoke and mirrors—by that I mean some atmosphere, with incense or candles burning, a large mirror so that he can watch his technique, some whipped cream, chocolate, sex toys, even a surprise or two. Maybe even a third per- son. As I said, they'll try anything once.

On the other hand, if the scales are out of balance, there's no telling what attitude you might be met with. Timing, chemistry, and mood are everything with these complex, thoughtful creatures. If they agree, strike while the iron is hot!

Money Matters

If you are in a relationship with a Libra, well, God bless you! You'll need all of the blessings you can muster with a Libra, who spends money with reckless abandon. Image is everything, you know. When it comes to spending money, Libra is second only to Leo.

If you're dating or considering marrying a Libra, one thing's for sure: You'll understand her philosophy about money early. As one Libra sister put it, "Money is to spend, not hoard. What's the point?" Even if there comes a time when the Libra has to make a de- cision about what to invest in or what money market account in which to get involved, it's going to be a back-and-forth struggle for them. So please make the decision so that they can avoid putting themselves, and you, through their mental masturbation. It's called cruel and unusual punishment.

Libra people expect to have a lavish lifestyle. If they can't afford the clothes and car, and are living beyond their means, the public will never know. The credit cards will be *way* past their limit. The Li- bra brother is the one who gets indignant when his credit card is declined, knowing good and well that it would be a miracle if he could charge another item. If not, he'll write a rubber check and worry about the consequences when he gets his overdrawn statement in the mail.

The Libra sister believes nothing, absolutely nothing, is too good for her if she really wants it. She shows very little prudence or caution when it comes to her purchasing power. She will buy expensive clothes, furnishings, and car to boot without a moment's hesitation, and worry about the consequences later.

Although Libras want perfect balance in their lives, balancing the checkbook is an exercise in futility for them. They're into immediate gratification, not long-term saving and investment.

Once they get married, then they are a bit more conservative about spending. A married Libran won't spend the children's allowance, but the single Libran would, along with yours, her parents', or anyone else's foolish enough to oblige.

As these air signs mature, they come to realize the importance of investing and saving. But if there is a choice between that killer must-have outfit and cashing in the savings bonds, well, there's always next payday for you to buy more bonds.

One reason why they don't pay attention to saving money is that they must be in the mix with the very best outfit, best car, biggest house that their money can buy. They must be admired and looked up to for all of their material trappings. I know, it's superficial—but to Libras style and flair are more important than a financial portfolio. You see, you can't carry the portfolio around and show it off. However, you can be dressed to the nines and be admired by the masses.

Here's a suggestion: If you can show the Libra how investing money and saving for the future can yield even greater benefits and make it possible to buy a bigger house or a more expensive car by doing so, then you may be on to something. It would help if the financial returns could be instantaneous. And while you're in your convincing mode, you need to have a financial planner there, too, so that a payroll deduction plan can be worked out on the spot, before Libra's mind changes.

PAMPERING TIPS FOR LIBRA

✳ Plan a romantic picnic with tablecloth, china, and wine—with glasses, of course. A remote area is best, if you get my drift.

✳ When you're trying to pamper your Libra, the more lavish, the better. Champagne in the bubble bath or chillin' at a luxury hotel in a Jacuzzi sipping the bubbly works.

✳ Libras must have peace and harmony. Any out-of-the-way hideaway will work so that your Libra can relax. But other details like finding a baby-sitter and canceling appointments must be addressed, too.

✳ Pampering for the Libra also means having your undivided attention. Turn the telephone ringer off, unplug the answering machine, and create that haven at your Libra's place, with fun, food, and frolic.

✳ A cruise or trip out of the country—let's say, Paris, France. Librans love romance, intrigue, and mystery. Any trip to a place that these air signs haven't explored before is pampering enough.

✳ Libra wants to be appreciated. Arrange to have a family or church banquet to commemorate some special event in his or her life. Your Libra will be forever grateful.

✳ Arrange for a manicurist, a masseuse, and her favorite hairdresser or his favorite barber to make a house call! You'll definitely be in da house!

✳ Keep your Libra supplied with her favorite things. For example, if your lady Libra loves chocolates or has a favorite perfume or cologne, make sure she doesn't run out.

✳ A gift basket that includes all of your Libra's favorite things will be most appreciated. Bubble bath, candles, food coupons, and coupons for chores around the house will help you redeem yourself!

✳ Once all of the trappings are in place, then it's time to arrange for the roving musician at the most elegant restaurant that your checkbook can stand. And while the music plays, read your favorite love poem to your Libra to top the evening off.

GIFT IDEAS FOR LIBRA

- ❉ Libras love the finer things of life: The more expensive the gift, the better.
- ❉ Expensive jewelry like earrings, bracelets, pendants, or bangles works for the Libra, who loves jewelry.
- ❉ Your artsy Libra loves plays or community theater. Season tickets for the arts will always work.
- ❉ Original artwork and signed and numbered framed prints are winners. Libra's furnishings are upscale and these gifts will complement his home nicely.
- ❉ Libras love to travel. Buy the tickets and include the string bikini or the French-cut briefs. Make the whole affair a surprise. Libras love it when they don't have to make decisions.
- ❉ Libras look for quality and class when it comes to gifts. A handmade gift like a desk or a sculpture will have your Libran purring like a kitten.
- ❉ As long as the social calendar isn't bulging,, books of fiction, self-help, romance, and mystery make great gifts.
- ❉ A surprise party will have your Libra chomping at the bit. The Libra likes nothing better than to be the center of attention.
- ❉ A set of luggage for the special trip the two of you are planning is an ideal gift. Your Libra would not be caught dead with luggage that doesn't match!
- ❉ Sterling silver or fine crystal or china for the home makes your companion feel special. Your Libra thrives on beauty and luxury.

Scorpio

(October 23 to November 21)

SYMBOL: THE SCORPION

Positive love traits: Passionate, sensual lover and confident partner; one of the stars of the freak show.

Negative love straits: Insatiable lover; may be kinky and sadistic.

Ruling planet: Pluto is associated with regeneration and obsession.

Word to the wise: Once you're involved with a Scorpio, there's no turning back. Total possession is the goal here.

You'll be automatically drawn to this water sign—not romantically at first, but just out of curiosity. Scorpios are usually overly friendly or totally distant upon first meeting, but their calm outward appearance masks the inner struggle of this water sign. Uncovering the mask and understanding Scorpio's core are chores you may not want to tackle.

Their ruling planet is Pluto, which is associated with regeneration and obsession. Not only can they bounce back from traumatic situations in their lives, but they're usually intrigued by the challenges. They're obsessive about love relationships and protecting loved ones. Remember, folks, if you get involved in a relationship with a Scorpio, you'll be expected to call in two or three times a day. The Scorpio plans to know your every move. If you fail to call, you'll be questioned—excuse me, interrogated.

For Scorpios, passion and emotions rule every aspect of their lives whether it's work, play, family and friends, or personal challenges. Although these water signs present a placid exterior, things are often rough and choppy inside. Only a few will be privy to Scorpio's inner workings and deep, dark secrets. If you're clamoring to know more, be careful what you ask for. With a Scorpio, you just never know what you may find.

If you're interested in getting to know this sign, be genuine, straightforward, and direct because the scorpion can spot a phony a mile away. People born under the sign of Scorpio are highly emotional and intuitive. If you're prevaricating and lying, you can forget it! On the other hand, they are very mysterious and private people. They will read you like a book, but keep their own cards close to their chest.

You won't have any trouble locating Scorpios; they are usually surrounded by interested suitors. They are people persons; you'll find them at card parties, sports bars, out camping, clubbing, or any place where there are lots of people. Then again, they may be totally reclusive, only emerging to work or obtain the necessities of life.

Their symbol is the scorpion, which, as you know, is a member of the spider family. Spiders make most folks run for cover; the scorpion's pinching claws and long tail with the poisonous sting at the tip go even further, signaling that a scorpion's wrath can be deadly.

Scorpio is the sign of extremes. Scorpios are very vengeful if they feel you have crossed them in some way. A Scorpio who found out that his wife, also a Scorpio, was sleeping with his best friend, and had added insult to injury by using *his* credit cards for the hotel charges, decided to enroll in martial arts training. In his rage, he drove his hand through a mirror—but he also went on to become a black belt. "I took up martial arts because I planned to kill him," he said, but after several years, thankfully, the vengeful Scorpio abandoned the idea. On the flip side, scorpions can be the most devoted, generous, loyal, and gentle people you'll ever meet. That's what makes them so intriguing. You know the potential for danger, yet that's what keeps you drawn to the relationship. There won't be any gray areas: Things are pretty much black-and-white—which is also a favorite clothing combination for them. It's feast or famine with these water signs. Scorpio people are very outspoken. If you don't want to hear the painful truth, don't ask. Sometimes, however, things will just pop out of their mouths. Of course, most times, the

Scorpio is not trying to hurt your feelings. That's simply the way they are.

Both the men and the women have brilliant minds. Scorpio people have definite goals regarding career, relationships, marriage, and children. When you're on a date with a scorpion, initially she is very quiet, but she is definitely assessing your qualities, strengths, and weaknesses. By the date's end, the scorpion usually knows if it's going to work. "Dating is kind of like applying for a job. A person applies for CEO, but may only be qualified for the position of clerk," said one scorpion brother.

You might as well get this message into your head now before going any further. Here's the deal. If you end up totally smitten by a Scorpio, this behavior will come as no surprise. The Scorpio understands early on the effect that he or she has on would-be suitors. But just because you're impressed, this doesn't mean that they're impressed, too. So get over it!!

THE SCORPIO MAN

The Scorpio brother will be a challenge that will take you from one end of the relationship spectrum to the other. He's more than a handful and understands his effect, either long-term or short-term, on women. He's passionate and emotional, he'll cry with you, hold your hand, rub your back, and hang on to your every word. On the other hand, he's vindictive, prone to jealous rages, moody, and secretive. While you're trying to figure out this man of mystery, with his layers and layers of complications that you won't ever fully understand, you'll probably end up in a hopeless head-over-heels-in-love relationship.

However, he may also feel compelled to accommodate another woman, his philosophy being "There's plenty of me to go around." If another relationship evolves, he'll expect you to be loyal and faithful and not question him. Of course, you could never pull the same stunt and live to tell about it. I know it's not fair, so you decide how to deal with it. You may know that the relationship is potentially troublesome, but you continue to see this man or build a relationship with the brother in spite of yourself, knowing that you shouldn't.

For example, a Scorpio attorney mentioned that his best relationships in the past were with Virgos (four of them) because, according to him, Virgo women want to please 100 percent. But that's not enough for Mr. Scorpio: "I find it very difficult to stick with one woman." Each of the three women he deals with presently has characteristics that the other doesn't have. Mr. Scorpio obviously feels that he's all that they need.

That's not to say a Scorpio can't be faithful. But you need to understand the potential screwups in the liaison. Actually, Scorpios would never trade true love just to knock the boots. It simply means women will find him attractive, oh, so masculine, passionate, sexy, confident, and presumably the kind of man women dream about.

If marriage is on the horizon, plan to have at least three or four children. Scorpios are breeders. In fact, if possible they will spend most of their waking hours in bed. They also love children and will be demanding but effective fathers.

The Scorpio very definitely wants a meaningful relationship. He can be a devoted and faithful person, but this complex, secretive man is very hard to get to know. What you see on the surface is exactly what he wants you to see. For example, he might have several different types of vehicles, including a worn-out old Fred Sanford–type truck, a convertible that was headed for the junkyard before he refurbished it in his spare time, and the Benz or Jeep to attract the ladies. You won't be able to detect where he is or what he's doing and with whom.

He's sensitive, strong, but rarely silent. You will hear his opinions whether you want to or not because he's an intelligent man who has a working knowledge of most things. And pay attention: Scorpios value their own opinions. Besides, they figure you can learn a thing or two from them.

The Scorpio man has an intensity that you will sense immediately. His outward appearance will appear calm, controlled, and placid, but inside, an eternal flame burns to warm the hearts of many, including you. For example, when a Scorpio brother introduced his new Pisces friend, he was totally oblivious to the negative vibes Ms. Pisces picked up from one of his female friends. Turns out, the female friend wanted Mr. Scorpio for herself. She was playing a waiting game and wanted the Scorpio to notice, but he was clueless about her feelings.

Most Scorpios feel that they can do most things. Their egotism propels them to test themselves far beyond the realm of most possibilities. Consequently, they will want a companion who can stand toe-to-toe. In other words, you must have a full life, with your own set of accomplishments, because you won't be able to ride on their coattails—not for long, anyway.

When the Scorpio brother enters a room, he may not be the one dressed to kill. He may have on jeans, cowboy boots, or even polyester, but don't let that fool you. This brother is a master of deception. If you're turned off by his appearance, don't be so hasty: He probably has more money in the bank than anybody in the room. Plus, his appearance may only be a test to determine your reaction to him based on his clothing. Everything the Scorpio says or does is for a specific reason. Every innuendo, gesture, look, or movement has an ulterior motive. The scorpion makes the most of every moment.

For example, one Scorpio brother who takes the dating game seriously said that he uses a selfishness test. He knows right away if the woman is selfish if she doesn't reach over and unlock his door after the Scorpio has opened the car door for her. "Based on my experience, there's an 80 percent probability rate that that's true," he said.

His temper is a force to be reckoned with as well. For example, a highly successful Scorpio brother with three insurance company offices got into a serious altercation with his live-in companion. A scuffle and shouting match ensued and the couple broke up. The companion later filed a civil suit for battery. The jury found the Scorpio brother guilty and, since the charge was a felony, he lost his businesses.

Even something as minor as a companion preparing dinner can end in disaster. An outspoken Scorpio man describes the dinner his companion made. "She made this lasagna and there was grease floating on it. I said to her, 'I can't eat this, baby. This is like a candle.' I lit up a match, threw it on the food, and it caught fire. She said, 'I can't believe you did that!'"

If you decide to have a relationship with the scorpion, or, better yet, if he decides to have a relationship with you, the courtship will be as unique as his personality because every date, including the sex, will seem as though it's your last. And sometimes it is. If you're left holding the bag, without so much as a word of warning, it may be a relief to you and a blessing in disguise. In short, you ain't gettin' out of the relationship until he decides it's over—and even then, he'll expect to come back into your life at will for a secret rendezvous at any point. And you'll probably be tickled to death to hear from him. He knew when he called what your reaction would be.

THE SCORPIO WOMAN

This sexy creature is going to be a real challenge to get to know. Rule number one: Don't make any assumptions that the relationship is going full speed ahead. You may think all is well because Ms. Scorpio has orchestrated the courtship or given you the high sign, and that may be exactly what she wants you to think. That's how powerful this Renaissance woman is. Once she sets her sights on you (after you've passed her checklist of requirements), you're history. All she needs is a few minutes to get your attention, and her hypnotic and magnetic appeal will draw you right to her. At some point, though, you won't know which way is up.

For example, a Scorpio woman explained that a man she met in high school insisted on a relationship with her that only lasted for three months. But he hounded her for the next two years. "He had enlisted in the military and wanted to send for me in every location where he was stationed, professing undying love. It was almost like he was stalking me. I tried to break it off, then finally I had to ask him, what is it you want?!"

Both the men and women of the sign have a penetrating look, and when their eyes are on the prize, their stare does not waiver. Eye contact is very important to them. When you meet the Scorpio sister, the sparks may be flying, but don't jump to conclusions the next time around or you'll be the loser. A Scorpio woman from D.C. met a tall, dark, handsome Haitian brother at a party. The two were attracted to each other and there was definitely chemistry there. The next day, the Haitian had his assistant call to arrange a date.

"No way, José," said Lady Scorpio. "The brother was a little too big for his britches!"

Brothers, beware: Although Scorpios can be overbearing and pushy, they are definitely turned off by the know-it-alls of the world. As one Scorpio woman put it, "I can't stand a man who is authoritative and overbearing, who treats me like a dumb bunny."

In order to get the attention of the Scorpio sister, you're going to have to be unique and original in your approach. And listen, brotherman, this has to be ongoing, not just after you've scored. Scorpio sisters are high-maintenance and will tell you so.

A Scorpio college professor recalls a potential mate taking old photographs of the two of them together and writing beautiful erotic messages on the back of each photo. He would then mail them back to her on an ongoing basis. The two of them were in a long-distance relationship, but keeping in touch via the erotic messages was just the kind of titillation the Scorpio wanted and thrived on.

The Scorpio sister will expect your undivided attention. You see, she is loyal, devoted, and passionate and will expect no less from you. She wants a real man in every sense of the word. She wants a man who has opinions and passions about life and who is willing to stand his ground on matters of importance to him.

The Scorpio sister is very demanding and affectionate and her emotions run deep with the man she loves. She gives 120 percent in return. In an era where there is a shortage of men in general, and black men in particular, Ms. Scorpio will continuously have *her* man in da house. She can't stand for her man to be a pushover, but she won't be told what to do either. By all accounts from the brothers who are in relationships with Scorpio women, there are few complaints.

For example, a Scorpio administrative assistant has three men—two Virgos and a Cancer. Each calls every day. She no longer dates the first Virgo, the father of her 30-year-old son, but he comes around daily. He even feeds the dog. The other Virgo is her official companion. But the Cancer makes her laugh and wants to get married. Well, now.

When the Scorpio is hurt, either by her companion or another loved one, the sting can be deadly. The Scorpio woman deals in extremes; there is no middle ground. In one instance, a Scorpio woman who had long since ended a relationship with a companion of twenty years didn't take kindly to his effort to rekindle the flame because the brother lived with another woman. The Scorpio sister told him in no uncertain terms, "Take your penis [I can assure you she didn't say penis!] down to your woman's house where you live and screw her and don't come back!" Of course, the brother came back.

In another example, a Scorpio female in college went out with someone she termed "a sex-starved medical student." "I had no intentions of giving him any, anyway, so he practically tried to rape me. No more med students for me!"

The scorpion female will forever keep you guessing about her intentions and motivations, or the whys and wherefores of the relationship. In her mind, it keeps the relationship from getting boring. For example, a Scorpio sister gave her companion a coupon to redeem for a night of sex, dinner, and dancing. The coupon, which was created by her, complete with caricature in sexy underwear, included a deadline date. He missed the deadline because when the dude tried to redeem the coupon, Ms. Scorpio was out of town. Of course, the Scorpio showed very little sympathy: After all, he'd had three weeks to redeem the coupon before she left town. Oh, well.

Scorpios can sometimes have difficulty leaving a relationship because they will want to pop back into your life whenever the mood strikes them. For all practical purposes, the relationship isn't over until *they* want it to be. For example, a Scorpio tried to forget an old boyfriend by going to bed with another person. However, it backfired because during the encounter she realized that she was still in love with the old boyfriend. The date was a disaster after she started crying. Of course, she couldn't tell her escort what was wrong.

And don't expect the Scorpio sister to be at your beck and call. It ain't happening! The Scorpio woman must have "her" space, freedom of movement, and time to reflect. She will definitely expect you to check in, but when she's on hiatus, leave her alone. She's hiding and trying to rejuvenate. So you need to rest up for the impending sexual aerobics you'll find yourself embroiled in after she returns.

GUIDE TO A LOVE CONNECTION

Scorpio and Aries

Constant confrontation is a way of life for these two. Of course, they are the stars of the freak show in bed, where they keep reinventing themselves between the sheets. But here comes the but. Two domineering people in the relationship are a no-no, and neither is backing down or giving in. Scorpio's obsessive and possessive approach to the relationship has free-spirited Aries ranting and raving and demanding space. Aries is not about to let Scorpio control or dominate. Scorpio's fierce determination leaves the two in a battle of wills. They spend entirely too much time arguing and not enough time nurturing and supporting the relationship. So the bottom line is, move on and the two of you will be happier.

Scorpio and Taurus

These two are opposites, meaning the physical side of this relationship is already made in the shade. But wonderful sex has a tendency to cloud one's judgment about the feasibility of the relationship. Scorpio wants to totally possess stubborn Taurus. Taurus has his own ideas about the relationship and he wants to run the show. So does Scorpio. Scorpio's passions run hot and cold. While Scorpio goes off on jealous rages, Taurus's resentment festers. Both are highly motivated by money and work hard to achieve security, Taurus more so than Scorpio. If this couple wants to be involved in a constant standoff of wills, then maybe this relationship will work. Otherwise, forget it, except for the sex.

Scorpio and Gemini

Both are amused and interested in the novelty of the relationship at first. Scorpio is possessive, jealous, and overly attentive. Gemini, though intrigued by Scorpio's devotion, is changeable, flighty, and constantly in search of new adventures. Scorpio wants to control and dominate the relationship. Gemini won't be controlled and is highly unpredictable about his or her comings and goings. Scorpio yells a lot and makes demands. Gemini floats through life unscathed by Scorpio's demands. Sexually, however,

Scorpio's intense sex drive, along with Gemini's curiosity for trying new approaches, finds these two spending most of their time in bed. Incompatible as it may all seem, Gemini will realize very early that it ain't going to work. Gemini will be in the wind before Scorpio knows what time it is.

Scorpio and Cancer

These two water signs are highly emotional, passionate, and sympathetic to each other. They do a lot of crying in their beer. But, hey, if they like it, no problem. Scorpio is a control freak and wants to totally possess his mate. That's fine with Cancer, who sees this approach as nurturing. Insecure and moody Cancer broods about the lack of appreciation on the job and problems with family members. Scorpio is right there with a listening ear. Both are homebodies, and financial security is uppermost in their minds for the future. Cancer cooks and Scorpio wolfs down his morsels while hanging on Cancer's every word. Sexually, the encounter makes these two inseparable!

Scorpio and Leo

Scorpio's jealousy and possessiveness annoy Leo to no end. Leo's need for an admiring public makes Scorpio furious. Scorpio wants to be at home with Leo making whoopee, while Leo wants to be surrounded by people at social gatherings. Leo thinks Scorpio is a tightwad. Leo, the lion on the throne, wants a lavish lifestyle with luxurious surroundings. Scorpio wants to dominate and ascertain where Leo is every minute of the day. With a busy and bulging calendar, Leo simply doesn't have time to check in every hour on the hour. The sexual delights that these two share in the boudoir will not and cannot hold this pair together. Get over it!

Scorpio and Virgo

Sensuous Scorpio puts a few things on conservative and skeptical Virgo's mind. Virgo, with her practical approach to life, is hard to impress. Enter sexy Scorpio, and, well, now, you have a new ball game! Scorpio's determination, possessiveness, and passion have insecure Virgo feeling needed and appreciated. Sexually, as long as Virgo is attentive and teachable, there shouldn't be any problems in the bedroom. Scorpio, of course, is the freak; but catch Virgo on a good day and the erotic and quirky behavior introduced by Scorpio will be met by eager Virgo. Both are money-conscious and work hard to achieve their goals. Both are homebodies, Virgo more so than Scorpio. This coupling has the makings of a very rewarding relationship.

Scorpio and Libra

There's no problem when it comes to the physical connection; both can go toe-to-toe with each other in the sexual arena. Scorpio is constantly frustrated by Libra's lack of attention. Libra is attentive, but not to Scorpio's standards. Those standards call for several phone calls daily, along with the touchy-feely encounters. Libras must be free to explore their own goals and dreams. Scorpios want those goals and dreams to be their own. Libra is a social butterfly. Scorpio pouts at home while Libra is in the mix at receptions, happy hour functions, and community stuff. Libra is a flirt by nature, which infuriates Scorpio. Money matters widen the gap even more. Libra is the spendthrift. Scorpio holds on to a dollar till it hollers. Go figure! Give it up, folks.

Scorpio and Scorpio

Sexually explosive is putting it mildly with this dynamic duo, but both have hair-trigger tempers. Both are jealous and controlling and expect your undivided attention, 24 hours a day, 7 days a week. The conversation will go like this: "Why didn't you call me after lunch and at dinner to let me know where you were?" "I talked to you this morning and expected you to call me later and let me know if anything changed. Nothing has changed." "But why didn't you call me? I expected to hear from you!" Huh?! In short, the affair will sizzle, but the marriage will fizzle. Both will be beyond exhaustion in the relationship.

Scorpio and Sagittarius

Scorpio simply can't understand why Sag is constantly running off in several different directions without consulting Scorpio first. Sag doesn't see the point in doing so. The life of the Sag is not changing regardless of who the companion is. Scorpio's obsessive need to control has wandering Sag unimpressed and contrary, just doing what Scorpio despises. Once Scorpios understand that Sagittarians will not be harnessed, controlled, or dominated, the hot sizzling affair that these two embarked on with reckless abandon is over. Scorpio will retreat to brood in his corner. Sag is off and running in another direction. Sag is the first to realize that the fat lady has sung.

Scorpio and Capricorn

They provide great stimulation for each other in more ways than one. This combination will be a battle of wills. Scorpio's possessiveness and jealousy have Capricorn amused because the goat is faithful to a fault. Capricorns simply don't have time to figure out who's on the telephone if there's more than one companion in the mix. Scorpio's insatiable sexual appetite provides Capricorn with just the relief that's needed. Both are security-conscious and want the finer things in life. As long as Capricorn's long hours on the job are really on the job, Scorpio is content. Capricorn's stubbornness frustrates and irritates Scorpio. The ranting should be kept to a minimum if these two want a fulfilling life together. And that notion is very possible!

Scorpio and Aquarius

These two will spend most of their waking hours in the bedroom. Aquarius is an air sign; freedom and independence are all-important. Scorpio's jealous and controlling nature sends Aquarius running for cover. After this duo emerges from the bedroom, there won't be much to hold them together. Scorpio's controlling nature will be a turnoff for Aquarius, who's involved in so many projects that he simply won't have time to check in three times a day, much to Scorpio's dismay. The demands of Scorpio will have aloof and distant Aquarius looking for other outlets. If Aquarius is boxed into a corner, he will simply disappear. And Scorpio, you can't control what you simply cannot find. The two of you are better as friends than as lovers.

Scorpio and Pisces

Stay away from the champagne, wine, and cognac; they can be detrimental to the relationship. These two are so emotional and into crying in their beer, there needs to be an assessment of what's up. That doesn't mean that the romance is not on. It is! These two water signs are so into each other that they have to get a sanity check. Both are romantic, passionate, and devoted in the relation-ship. Scorpio is possessive, but that's okay because Pisces wants to be possessed. Pisces loves a take-charge kind of person. Scorpio dominates and wants Pisces to check in every hour on the hour. Once these two find each other, the close encounters of the one-on-one kind are so on that they won't want to come out of the confine-ment to deal in the reality mode. Do I hear wedding bells?!!!

ROMANCE AND THE SCORPIO

Scorpios are mysterious and very private people. Therefore, any dates or encounters that promote a private and secluded setting will yield the results you want. In other words, if you want the at-tention of the Scorpio, timing and location, and sexually provoca-tive clothing, get their attention.

Scorpions guard their privacy. You won't be able to just show up unannounced. On any date, she will want to know all the particu-lars. She will definitely be impressed with all your preparation and planning. But she'll want to know where the date is going to take place, the principal players, if any, and the occasion. This will enable her to dress up to be the center of attention with a provocative, low-cut spandex dress that lifts and separates. When the power-house of the zodiac emerges in the killer black dress, you'll be in love from that moment on. But for the scorpion, it's all part of the plan.

Scorpios are used to having lots of suitors and impressing lots of people. For the Scorpio, the attitude is "Been there, done that!" In short, just because you have discovered Ms. Thang and Mr. All That, it doesn't mean that they are going to be impressed with you. This water sign already knew early on that, yes, he had it going on and yes, this would be simply another feather in her cap, another notch in his belt!

If you're going on your initial date with a scorpion, keep the hair weaves, color contacts, and body piercing to a minimum. Scor-pios have very little tact, and what you may perceive as a turn-on may be a turnoff for him. He will definitely ask, "Is that your real hair?" or "Why do you feel that it's necessary for you to wear blue contacts?" A Scorpio woman was dating a very accomplished dentist. "Into the fifth or sixth date, the question just popped out of my mouth: 'Are all those teeth yours?' He answered, 'No,' very quietly. And that was the end of our romance." The dentist was in a no-win situation. Listen up, brothers: Having your hair lightly texturized is okay, but the Rev. Al Sharpton look may be viewed with a dubious eye.

Romance with a Scorpio will be carefree, fun, and exciting. The key is to simply be ready when she comes breezing into the room like a whirlwind, late, talking on her cell phone and expecting everything to move without a hitch. When you're on a date with a Scorpio, he can make the simplest of things romantic. If you happen to be out of doors on a starry night, he may suggest that the two of you get a bottle of wine, sit in the grass, and search for the constellations, admiring the moon and stars as he admires every inch of you, as well. The Scorpio's piercing stare doesn't waver. And it will seem like he's looking through to your soul or your very essence. The magnetic attraction of scorpions is unmistakable. You'll definitely stand up and take notice with these sexy, daring creatures.

A Scorpio trainer from Ohio commented that her ideal romantic date was a candlelit dinner, a good movie, or a getaway weekend at a resort cabin in the spring or fall of the year. And don't forget Luther Vandross, some wine, nice, crisp, clean sheets with good pillows. Her Leo husband, who complies, keeps a smile on his face.

A Scorpio nurse describes her most memorable romantic encounter, which began with a hot bubble bath. "My mate had a nice hot bubble bath waiting for me after work. He fed me in the bubble bath and then bathed me."

Intimate talks, taking trips together, and frequent calls to say "I love you" are at the top of this water sign's priority list. If you're dating a Scorpio or married to one, you'll have to check in frequently, because he or she will want to know where you are at all times.

Both the male and female of the sign will go that extra mile on a date, but they will expect the same in return. A Scorpio teacher described what gets her romance on: "An exclusive restaurant where a different wine is served with each course, topped off with a single rose and a walk—hopefully, near water."

On the other hand, scorpions can assess if the sparks are there within a couple of hours of the initial encounter or the first date. A Scorpio teacher commented that one of the biggest turnoffs is "someone who kisses with their mouth wide open and seems like they're going to suck in your entire face." If you can't get past the initial kiss, you're history. This may seem trite to some, but the Scorpio wants the total package and the kiss is the catalyst for what's to come. Get it?

And Scorpio will know in his heart that the relationship is going nowhere fast because of his innate ability to cut to the chase by assessing you and your situation and how it will mesh with hers. For example, a Scorpio from Wisconsin contacted a singles video dating service. His first and only date from that effort was a woman who constantly talked about sports and taking trips with her mother. As she talked, the Scorpio thought this woman's mother would be all in their business, among other things. As his date sat fixed in front of the television at the bar mesmerized by a football game, the Scorpio brother knew it wouldn't work. "It was like going out with a guy," he said.

Intelligence for Scorpio is also a turn-on because foreplay starts with stimulating conversation. While you're giving opinions about current events, the state of the economy, racism in America, or international problems, the scorpion is making mental notes, noticing your every movement and gesture. For example, a Scorpio woman reluctantly agreed to a blind date at the urging of a family friend. "Before we went on the date he explained that he ate peanut butter sandwiches before going out to dinner. That should have been a clue! His favorite pastime is sitting in the front of the TV all of the time." What she found was a short, round, overweight, middle-aged man who could talk only about the prime-time shows on television. Hello?

If you're dating a Scorpio and you happen to entertain the thought of dating someone else, she will sense it right away. Word to the wise: If you're trying to leave, you'd better do it in a subtle way. In an effort to stay on top of every call or innuendo, a Scorpio woman asked about a telephone call that her live-in companion had received from another woman. This happened after he had brought home a rose and card. Scorpio spoiled the moment by quizzing him about the call.

Scorpios play for keeps. Even after the relationship is over, he will expect to pop back into your life whenever the mood strikes him. You'll open your heart in spite of yourself and readily accept a phone call, giggling all the while. Afterward, you'll scold yourself about being so receptive. But get this: He already knew when he dialed your number that you would be glad to hear from him. There's no escaping the magnetism of Scorpios.

As one Virgo man put it, "A Scorpio woman can be a cold-hearted bitch." And the Scorpio will be the first to admit it. A Scorpio may summon you over for sex one night and treat you like a stranger the next day. Although you might declare that you don't do one-night stands, don't be alarmed: It was simply a booty call and nothing more, so get over it.

Scorpios have a vivid imagination. By the time they have thought of all the titillating ways to arouse your interest, they may take it right there against the wall as you enter the apartment. It's a turn-on for them. Don't despair; the night or the week will be full of impromptu maneuvers like this. You see, she has worked herself into a frenzy of anticipation. The sexual encounter is an all-day process that starts the moment they open their eyes and realize there were big doings today!

One Scorpio, who sends his wife erotic stories by e-mail, detailing exactly what he plans to do to her once they are alone, arouses himself in the process. So by the time they finally arrive home together, he's good to go. "I'll get so horny while I'm sending her e-mails. I wish she didn't work so far away. We could slip away."

SEX, SEX AND MORE SEX

GETTING THE GROOVE ON . . .

Scorpios are constantly in search of that next plateau of sexual adventure. Married or single, male or female, short or tall, big or small, the approach is the same: to "get off" as often as they can. For example, one Scorpio brother, then a senior in high school, made it a personal mission to have sex with the overweight girls as well as the Plain Janes. His philosophy was twofold: to get and to give as much sexual gratification as he could. "Why should they miss out on all the fun?" says he.

Now, folks, before you get bent out of shape by the possibility that the Scorpio doesn't have a faithful bone in his or her body, let me reassure you. These water signs can definitely be faithful, but the bottom line is, their sexual desires must be satisfied—and often. And they will stop at nothing to achieve this goal. If you're the companion or the spouse, your energy level may be too low to keep up. Then, in the back of your mind, you may be relieved that someone is stepping in. Just kidding!

Getting the groove on with these water signs will be easy because long before you decided to pursue or engage in a relationship with the scorpion, he will already have sized up the situation. So now it's time to just do it. With this feast-or-famine sign, Scorpios can take you to the height of sexual pleasure like no one else or bring you down when they become reclusive and noncommunicative. Their sexual behavior knows no limitations. Even if you beg for mercy as he slaps your buttocks or she bites your penis, it will only turn them on.

Scorpio people love erotic talk and talking dirty. But it is most important to both the men and the women that there be a connection between the two parties—an unspoken understanding of what each wants emotionally, mentally, and physically. A Scorpio brother who prides himself on engaging in over-the-top sex wants the woman to come to bed with an open and adventurous spirit and just go with the flow. However, the Scorpio man is not going to be controlled in the bedroom, so he definitely has his pet peeves. "I don't like a woman to come to me with a laundry list, saying, 'I want this, this, and this.' Sexual moves have to be reciprocal. If you want a gigolo, you should have paid for dinner and then paid me." Are you listening, ladies?

By the way, guys, when you're disrobing, don't forget to take your socks off, as well. The Scorpio sister likes to look at the total package, and having your socks on is a turnoff and a distraction. I hope you don't wear the little garter-type contraption to hold up the socks that have lost the elasticity. A definite no-no.

After you parade around in your French-cut bikini leopard-skin briefs, you'll be ordered by the lady Scorpio to come hither. A favorite position for the Scorpio sister is the woman-on-top position. This way she can control what's going on better. This position also gives her a sense of power over her partner.

And power and control are what the scorpion seeks. He sees nothing wrong with adding a little S & M to the mix, as long as you don't run away screaming and threatening to call 911. Ease up— you might be totally intrigued and call him for the next encounter. No matter what, Scorpios are definitely not judgmental when it comes to sex—and or any other area for that matter. But they are opinionated when it comes to what they want in the bedroom.

If you're lucky enough to end up in bed with a lady Scorpio, you'll be whipped, both literally and figuratively. The Scorpio sister loves to wear sexy underwear or lingerie. Her goal is for you to remember the night, the day, or the evening with fondness. Soft music, erotic food like whipped cream, chocolate syrup, or strawberries will all be a part of the set. Once you enter her boudoir, your sexual experience is totally in her hands. So you need to get some rest before your date. Trust me on this.

A scorpion engineer explained his requirements: A woman has to be able to keep up with him by being able to run a mile and a half, and not for physical fitness. "If you can run a mile and a half, then you're in condition to have sex with me," he said.

Unlike other signs of the zodiac, the Scorpio libido is always in overdrive. A Scorpio woman from Milwaukee decided to end a relationship with a man who developed a job-related lung condition. The Scorpio decided that if anything happened, she didn't want to have to call 911 while they were engaged in wild and crazy sex. You see, she had no intention of toning down her approach to lovemaking. Well, all righty, then.

When the sex drive revs up, it's full speed ahead. It doesn't matter how big, small, short, or tall the Scorpio is, the approach is the same. All Scorpios drip sex appeal. A Scorpio from Milwaukee described a Scorpio friend who was "five by five," almost as tall as she was wide at 5 feet, 4 inches and 350 pounds. During sex, the overweight sister would simply lift up the fat layers around her stomach so her mate could find "it." One time the woman's companion, a man of about 60, had trouble catching his breath after the scorpion dropped the layer of fat on his head while he performed oral sex. She had become so aroused that she threw up her hands in pleasure. The man, who had trouble breathing, was ordered by Ms. Scorpio to complete the job. "Just where do you think you're going?" she asked.

A Scorpio sister complained that during sexual intercourse, her sexuality and moves intimidate men. "My sexuality makes them worry about pleasing me, so the penis goes soft. This has happened to me with three different men and I don't know what to do about it." Ms. Scorpio decided to take a break from the frustration, and she's not dating presently.

One point here: If you're planning to have sex with a scorpion, you need to get your rest because you're in for a long, exhausting, yet exhilarating night. For example, a female Scorpion who invited her lover over to her house for the first time told him that he had to keep going although he was exhausted and tired. "Where are you going? You're not through until I say you're through!" Okay then!

EROGENOUS ZONES . . . SOME PHYSICAL, SOME NOT

Sexually, Scorpios need very few maneuvers to get them aroused. The mere thought of sex arouses them. Their erogenous zone is the genital area. Any moves in that direction will turn them into insatiable wonders instantaneously. The Scorpions will try anything once; there are no real taboos in the sexual arena.

With a Scorpio, a turn-on in the bedroom could be anything from sex toys to a partner with gas. Sounds strange? I needed clarification about the gas factor, so I asked if the turn-on was intermittent farting, knowing that gas from indigestion could be painful, the smell, or all of the above. "My goal is for my companion to be so immersed in the sexual experience that all of her inhibitions are gone. Consequently, the passing of gas would be last vestige of reserved behavior." It became such an issue that his mate would call him and say, "I have gas" which would be an automatic turn-on. Go figure!

A Scorpio woman from Washington, D.C., said what drives her

wild are the brothers who take their time and work slowly from the toes up! Yo, are you listening, brothers? Foreplay is essential for both the men and women of the sign. They want the total experience, which includes the long, deep, passionate kisses, the kissing of the entire body, along with the waves-washing-up-on-the-shore syndrome.

The 69 position works for them. However, any position that maximizes the sensation of the genitalia is good to go. Oral sex is absolutely essential to the sexual experience for these water signs. For example, a Cancer woman who was once married to a Scorpio complained that her husband wanted oral sex during the encounter most of the time. "I believe my ex-husband wanted to see if I would get lockjaw after so long."

With a Scorpio, never say what you will or won't do during the sexual experience because when you get to the fever-pitch level that your Scorpio lover plans to take you to, you just never know. The main approach is to keep an open mind. If not, keep your car engine running or a cab waiting! Just kidding!

Scorpios are water signs: Any sex play, intercourse, or foreplay performed in, near, or on water creates the maximum effect. Scorpios love to have sex in the shower, in the bathtub, in the Jacuzzi, on the beach, in his lab during working hours, or even behind an oak tree in your mother's backyard. Also, sexy lingerie is a great stimulus, but you won't be able to determine how long you'll have the outfit on. It may only be for a few minutes. A full body massage after leaving the hot tub, where the sex was probably initiated, is a turn-on. Even a compact disc with nothing but the sound effects of rain and thunder is a great aphrodisiac for Scorpios.

Understanding what turns scorpions on is essential. They don't mince words, and if it ain't happening, you'll be told. "Fumbling is a turnoff. Nothing is worse than a man who doesn't have a clue about foreplay, and a person who expects more than he's willing to give," a lady Scorpio declared.

One Scorpio engineering student liked to have sex with his girlfriend while he was studying. "The harder the engineering problem, the hornier I get." His companion complied. Sex clears your head so you can work on solving the problem.

PLAIN OL' SEX AND NOTHING MORE:
WELCOME TO THE FREAK SHOW

Here's the deal. Scorpios are definitely one of the stars of the freak show.

In general, Scorpios want an emotional commitment as well as a physical connection. They simply must have intensity in their lives and their sex lives are no different. If by chance the Scorpio is between relationships, there's a good chance that sex for sex's sake might happen.

For these sex-driven creatures, booty calls are always in order. And don't get your feelings hurt if you plan to have more than just sex. When Scorpios want sex, they want it whenever, however, and definitely wherever. They will tease you over the telephone so that you will be ready to drive right over and have sex in the car, even during daytime hours.

Yes, the scorpions will step right up to the plate and have sex even if it's a one-night stand, and will expect the mate to enjoy it, be emotionally connected, and make plans for the next sexual encounter without so much as a hint of a complaint.

And because Scorpios are ultrasecretive, for the most part, there won't be any problems having an afternoon delight or a nooner. They simply relish the secret romp or freak show or one-night stand. As long as good sex is involved, it's not a problem!

MONEY MATTERS

Scorpios are very frugal. They will secretly save their money and retire to an unknown place, like Florida, the Bahamas, or the South Seas without so much as a good-bye. In fact, scorpions love deception and being people of mystery. You can never judge them by what they're wearing or the material things that they own. Nine times out of ten, Scorpios have more money in the bank than most of the people present in the room. Usually, their possessions have more to do with making loved ones comfortable than with what the Scorpio aspires to have.

For example, a male scorpion who owned his own public relations firm would constantly pick up the tab no matter how many people were present at the table. When he was asked why he would consistently do this, he commented that "money is meant to be spent, and after I spend this I will get some more." And Scorpio people definitely will. Scorpios are resilient and resourceful and know, either instinctively or from research, the smart money moves it takes to retire early. You see, these water signs will live in the lap of luxury.

When shopping for clothes and other items, the Scorpio doesn't mind looking for the bargain, buying the used car, buying the manual to install his new toilet or hiring someone at a cut rate as the handyman. There's a dual purpose here; he figures by hiring the handyman, he provides this person with a job. The money that's saved will be put to good use in investing, helping a family member, or hidden away in the cookie jar.

The Scorpio won't simply be satisfied to handle money matters based on what is told to her or advised. The Scorpio will want the background, the hidden meaning, and the reason behind what the investments or the business venture has to offer, and the total analysis. She will want to know all of the key players and where all of the pieces of the puzzle fit.

Scorpios are the power people of the zodiac. Having money and building a foundation are always uppermost in their minds. Now, if you're dealing with a scorpion and wonder why there is very little money and he is constantly borrowing from you, what is happening is, he's probably paid a friend's property taxes to keep him from los-ing his house or helping someone pay her son's college tuition from the semester before as a condition for getting loan money for the current semester.

And what about saving for the children's college education or early retirement? The early retirement plan may never happen be-cause the Scorpio has usually figured out how to retire by age 50 without worrying about the retirement home. His early retirement doesn't need an abode with picket fence and daisies growing in the yard. This sister will be far too busy to concern herself with coun-try living and gardening. Scorpios are about living life to the fullest. This is the sign of extremes, you know. There is never any middle ground with these intense creatures. It's either all or noth-ing with them!

PAMPERING TIPS FOR SCORPIO

✳ For the men, save the aesthetic surroundings. Pampering means agreeing to their demands—sex, sex, and more sex!

✳ Scorpios are homebodies by nature. So your plans should be centered around home—like dinner at your place that you prepared, with you for dessert.

✳ Pampering a Scorpio means having your undivided attention, 24 hours a day, 7 days a week. So plan ahead.

✳ Create an island for the two of you in bed where everything is at your fingertips—wine, music, food, condoms, etc.

✳ Scorpios love to be in water and near it. Plan a getaway weekend with a Jacuzzi and you probably won't leave the room the entire weekend.

✳ You can't ever go wrong with a full body massage, followed by a hot-oil treatment. You might not get to the entire body!

✳ Surprise your companion by outfitting yourself in a Xena, catsuit, or edible underwear. He'll love every minute of it!

✳ Surprise your lover by hiring a temp to help him get a jump on his paperwork and thus have more time for the two of you.

✳ Plan an outing fishing, boating, or hanging out near water. It'll relax and calm your intense scorpion.

✳ Find a manicurist who makes house calls. Your surprised but grateful Scorpio will delight in any service that she doesn't have to leave home to enjoy.

GIFT IDEAS FOR SCORPIO

✳ Both the men and the women love jewelry. Dangling earrings for the woman or a gold bracelet for the man works best.

✳ Buy a hot little black dress with splits and plunges in all the right places. Black is a favorite color of Scorpios.

✳ Sexy teddies and thong underwear for the women and those cute French-cut leopard-skin bikini briefs for the men will definitely get the party started!

❀ Scorpios love connecting with the metaphysical and spiritual world and Old World philosophies. Any books on the subject are a sure bet.

❀ Sex toys—including vibrators, S & M costumes, porno videos—make great gifts for Scorpio because sexual enhancements are always welcomed.

❀ CDs of slow-drag oldies are great for the Scorpio brother, who usually takes his own music wherever he goes.

❀ A bottle of her favorite cologne or rare perfume is a winner. (But please don't get the drugstore brand.) If you don't know, then you need to ask somebody.

❀ A framed picture of yourself in a swimsuit, shorts, or bra and garterbelt will delight him and keep him "up and coming."

❀ An engraved flask with his name or pet name is a winner. Scorpios love personalized gifts.

❀ Give your Scorpio woman diamonds or, if the funds are low, her birthstone ring, and she'll stand up and take notice.

Sagittarius

(November 22 to December 21)

SYMBOL: THE ARCHER

Positive love traits: Traditional lover, confident partner, methodical and arduous; one of the participants of the freak show.

Negative love traits: Prone to bisexuality; may be sadistic or inconsiderate; a penchant for anal sex.

Ruling planet: Jupiter is associated with good fortune, optimism, expansion, and abundance.

Word to the wise: Sag people are the flirts of the zodiac, so if you're prone to jealousy, you'll be licking your wounds a lot.

When you first meet Sagittarians, you'll be intrigued by their vast knowledge of things and you'll laugh a lot. However, Sag people can be somewhat puzzling at first. You will continually ask yourself, "Why did she say that?" or "Why did he do that?" Save yourself some time. You won't get an answer because they don't know why they do what they do—most of the time, anyway.

The symbol of the Sagittarian is the archer, and the arrow is pointed straight at its target. The Sagittarian pulls no punches and basically tells it like it is. Sag people are very blunt—some would say tactless. But it's never an attempt to hurt feelings. Sagittarians are seekers of the truth. For example, a Sag public relations director told her Taurus husband that if he didn't buy some suits that fit properly he was going to eventually resemble a man who looked like he was in his third trimester of pregnancy. Because he was trying to wear the same size as he had years earlier, his belt was well below his stomach. His shirt buttons were about to pop off. The husband ignored his wife's prediction, but weeks later bought several new suits.

Sag's ruling planet is Jupiter, which is associated with expansion, good luck, and optimism. Both luck and a thirst for knowledge play major roles in the success of a Sagittarian.

You will find the Sagittarian where new technologies are being explored. The Sagittarian has a keen interest in computer technology, including repairing, building, or selling computers. You'll also find them on the Internet. If you're in an Internet chat room, the Sags will dominate the conversation. They talk just to hear themselves talk. But for the most part, it's some heavy-duty stuff on a variety of subjects.

They love the great outdoors and love to travel, even if it's only to the neighboring town. Camping, horseback riding, biking, and all types of outdoor activity get the attention of Sagittarians, who are usually in search of their next adventure.

Physically, Sagittarians are at two extremes. The men are either short with broad shoulders or tall and willowy, even athletic-looking. The women are either thin or making significant strides toward obesity. Sagittarians have nice oval faces and well-shaped heads. The men can even wear the bald look without stares of disbelief.

Sagittarians are restless and need constant mental stimulation. They are very much interested in higher learning and exploring new territories. They enjoy the challenge of solving a problem more than the problem itself, just as the chase is more interesting and challenging than the capture. To maintain a Sagittarian's attention, keep the mental challenge and flirtatious exchanges going, but never surrender totally because they will soon seek the next challenge.

Sag people are fire signs, which means that like the element of fire, they're unpredictable, feisty, aggressive, impulsive, and hard to control. To put it bluntly, it's going to be their way or no way at all. But in general, Sag people are friendly and easygoing. It takes a lot to get them riled up, but once that happens, you've got problems. They will go off on everybody they see. After the tirade is over, the Sag's disposition is sunny and bright. In fact, they might not even recollect all of the details of what happened.

Basically, Sag people are not the great clotheshorses of the world. Although black folks love to jump sharp whenever there is the slightest opportunity, Sag people are pretty much casual dressers. The Sag brother would prefer to spend his money on a new computer than a new Armani suit. The Sag sister likes to dress, but there will definitely be a limit on how much she will spend on one outfit. She's got to have the extra money for her many trips out of town.

As for hair weaves, blond hair, nose rings, color contacts, or tattoos, the Sagittarian may be curious about such, but certainly not to the point of being turned off or distracted. Usually, Sag people are pretty much open-minded about such matters.

As long as Sagittarians can enjoy a good laugh and do what they enjoy hassle-free, you've got no problems. However, Sag people hate to be bored, so keep the conversation, activities, sex, and surprises coming hot and heavy. You'll have very few complaints from this optimist.

THE SAGITTARIAN MAN

When you first meet this dynamic and intellectual person, you can't help but be intrigued. He's full of self-confidence and has no inhibitions about getting to know people from all walks of life. From the chairman of the board to the street sweeper or the homeless, the Sag brother has few problems conversing, so striking up a conversation with this brother will be a snap.

If by chance you notice this brother and he's decked out in what you deem as a suit from JCPenney or Montgomery Ward, don't be too hasty in deciding that he's Steve Urkle's first cousin. More than likely this brother has more than one college degree, owns his own business, and is smarter than most. Things like the Pee Wee Herman suit can be changed. Besides, he's the jeans and jogging suit kind of guy unless he's a white-collar worker. This brother is not at all interested in the total look—only the total checkbook. And that includes investing money wisely and being scrupulous about not overspending.

When this brother finally falls in love, the sky will be the limit. He will lavish you with gifts, make extensive travel plans, and keep the surprises coming. And if you want to keep his attention, you had better have some surprises of your own. Don't be boring.

The Sag brother has a great sense of humor. He laughs with reckless abandon, and you will too. But the Sag brother is a free spirit and you'll get that sense about him very early. For example, if the two of you go out for drinks, don't think that your tab will be his tab. You need to have some cash or some credit cards handy. He will look at the unofficial date as simply an impromptu exchange without any commitments. And initially, there won't be any leanings toward a long-term relationship.

The Sag brother is not overly concerned about looks, whether you have a hair weave, or even if you're overweight. And regarding weight issues, Sagittarians can be rather chunky too, so it would be like the kettle calling the pot black. The hair issue is in the same vein. As one Sag brother put it, "If you're bald or if you're losing your hair, you need a wig or something." Besides, they're more interested in issues with far-reaching implications, like computer technologies, the effects of institutional racism, and AIDS research.

Sag men are certainly attracted to good looks, including fine, voluptuous creatures and big-legged women. They're generally leg men, butt men, and breast men, but you've got to have much more to sustain the interest of the Sag. As one Sag brother put it, "Although we place a lot of importance on physical beauty, if you can't stimulate my mind, we probably won't do anything together."

Sagittarian men are very popular with the ladies. They will make you laugh, counsel you on your love life, and even offer to have sex with you on a no-strings-attached basis. These fire signs are generally accepting of any of your vulnerable spots or character flaws. They don't tend to be judgmental. Their motto is live and let live. They're not interested in making you over and they expect the same treatment from you. Let's get something straight now: A Sag man is his own person and will always be a bachelor of sorts, even when he's married.

This brother is a natural flirt. He's always complimentary to women. It makes no difference if you're his friend's wife, the pastor's wife, or the boss's daughter; his appreciative eyes don't discriminate. He's going to be enthusiastic when he picks you up for a date, and once he arrives at the event, the appreciation for the ladies will continue. The fact that he's also interested in Ms. Thang across the room has very little to do with his interest in you.

If you're lucky enough to keep up with his whereabouts long enough to get married, then congratulations. These rolling stones are not really the marrying kind. They either marry very early, like in their early twenties, or very late. Like Virgos, Sagittarians are the confirmed bachelors of the zodiac. They learn all the areas of domestic life and can cook up soul food to compete with the best of them. But remember what attracted you to this fascinating creature in the first place, hold on tight, and don't let go.

As a husband, he'll be as attentive as he can be with two careers, community work, and hobbies like building model airplanes, being the Little League baseball coach, and mentoring teenage boys. You'll simply have to take a number like everyone else and get in line.

The Sag brother will cook for you, take long walks with you, plan surprise outings. But as one Sag put it, "Use your tongue—talk to me!" The Sag insists on open and honest communication. Even if the truth hurts, his motto is "Spit it out."

Sagittarian men are not looking to accumulate a lot of sexual conquests, either. One put it this way: "When you take a woman's virginity, she's looking to marry you somewhere down the line."

The Sag brother will be forever on the prowl. That doesn't mean he's going to have multiple affairs—not right away, anyway. Just kidding! He simply has to keep his flirting skills honed and ready. He loves the games people play with the teasing, flirting, and propositioning. His optimism and enthusiasm for any area of interest he undertakes find him wanting to be a part of the mix, even if he's married. So don't be a nag. That's a pet peeve with Sagittarians. They won't hang around long for that.

And if by chance the handwriting is on the wall and you know the relationship is not going anywhere, then the Sag will be just as relieved as you are. Don't think you have to break it to him gently. For example, a Sag brother tried to persuade his girlfriend to leave her house to enjoy an impromptu rendezvous with him. When he showed up at her house unannounced, she explained that she was expecting her cousins and couldn't leave. Undaunted, he patted his butt at her—in jest, of course—then left. Although she never forgave him for his indiscretion, it was fine by him, for he never called again, and it was a mutual parting of the ways.

As fathers, their happy-go-lucky nature will spill over to their children. He'll go camping with his son and daughter, and spend more play time than serious time with them. Sagittarians create the ideal setting for a son or daughter to take all that life has to offer. You see, they'll be getting firsthand knowledge about life's lessons from the master himself.

THE SAGITTARIAN WOMAN

This dynamic, independent, fun-loving sister is going to be a real challenge for anyone to get close to or develop a relationship with. She's the adventurous type. The Sag female must have spontaneity and creativity in whatever is happening in her life. If you're thinking about renting videos and popping popcorn on your first date, you may not have a second date. On the other hand, sometimes a quiet evening as an alternative to her helter-skelter life can be inviting. Just don't make it a habit every Friday night. Whatever the approach with the Sag sister, it's got to have pizzazz and excitement.

The Sag is fiercely independent and has a wild streak. She may even do a tabletop dance if it strikes her fancy. But she pays her own way and she makes her way. This woman is not one to be controlled by your set of rules and regulations. Her response to the plans that you have developed for her life will be "Later, baby. You need a life, because I've got one."

Oh, by the way, if you don't want the painful truth, don't ask your Sagittarian mate. She'll even tell you if you *don't* ask. But one word of note here: Her intent is not to hurt your feelings. She's the seeker of truth and she's going to be honest if it kills her. And that thought will cross your mind, too, before the relationship is over.

She's moody, erratic, changeable, and somewhat mysterious, and she will keep you guessing about what to expect next. For example, a Sag sister from New York decided that the only way she was going to get over her love jones with her longtime companion was to leave the country. The situation had gotten to the point where she was possessive and obsessive about him and the relationship. Ms.

Sag moved to Europe for two years and supported herself by singing cabaret-style jazz. During one of her shows in Switzerland, she met an African man and later married him. Thus, the Sag's way of getting out of a relationship.

When you're at a party and there's a lot of commotion going on and a crowd is gathering, that commotion may be Sister Sag agreeing to a spontaneous medley of Anita Baker or Toni Braxton songs, or she may be retelling the details of a broken engagement. For example, a Sag woman decided a few days before her wedding that she wasn't marrying her fiancé of two years. The engagement ended after her fiancé accused her of flirting with her own cousin! She decided right then and there, she was not going to live with a man for the rest of her life who was jealous and controlling.

Her sense of humor and unabashed personality can keep any suitor hanging on her every word. This good-natured, fun-loving person has her own life and lives it to the fullest. With the Sag, the need to know is an ever-present force in her life. So you'll need to know about current events and who the president and vice president of the country are.

For the Sag, intellect is more important than looks. Still, a Sag sister took exception on a blind date. "I went on a blind date and met a man who weighed 450 pounds, but he was a sweet guy and a smart guy. It hurt to know that I couldn't get past his weight. He was a decent guy, too."

Before you take a Sag woman to bed, you don't have to fret over whether you're going to have to profess undying love. The sexual encounter to her is simply one of the many experiences that she plans to have during the day. It's no big deal. In fact, you may even be turned off by her indifference. But you must also realize that if she consented to be your bedmate, that's noteworthy in and of itself. Don't press your luck, buddy.

The Sag woman expects you to be honest because she tries very hard to be forthright and open to communication in a relationship. But the Sag is nobody's fool, and if you try to have an additional companion, along with a history of lies, you will be minus your Sag sister. For example, a Sag author caught her husband in bed with someone she thought was his cousin—that's how her husband had introduced the woman when she had been to their house previously. After the Sag caught them, she stood at the door of the bedroom for a while, ready to do battle with her husband, the "cousin," or both. Luckily, there was no bloodshed.

Another Sag sister also witnessed her husband trying to get his girlfriend to spend the night at the Sag's house. The husband thought his wife was still out of town. Earlier that day, when Ms. Sagittarian had arrived unbeknown to her husband to a spotlessly clean house, she immediately became suspicious. She hid in one of the bedrooms and listened to her husband tell his girlfriend that he and his wife had split up. The couple was eating when Ms. Sag came barreling into the living room, creating a scene, yelling, and turning over burgers and fries all at the same time. Needless to say, the husband is history.

If by chance you're invited over for dinner, you'll be in for a treat. She's an excellent hostess. The meal will be good, although it may be ordered in. Although she can be a good cook, the domestic scene is far too boring. She simply can't get excited over meat loaf and potatoes.

There won't be any stringent rules or regulations in a relationship with a Sag sister. Although independent, she loves flowers, champagne, and stimulating conversation, along with an intimate backdrop. Her big issues are that you not be boring or suffer from body odor. You will be told about both matters in no uncertain terms. For example, a Sag woman had met a Taurus brother from the Midwest. Taurus wined and dined Sag until she all but felt obligated to give the brother some. During the dating process, there weren't any sparks on her part, but apparently for the Taurus, there was great potential. When they made it to the bedroom after a lavish candlelight dinner, he began to undress her while talking dirty. She settled back for what she thought would be long and loving foreplay. After the two were partially nude, the Sag sister noticed that homeboy had stripped down to his boxers, but had on his shoes and socks. When Ms. Sag inquired about both, no explanation was given, except he reluctantly took them off. By the time the brother had carefully placed his socks and shoes at the foot of the bed, his foot odor overpowered the burning candles and the scent of cologne in the air. Said the Sag, "No wonder you didn't want to take off your shoes. Have you been to the doctor?" Poor guy, he didn't get anything but hurt feelings.

GUIDE TO A LOVE CONNECTION

Sagittarius and Aries

These two fire signs are very well matched. Both love to try new and different things and are very spontaneous people. Both are prone to rant and rave. The key is, they recover and forgive and forget quickly. Sexually, it's on. Sagittarius is receptive to any new sex tricks that Aries throws in the archer's direction. Sag's lack of tact gets on Aries' nerves. Aries is prone to spending sprees, and Sag spends impulsively. Both love life and the many friends they have. Both are intelligent and can talk for hours on a variety of subjects. They can definitely entertain each other and hold the other's interest. If these two can get beyond the hurt feelings and impulsive behavior of the other, this relationship can definitely work.

Sagittarius and Taurus

This pair is a work in progress most of the time. They desperately want to remain close because of the good sex, but that alone will not sustain this relationship. Taurus will find Sagittarians' creative lovemaking a plus—but don't get too kinky. Sagittarians have a devil-may-care attitude about most things. Life's a beach for them, while Taurus plods through life calmly and systematically. Taurus is just too slow for the energetic, just-do-it Sagittarian. Taurus sees Sag as tactless, careless, and undisciplined about money matters and building for the future. This drives "show me the money" Taurus to drink. Taurus must be in control and Sag is out of control, or so Taurus believes.

Sagittarius and Gemini

These two opposites of the zodiac have no trouble finding each other and getting it on. Sexually, this pair won't have a problem in the world. Neither is emotional and inclined to want the waves washing up on the shore in the background during a relationship. Sag's lighthearted approach to union annoys Gemini, who is more analytical and serious. Sag is the intellectual of the two and bores Gemini, with all of his platitudes and theories of life. Both are social creatures and love being in the mix. Both are involved in too many other activities to put the time needed into the relationship. Sag is a flirt and Gemini has a roving eye. When they hear the fat lady warming up, they'll usually be long gone. No hard feelings for either.

Sagittarius and Cancer

Both have a great sense of humor and keep each other in stitches. These two will need humor, and much more, to get them through this liaison. Sexually, Sag remains curious about the passion and romance Cancer brings to bed. Cancer is emotional and insecure, while Sag throws caution to the wind and faces life head-on. Sag's mental agility and insatiable appetite for knowledge leave Cancer feeling neglected. While Cancer licks her wounds, Sag is hanging with his homies. Cancer wants to feed, pamper, and spoil Sag, and she wants him at home with her. Sag is too much of a free spirit to be interested in the boredom of domestic life. Although this pair has mutual respect and genuine affection for each other, both become frustrated in a relationship that's as short as a boy's summer.

Sagittarius and Leo

These two fire signs sizzle, provided they're not involved in some heated discussion. Both are headstrong and must be in control. Leo tries to make Sag bow down before her throne. Sag ain't having it. He's his own man and his manliness and intelligence excite Leo. There won't be any dummies in Leo's life—not for long, anyway. Both love to travel and explore and are receptive to whatever adventures await them. The bedroom scene is just as exciting because Leo knows how to keep reinventing herself with romantic rendezvous and playful acts of love in the boudoir. These two are never bored, not with each other, anyway. A more-than-satisfying affair. If these two plan to marry, Leo must not have control of the checkbook!

Sagittarius and Virgo

Why are the two of you reading this section? Virgo's constant nagging and attempts to mold Sag won't work for a minute. Sagittarius is ready to explore the whole world without any inhibition,

while Virgo simply wants Sag to come into her world of home, security, and stability. Sag admires Virgo's predictable behavior and
devotion. Admiration is one thing, but wanting to be a part of that
mix is another. Both admire each other's intelligence. Sexual matters are stalled before they can get off the ground or in the bed. Sag
has very little patience for Virgo's reserve and timid self in bed. Sag
wants to play and romp without any perimeters, while Virgo wants
to discuss the matter first. You both need a break from this tor-
ture—now!

Sagittarius and Libra

These two might be onto something here. Sagittarius is intrigued by the glitz and glamour of charming Libra. Libra is always
interested in a meeting of the minds first, so the conversation will
be most stimulating. Both are people persons and love to entertain—Sag with her intelligence and Libra with his charm and so-
phistication. Regarding sex and romance, there are no complaints
here. Both love to travel and explore new places, people, and things.
Libra is the peacemaker and won't allow Sag's temper to come to the
boiling point. These two could have a happy marriage if Sag can
control the spending habits of Libra without hurting feelings. But
know this, Libra: Sag's lack of tact is certainly not meant to hurt,
harm, or hinder the relationship.

Sagittarius and Scorpio

Sagittarius is the happy-go-lucky sign of the zodiac. Scorpio's
emotional outbursts and passionate pleas for devotion will fall on
deaf ears. Scorpio, you need to chill and get over Sag's inclination
toward being unfocused. Scorpio wants total focus and commitment, while Sag says, "Look, let's just have a good time with very
few problems." Scorpio is left brooding and totally disenchanted by
Sag's aloof behavior. Once these two meet between the sheets, they
forget why this relationship isn't going to work. Sag is always looking for a higher plane from which to work sexually. And Scorpio is
always trying to reach the pinnacle of fulfillment, much to Sag's delight. But will sex alone make it work? No!

Sagittarius and Sagittarius

The breakup of this relationship is inevitable. They are the flirts of the zodiac. That's why they found themselves together in the first place. But the flirting is not going to stop with the two of them—and that's when the problem begins. Pure and simple, they are too busy with their many projects to give the quality time it takes to maintain a relationship. They also have biting tongues. It's called being tactless. And they are both in trouble if the verbal as sault is directed at each other. These two companions will be the first to agree that it's over. They'll shake hands, come out smiling, and the split will be without incident. Low-maintenance partici pants.

Sagittarius and Capricorn

I don't know how these two came together. Maybe it was be cause they admire the characteristics of the other. Capricorn knows in his heart of hearts that the Sag of his life is far too out there for Cap's way of thinking. This relationship will definitely need work. They are too different to find any common ground. Sag's life is lived with reckless abandon on the fringes of frivolity, running in twenty different directions. Sags simply enjoy life. Capricorn's life is scheduled, orderly, and practical—and for the most part, spent at home or at work. Sag will respond, "Excuse me?!" Sag is initially taken with Capricorn's take-charge demeanor. But when Capricorn starts putting everyone on a schedule, that's when things change. Sag is not the one!

Sagittarius and Aquarius

When this fire sign–air sign combo is together, there's a bon fire a-blazin'. Both enjoy life to the max and are always seeking new adventures in life and in each other. Believe me, when these two are together, there's never a dull moment. Aquarius will show Sagittarius a thing or two in the bedroom. But Sag is undaunted and soaks up all that this humanitarian has to offer and then some. Sagittarius's upbeat personality and dry humor keep Aquarius laughing. But bear in mind, Sag, that Aquarius can laugh all the way to the bank. They will spend money recklessly, be it yours or their own. A hot-to-trot affair and a lasting marriage, provided Sag's flirtatious nature doesn't annoy Aquarius too much.

Sagittarius and Pisces

This pair spends most of the time honing their sexual skills together. As long as Pisces is a willing participant, Sag will be right there stroke for stroke. Trouble is, Pisces is the homebody of the two and wants her mate confined to quarters—his, of course. Unlike Sag, she's not the social butterfly unless she has to be and is unimpressed with Sag's life-of-the-party antics and flip-with-lip attitude. Sag is intellectual and worldly and wants Pisces to be gung ho too. Pisces' interests are artistic in nature and her approach bores Sag. Pisces' insecurities and lack of get-up-and-go have Sag seeking other outlets. They're the flirts of the zodiac, so finding other playmates is no problem. Oh, well.

ROMANCE AND THE SAGITTARIAN

With Sagittarians, romance can be somewhat unconventional at times. They will want to know you on an intellectual basis first to determine what's in your head. And if there's nothing there in the way the Sag perceives that it should be, then you'll be told.

Sag brothers are not necessarily interested in candlelit dinners with all of the trimmings. For them it may be a casual encounter at a steak house, followed by a walk in the moonlight under the stars. There won't be waves washing up on the shore, hair blowing in the breeze as you look wistfully off into the distance. In fact, the only hair that may be blowing is your own as you put your bottom lip over your top in frustration and blow until your bangs fly up.

Sag sisters, however, prefer the traditional fare of a cozy restaurant, flowers, and good wine (not Boone's Farm), and of course, that all-important conversation on areas of substance.

If you're going on a date with a Sag woman and she volunteers to pick you up, check the gas gauge. If not, you may be pushing the car to a service station while she steers. She'll be laughing all the while about what happened and how she simply forgot. She was so busy with meetings, her two jobs, and running errands for a parent that getting gas was the last thing on her mind. You won't be amused, though. Oh well, there goes the romance.

If you want to get the attention of the Sagittarian, you need to plan an adventure of sorts. Sag people love the unique, off-the-beaten-path kinds of activities. For example, surprise him or her with a weekend getaway. Don't allow him to pack. Explain that where he's going, he won't need any clothing. Disconnect the phones (keep the cell phone in the car in case of emergency), take camping equipment, a flashlight, food, you, and only the spoken word. He will love it. (And try to go camping when the bears are hibernating!)

Also, if you're living with a Sag, pulling your weight with household chores is a big turn-on for her. After all is settled with your help, the romance can definitely start unless one of the children starts bawling or the dog jumps in the middle of the bed. Sagittarians are animal lovers.

Sometimes the Sag suffers from naïveté and acts too impulsively in relationships. Usually, if he determines that he's found his soul mate, he won't waste too much time playing a cat-and-mouse game about the situation. For example, a Sag gay brother met his Scorpio lover while visiting Washington, D.C. Intrigued by the attention of the Scorpio, the Sag took Scorpio at his word, sold his antique business in Louisiana, and moved to D.C. By the time the Sag arrived, the scorpion had had a change of heart.

In addition, talking, dancing, and kissing are also a big deal with Sag. These maneuvers will have your Sag leading the way when it's time to retreat behind closed doors. After hearing about how blunt and unemotional they are, you're probably having second thoughts about pursuing a relationship. Sagittarians, however, like romance and the whole package. But because they're so preoccupied with all the thoughts roaming around in their heads, they can be a bit distracted. But, hey, trust me: You don't want to miss this adventure.

A Sag bookseller remembers one of her most romantic dates was when her mate put together a collection of songs on tape by the artist formerly known as Prince. Later her companion gave the Sag Prince concert tickets. Are you getting the picture now?

Another Sag attorney living in Los Angeles remembers a romantic evening with a date who wanted stimulating conversation, and atmosphere, too. "He wanted to talk to me, so he took me to a plush hotel and gave me a massage. We had wonderful conversation and lovemaking."

Here's another idea of romance from a married Sag, who says her Leo husband tries very hard to keep the romance fresh by taking her on trips out of town. "We enjoyed a night out on the town going in and out of little cafés, clubs, et cetera. The night out ended with dinner on the beach and a stroll for dessert," she said, recalling one of the most memorable trips.

One Sag brother explained that slow-drag music, a meal that he cooked, a long walk under the moon, candles, drinks, and the spoken word is the stage for a dynamite weekend. By now you're understanding that communication is one of the main ingredients for getting the attention of the Sagittarian.

Sag men enjoy creating an unusual date for a potential mate or companion. For them, cooking a meal is no big deal. But for women who haven't encountered men who can cook, it *is* a big deal because these brothers can burn! In the case of one Sag male, the woman obviously missed the boat with his culinary skills. The brother recalls a most disastrous romantic encounter: "A woman stood me up for a date after I spent a good two hours cooking dinner for her."

When the Sag is in love, or thinks she is, she'll be devoted to a fault. The warnings of overprotective parents on abstaining from sex or avoiding sexually transmitted diseases will fall on deaf ears. For example, a Sagittarian college student from Milwaukee would travel home during the week during her freshman year at a predominantly white university to see her boyfriend. The Sag was so brazen, she would even ride the bus past her own house on these weekday excursions. She was easily recognized in her distinctive reddish orange coat. At one point during the weekly visits to the boyfriend's house, her aunt got on the same bus that Ms. Sag was on. Ms. Sag's rationale was that she had grown tired of being the valedictorian, Miss Goody Two-shoes type and felt it was time to venture out.

She's daring and will take the relationship to the next level, if the companion is willing. So instead of being anal-retentive about the whole matter, just go with the flow. Don't worry about appearances—the Sag sure as hell is not the slightest bit concerned.

Even after the romance or love affair is over, Sags will expect to remain friends. They value friendships and want to remain in contact because to them you were a friend first, before all of this love stuff began.

One Sag brother was so popular with his former girlfriends, he had to change his address and phone number. He also told his new companion that the constant calls were from overzealous telemarketers and disgruntled former employees. The calls still continue, however. He sidesteps them very effectively and manages to keep the peace with his mate, too.

With the Sag sister, you'll be mesmerized by her general knowledge and gift of gab. She'll talk your arm off and still remain on the edge of her seat as you relate story upon story about your life. And while your head is spinning from all that's been said about a Sagittarian, don't freak. It's all good. To know a Sag is to love a Sag.

SEX, SEX, AND MORE SEX

GETTING THE GROOVE ON . . .

For the most part, there ain't too much regarding sexual matters that would shock or turn off a Sag. Maybe over-the-top stuff like handcuffs, corsets, or S & M, where an ambulance had to be called, would get the Sag's attention.

But sex with more than one person or even persons of the same gender would definitely have possibilities. You won't find these fire signs showing any prudish or reluctant behavior. If they are shaking in their boots, you'll never know it. If Sag people are interested in any area of their lives, they put themselves into it. They want the total experience. Therefore, they want the total experience in the bedroom too. As long as the parties involved are not bleeding or crying for help, it's okay with the Sag.

Mental foreplay is a big turn-on for Sagittarians. There definitely must be talk and laughter before any serious sex or heavy breathing commences. A Sag wants to hear about your day, and she wants to tell you about her meeting. He may want to discuss a potential business venture with you or discuss current events. And please, if you're dealing with a Sag, read the newspapers and pay attention to current events. That is simply a must for these mental creatures. Ignorance is the quickest way to throw cold water on the fire.

The mental foreplay also includes talking dirty and communicating your feelings without feeling inhibited. Sagittarians are always turned on by an open, honest conversation. They don't like to be in suspense about anything. They want to know as quickly as you can verbalize or visualize it, as the case may be.

Knocking the boots under the stars or while traveling by car is definitely something the Sag could get into. They love the outdoors. These two areas for them are a winning combination. Also, the possibility of getting caught adds extra titillation and enhances the erotic experience. Remember the song "Feels so good when you slip and do it?" That song could be the anthem of the Sag.

Sag is constantly full of surprises. During the initial getting cozy phase, don't be surprised if the Sag brother asks you several questions before you adjourn to the boudoir. He may ask you about what type of foreplay you prefer, or he may ask you if you have orgasms. There are several reasons for the latter. One main reason, though, is that your answer will give him an idea of whether you're in touch with your sexuality and whether this encounter will be a waste of time. The Sag doesn't have a whole lot of time. And he wants this encounter to be a memorable one, even if he has to bombard you with a lot of preliminaries.

And to those hopeless romantics out there, this may be a total turnoff as you're thinking the approach is too matter-of-fact and emotionless. But consider that the Sagittarian's inquisitive mind and compulsive need to know are at work here.

For the Sagittarian woman, the approach to sex can be a little off-putting to men who believe that they should run the show. The independence of the Sag woman also carries over into the bedroom. Yes, she can be a highly sexual creature and creative when it comes to the bedroom. But she also has a very logical approach to lovemaking. She doesn't always expect bells and whistles each time she has a sexual encounter. Her favorite part of the action is the actual intercourse and the intimate or animated talks afterward.

The Sag brother will want to try new positions, different locations, and enhancements like sex toys to get you interested. The Sag man also enjoys watching sex videos, role playing, or any other off-the-beaten-path move that might be suggested. The trick is to tweak his curiosity. Both the men and the women want sex often. However, the quality may be lacking. In an effort to create a sexually creative encounter, the Sag must make an effort to "take the time and do it right"! And if that's not the case, then by all means, it's time to talk about it. They love to talk and they will also listen. They also have a preoccupation with the anal thing. Sagittarians love anal stimulation. That's not to say that they want to be poked in the rectum, constantly. But manipulation of the area through caressing and mild penetration is appealing to them.

A turnoff for one Sag woman from Virginia is a man who wants to receive, but not give, and one who is too rough and seems to be self-absorbed. A Sagittarian male commented that many women subconsciously compare the current encounter with former lovers. "It's very odd. She can't seem to get past it."

Odors are a big turnoff. A hint of musty smells can be an aphrodisiac, but bad breath and strong underarm odor will send any Sag packing, man or woman. Oh, by the way, missing teeth, especially in the front, will pour cold water on any flame before it flickers. Sag's first question will be "How did you let your mouth get in such disarray in the first place?" The second comment will be "You need to turn your face to the wall because I don't want those bad breath fumes creeping into my nostrils." Both the men and women of the sign will take you by the hand and walk you to the nearest dentist. And despite all the embarrassing moments, you'll turn to your Sag mate at the end of the day and thank him for being open and honest about what transpired.

Good oral hygiene for Sagittarians is a must, for they love kissing and using their mouths as instruments for great foreplay. One Sag male had definite ideas about the mouth area: "I like to excite a woman with my tongue. I like to kiss. Some women don't like you to lick them in the ear, but it excites the hell out of me. I think it's very important to use your tongue."

Another turnoff for a Sag woman was a man who was unimaginative and didn't know the word "foreplay." "He lay on me with all his weight, moved his hips, and that was that," she said, shaking her head.

A Sagittarian from Memphis had a quirk that put him at ease before having sex with a woman: "When I was single, my main quirk while visiting a female was to lay my clothes beside the bed, just in case something went wrong and I needed to make a quick escape." Hmm. . . .

EROGENOUS ZONES . . . SOME PHYSICAL, SOME NOT

The erogenous zones for Sag people are the hips and thighs and all areas in between. Although they enjoy sexual encounters very much, many times a Sag is more interested in having sex with many partners over a single one. They're sometimes more into the experience of it all than the actual person who's involved.

Brothers, you need to be put on notice. The Sag woman is definitely turned off by seeing you in the nude while you're wearing black nylon socks! That's a no-no. And don't forget to use some lotion, baby oil, or, better yet, Vaseline on your husky feet, elbows, arms, and legs. And if none of the aforementioned is available, Crisco will do. Sag women explained that they don't like scratches on the body during lovemaking, at least not from husky feet! The Sag women of the world will thank you.

In addition to being turned on by the spoken word, a Sag sister explained that a turn-on is also the tone of the voice. "My honey has this deep, exquisite, baritone voice. When he drops it an octave and makes a request, I melt."

A Sag brother from Miami said he was turned off by a female companion with dirty feet. The sexual encounter didn't occur because he felt if the feet weren't clean, there wasn't much hope for the rest of the body.

Scents and sometimes odors are turn-ons for the Sag. However, body odor from not bathing is another story. One woman explained, "The morning after is good because we both have the scents of last evening on us. It's like a catalyst for more."

Sag people prefer the man-on-top position. But before getting to that position, the exploration will be varied, with a lot of experimenting. It boils down to whatever is acceptable between the two. Sag people love oral sex, and anal sex, too. A Sag consultant commented that off-and-on oral sex accompanied with anal stimulation drives her crazy in the bedroom. A Sagittarian man was very specific about what turns him on in bed: "a woman giving me oral sex, and licking my penis, testicles, and anus and sticking her tongue in my ear." Is this what is known as a tongue bath? Also, if you want the archer to stand up on his hind legs with delight, rub those thighs and hips. Lightly stroking the genital area and massaging the back, groin, and hips with oil—that's all that will be required with this fire sign. One Sag courier named two things that drove him crazy in the bedroom—naked woman and a bottle of baby oil. A Sag sister also explained that rubbing her hair, legs, feet, and hips drives her wild—in that order.

One of the big turn-ons for most Sagittarians is the use of oils on the body. Massages are all-important as well, because the Sagittarians have bulging schedules and there's nothing they like better than a long hot bath, followed by deep massages with exotic oils, good conversation, good food, and a good lay for dessert.

Plain Ol' Sex and Nothing More: Welcome to the Freak Show

The twelve signs of the zodiac fall into three categories: freak show participants, freak show sideliners, and stars. Sagittarians are participants, which means they will go along with about any maneuver in the bedroom. They will try anything once. They want to be in the know about most subjects and they figure there's lots to be learned in the sexual arena. They're not intimidated by new techniques or suggestions.

Sags' open-mindedness and liberal attitude will have them seeking ways of relieving stress without an emotional and everlasting commitment. They love the no-strings-attached approach to relationships because it definitely liberates them from the union. At the same time they don't have to weigh every move to make the union work.

Actually, the Sag will function better between the sheets when the expectations of where the relationship is going are not the main issue. Sagittarians are all about the fun of the sex play. They're the

realists of the zodiac and they don't need or expect a strong emotional bond during a sexual encounter.

So if by chance you meet a Sagittarian of either gender and you
can't resist asking for sex simply for sex, this liberal sign of the zodiac will probably give you a positive response. If the answer is not
in the affirmative, you certainly won't get your face slapped. You
may get a curious look or a throaty laugh. You may even get a totally unexpected response from the Sag sister, like "How about
every Wednesday afternoon?" That's hump day, you know.

MONEY MATTERS

If you're looking for a cheap date, you've come to the right place.
Sag people are very cautious about money when it comes to show-
ering their mates with needless gifts—practical gifts, maybe. In
fact, they're cheap when it comes to money that they consider is
spent in a wasteful manner. But then again, the money that they
spend on what they deem is worthy of the price is another story.

They will definitely spend money on what they consider important possessions. But what you consider important is probably
not important to the Sag. For example, you may want to have your
bathrooms remodeled. In fact, he might have promised to take care
of it next year. But then, unbeknown to you, he buys an extensive
computer system with a direct link to the New York Stock Exchange. In his spare time he researches commodities, stocks, or mutual funds. He figures that with this investment the two of you
could eventually rebuild your whole house. In the meantime, since
the Sagittarian has such a curious mind, he may buy a book on in-
stalling a shower and new toilet. Your bathrooms will probably be a
wreck for six months because usually he's already overextended
with two jobs and other projects before he starts yet another
"great" idea.

Whatever the Sag is interested in, he takes to the next level,
which means money is no object. For example, a Sag counselor from
Philadelphia was responsible for teaching young black mothers
about the skills of parenting. When the Sag sister sought information on black parenting tips from guides or magazines, she couldn't

find any published information. She decided to publish her own magazine on the subject.

When it comes to money matters, Sagittarians can also suffer from erratic and unpredictable behavior. Although Sag people are cautious about money, they can also be over the top and wasteful about it too. Sag people are ruled by the planet Jupiter, which is associated with good luck and optimism. You feel that Lady Luck is forever on your side. One downfall of Sagittarians is gambling. They definitely don't mind taking chances when it comes to gambling. They definitely will go out on a limb when it comes to taking chances with money because they're eternal optimists. Consequently, their positive attitude about money finds them with a devil-may-care attitude many times. But exercising prudence is the key. Don't overdo it.

Since education is a high priority with Sag people, investing in their children's education is a must. They have an insatiable thirst for knowledge and will try to impart the value of education to their children.

Saving for a rainy day is to a Sag's liking unless she stumbles upon some foolproof scheme that she can't resist. For the most part, however, Sagittarians will definitely do their homework when it comes to high-risk projects. But they can also be impulsive. Usually, their luck and optimism will have them okay with the venture. On the other hand, if you're a spouse or a companion of a Sagittarian, you may continue to fret and wring your hands over the feasibility of the projects. One final note: There will never be a dull moment with money or any other area of the Sagittarian's life.

Pampering Tips for Sagittarius

   ✳ If you can track down your Sag for some pampering, you deserve a medal. Suggestion: Lock him up and throw away the key. Then start your tabletop dance, Dr. Feelgood.

   ✳ Retreat with your Sagittarian to a secluded cabin in the mountains. It may be a good idea to blindfold him so that he can't escape.

   ✳ A surprise visit from a masseuse will work for your Sag.

High stress and multiple jobs are Sag's middle names.

❋ Plan a spa weekend that includes hiking and outdoor fun. Your Sag will thank you.

❋ A cruise would do wonders for your Sag. Once he is re-signed to the fact that there's no escape, then he will truly relax.

❋ Hit the highway with your Sag and see where the road leads. Your adventuresome Sag may want to stop on the side of the road frequently. Be prepared.

❋ Plan a picnic with all of her favorite foods. Then cap off the day with horseback or bike riding.

❋ A day at a trade show may sound boring to some. But discovering state-of-the-art gadgets and machines for the new millennium will excite and relax your Sag.

❋ Arrange to have your Sag's car serviced or washed, or get in a maid service to clean house for a day. Then take off to parts unknown.

❋ Show up at your Sagittarian's door with a prepared meal and his favorite champagne. Oh, by the way, a garterbelt and your apron are the only articles of clothing you need.

Gift Ideas for Sagittarius

❋ A puppy or a kitten will score major points. Sagittarians are animal lovers. You can skip the exotic pets like the parrots, snakes, Gila monsters!

❋ Any state-of-the-art gadgetry, computer, or video game is fine for your curious Sag.

❋ How-to books, books on science and religion, and even novels are great gifts. Sagittarians have an insatiable thirst for knowledge.

❋ Your Sag loves to travel, so a monogrammed garment or travel bag won't miss. Hey, don't forget to include the airline tickets!

❋ Practical gifts work for a Sag too. A cordless phone, an electric blanket, or even a pager is okay.

❋ Sagittarians love the great outdoors. Sleeping bags, outdoor lamps, a tackle box, or a tent are all gifts your Sag will appreciate.

❋ Hire a clown or send a singing telegram with balloons in tow to your Sag. Sagittarians have a great sense of humor.

❋ Any computer software such as accounting or calendar software that talks will be a welcome gesture. Sagittarians are futuristic in thought and deed.

❋ Season tickets to any spectator sport will work every time.

❋ A camera, video camera, portable radio, or CD player is a great gift for Sagittarians because these items will be used during Sag's many travels.

Capricorn

(December 22 to January 19)
SYMBOL: THE GOAT

Positive love traits: Conventional, arduous, and methodical lover; doesn't participate in the freak show.
Negative love traits: Selfish in bed; sadistic; may put love-making on a schedule, like 8:30 P.M. on Saturdays.
Ruling planet: Saturn is associated with limitation, restriction, obstacles, and discipline.
Word to the wise: Capricorns are immovable objects and resistant to change. This serious-minded sign is nobody's fool.

Capricorns are not social butterflies. Most of the time, you will meet this earth sign in a controlled setting such as work, church, health club, or fund-raiser for a day care center. The events or organizations in which they participate usually have some good-deed overtone to them. And so does the Capricorn's life.

This earth sign enjoys a variety of activities such as outdoor sports or anything where strategy is involved, such as tennis, chess, or basketball. Capricorns also love African art, plays, jazz concerts, biking, or kickin' back with a good book.

The symbol for Capricorn is the goat. The ruling planet is Saturn, which is associated with discipline and hard work. These mountain goats will work as hard as they need to, to reach the top in a career or any other area in their lives.

Capricorns are earth signs, which means they are down to earth, practical, and cautious. Capricorns are always the same: predictable, reliable, and grounded. These earth signs are far too serious for their own good, though. In their hearts, they want to be foot-loose and fancy-free, but they simply don't know how. For example, if you happen upon Capricorns in what they consider an un-scrupulous place like a casino or a booty bar, they will immediately explain that the only reason they're there in the first place is be-cause their out-of-town guests requested this type of entertain-ment.

Although serious, these down-to-earth people are also sensi-tive, strong, and caring. But for the most part, unless you've known them since childhood, their personal and private side won't be readily visible. You would have to be in their inner circle of friends or a person worthy of trust.

The physical makeup of a black Capricorn won't include too many distinguishing features. Capricorns are usually slim and ath-letic-looking, but physical size can run the gamut. Most of the time, Capricorns look considerably younger than they actually are. The jawbone is prominent, and they will sometimes have a habit of bit-ing down in a clenched-toothed manner. If a Capricorn brother is going bald, he won't wear a toupee; he feels that he should be man enough to show the real person. The women of the sign like a vari-ety of hairstyles, but most of them will be conservative in nature—a short cut, braids, a perm, or even dreads that are kept at a moderate length. Multicolored hair of blue, gold, and burgundy won't ever crown a Capricorn's head. They are far too conservative for any leanings toward what they perceive as nonsense. You would never see a Capricorn with locks of hair resembling Ru Paul or the fortress hairdos, which are so tall that trying to get inside of a car is futile.

If you're into the natural look, that's okay. But don't let a Capri-corn spot you in your nappy-headed state. The hairdo needs to be permed or natural, but not half and half (permed on the top and nappy underneath). The Capricorn brothers certainly don't like their companions to be between hairdos. And the Capricorn sister wants some sense of order when it comes to the hair. A hairdo like Maxwell, the singer, will leave you singing the blues after Lady Capricorn cancels the date.

Capricorns are friendly and, above all else, polite. But trying to get next to them will be slow going, to say the least. Trust, re-

spect, and honesty are the common denominators of all the relationships Capricorns are involved in, whether platonic or romantic. If you're interested in a Capricorn, then you had better buy a
new watch. Any dates or outings will be planned, scheduled, and
orderly, just like their lives. And on any date, they will expect you
to act appropriately, which means, for them, in a gentlemanly or
ladylike manner.

As spouses or companions, Capricorns are faithful without a
doubt. You don't have to worry about trying to keep up with their
whereabouts. Yes, these earth signs are usually involved in a variety
of activities, including meetings, travel, community service projects, or church-related stuff. But just because they're not in da
house doesn't mean they are hangin' out at a would-be companion's
crib. They simply don't want to deal with more than one companion.
They don't see the point.

THE CAPRICORN MAN

This brother is definitely the strong, silent type. Trouble is, you'll be
hard-pressed to see any emotion or vulnerable behavior from this
earth sign at all. He probably thinks that showing any emotion is a
sign of weakness, and he must be in control of all situations in
which he finds himself. He's forever weighing the pros and cons of
any impending relationship.

The Capricorn man may appear aloof and unsmiling, staying to
himself at a club or social setting, but women are intrigued by this
brother. Once when a Capricorn man was throwing up outside a
nightclub, a woman standing outside of the building tried to talk to
him in a more-than-friendly manner. "I don't mean any disrespect,"
he told her, "but this is *not* a good time. I don't want to get to know
you right now." Go figure!

At a party, the Capricorn will strategically place himself in the
background. He wants to be in the mix, but he prefers to fade into
the background to take it all in without being noticed. This way he
can assess how all the players and pieces fit. It's about being in control, you know. In short, this brother is not going to throw caution
to the wind and hit on any woman that he thinks looks good. That's
not how he operates. The moves will be slow.

For example, a Capricorn female who had been attending drug rehab meetings was approached by a Capricorn counselor, who told her that he had been watching her for an entire year and was interested in having a relationship. He told her that he had observed her demeanor, and the fact that she was not loud and boisterous and was intelligent and levelheaded. "I didn't realize that he had been watching me all that time," she said. "I was smitten."

The Capricorn brother has the front made. He's always dressed to the nines. He has the facade that he's Mr. All That, and to some women he definitely is. His appearance and his cool, calm demeanor indicates a man of mystery, someone most women would be curious about and want to get to know. But before the hot pursuit commences, there are a few points you need to know.

When you approach the Capricorn man, you need to be careful. He is very good at pretending that he doesn't realize you're flirting shamelessly with him. If you don't meet his long list of criteria as he's sizing you up, you can, for all practical purposes, skip this catch. He won't miss a beat as he notices your makeup, nails, hair, the missing button on your clothing, your eye contact, and even your teeth. If you're in a casual conversation with a Capricorn, you'll find yourself in an interview. And you need to try to speak correctly. A few slang words are permissible, but no dirty jokes in mixed company. You're probably asking yourself by now, "Who needs this stuffed shirt?" But believe me, his pluses definitely outweigh his minuses. He's got a great sense of humor, an earthy and pleasing personality. And once he trusts you and you're brought into "the fold," it will be fun.

The serious, no-nonsense side is what's visible to the outside world. Those persons privileged enough to see the other side—sensitive, strong, caring—probably have been around for years. Aside from what is seen, he seeks to do the right thing in most situations. For example, a Capricorn brother met a Taurus woman and they instantly connected. Although the Taurus woman was to have been his girlfriend on the side, Capricorn ended up seeing Ms. Taurus more often than his main squeeze. The relationship soon ended, because he felt guilty about having two women.

A Capricorn man who found himself in the one-night-stand situation ended up having to pay child support for a two-year-old whom he had never met. "It was a friend's birthday and we had been partying all day and half the night. I met this woman who flirted with me and that's all I remember. I woke up naked in her bed, apologized, and told her I was leaving." Although the Capricorn pays support, the mother insists that he cannot see the child unless she's present. The Capricorn told her he didn't want a relationship and explained he didn't know her. "Something happened, I'm sorry that it happened, and I'm paying for it." I'll say, it's called 18 years!

Capricorns generally marry very young or very late or not at all. Usually, they are so wrapped up in career-ladder jobs and being successful in the workplace that love, marriage, and long-term unions are delayed. In the Capricorn man's quest for prestige and success, he may marry for money and status instead of love and happiness.

He's definitely not above finding a wife who will enhance his career. His philosophy is, he can fall madly in love with a woman who will support him and enhance his career just as readily as one who won't. So if you're married to Capricorn, you were probably handpicked.

There won't be any waves washing on the shore with this down-to-earth sign. They're too practical to do impulsive things. However, the Capricorn brother definitely knows how to wine and dine and play the romantic role. For example, a Capricorn social worker surprised his companion with a picnic, complete with wine, music, and a meal that he had prepared, right smack-dab in the middle of his living room floor. The earlier plans of going hiking had to be canceled because of rain and sleet. Mr. Capricorn, who was not to be outdone, created the indoor picnic with dessert afterward!

To enhance the relationship, this earth sign needs, above all else, support and admiration from a companion. His ego can always use a little stroking, and you'll be the beneficiary by loving him in spite of himself.

Although he requires a lot from friends and companions in the way of loyalty and devotion, his serious-minded, do-the-right-thing approach to life finds him giving as much or more in return to loved ones. For example, a Capricorn brother decided to take a leave from his job to raise his newborn child. His Aquarian live-in companion knew nothing about child rearing, so he decided to become Mr. Mom, including the 2 A.M. feedings and the overall care of the baby until the baby was 18 months old. The Capricorn brother lived on his savings, while showing the mother the ins and outs of care for a newborn, until he returned to work.

THE CAPRICORN WOMAN

Don't make any assumptions with the Capricorn sister, namely, that this courtship will be a walk in the park. It won't! The notion of falling in love for a Capricorn sister is risky but serious business. And she doesn't intend to put her feelings and vulnerabilities out there for you to walk on.

Like most areas of her life, she will take her time about getting involved in the knee-deep, head-over-hills love affair. She is too practical and cautious for that. If by chance she's interested in you, you may be totally clueless until she feels that the time is right to make her move or give you the green light to make yours. (The process may take a year or more.) She will observe how you interact with others, whether you exhibit gentlemanly qualities and common sense, and, most important, whether you are drug-free.

If you're divorced, she'll want to know whether you have children and, if so, whether you pay support and are involved in the children's lives. At this point, you may feel like you're in a CIA interview. You are! But it's for her own central intelligence of understanding you! I know, you haven't even gone on your first date yet. But be patient because this classy lady is definitely worth waiting for. The Capricorn woman keeps a running list of requirements that she wants in *her* man and her standards are high.

And rarely will she settle for less than what she wants. But what she wants and what she gets in a relationship don't always come together. For example, a Capricorn female who met her husband while both were in the military thought that if she showed her husband total devotion and love his unreasonably jealous behavior would change. "The jealousy was driving him to be so possessive. He wanted to possess me totally. And I confused jealousy with love. He was even jealous of my girlfriends. I would see someone I knew and turn my head to keep from stirring up problems." Soon, the jealous rages turned violent and the union ended with a quickness.

The Capricorn sister will expect to be first in your life. But she is definitely a good catch with goals, aspirations, and self-discipline. In short, this high-maintenance sister won't require any more from her man than she's willing to give in the relationship. For example, a Capricorn woman from Chicago made an unwise move in a relationship and suffered the consequences. "I was the number one woman in a relationship with my mate. I later ended the relationship, but had a change of heart and wanted to come back. When I went back as the number two woman, I realized that it was a stupid and foolish move." After a little soul searching, Ms. Capricorn let the whole scenario fall by the wayside.

The Capricorn woman is ultrafeminine and will be impeccably dressed at all times, even when wearing jeans. (The jeans will be sent to the laundry.) Her body will be toned and her outfit will offer just the right degree of subtlety. When you first notice this woman with her head in the air and a removed look on her face, she will be dressed in a way that reeks of perfection. Her appearance will be ultraneat, hair freshly done, nails and toes manicured.

These women of the sign enjoy shopping for and collecting antiques, art, books, or items of value. When she shops for clothing, she buys quality instead of quantity. If she purchases a suit for $500, she knows that it will maintain its look over the long haul.

Capricorns have a great sense of humor and they love to laugh. Having a sense of humor is always a great quality because as uptight as the Capricorn sister can get with all of the demands of career, family matters, and her many other projects, she can always use a good laugh.

Although the Capricorn sister may project this tough, independent attitude, she is a sensitive, caring person who seeks true love. However, her mistrust of people sometimes has her waiting in the wings, never to take center stage in affairs of the heart. This earth sign is very ambitious and many times will totally immerse herself in her career or community causes, not allowing time for much dating.

After working hard all day in her leadership role at work or play, her biggest need is to retreat to the safety of her abode. Hopefully, her man is there at the door with a glass of wine and assurances that it's time to relax. She wants a strong, take-charge man whom she can rely on and put her trust in and who, like a bubble bath, will just take her away.

If you expect to have a relationship with a Capricorn female, there definitely won't be a lot of talk and production on your part. Capricorn females detest men who are braggadocios. "The worst turnoff for me with a potential companion is someone who tells me all they can do or have done—Mr. Been There, Done That. Don't tell me you're cold. Let me see it for myself. Show me," said a female Capricorn video director.

And show her is exactly what has to happen if you expect to enjoy more dates with this sophisticated lady. For example, this earth sign prides herself on indulging in very few excesses. More than likely she probably has a spa membership. If you lie, she'll know immediately. Phonies need not apply. For example, if you mention that you go to the spa regularly but have a beer belly that won't quit, your Capricorn lady will know you are only trying to impress. After she comments that your waist size is the same size as her hips, you probably won't mention exercise again.

A big turnoff for the Capricorn sister is being embarrassed in public. Image is everything, you know. For example, a Capricorn sister was in the grocery store with her live-in Scorpio companion, when she casually asked him to push the basket as she shopped and examined coupons. "Why should I push the basket? I'm paying for the damn groceries," he said, while pushing the basket away and storming out of the store. The encounter was the couple's last.

In another situation, a Capricorn sister was totally mortified during a chance meeting with her Aries ex-beau. During a date with a new potential companion, the couple stopped at a convenience store. Before her date could get out of the car, Mr. Aries pulled right up beside them, looked down in the sports car and over at Ms. Capricorn, and asked, "How are you doing?" Not only was the Capricorn embarrassed, she was wearing the outfit that her former companion had purchased for her months earlier.

Any man who can stand up to the independence and assertiveness of the Capricorn sister deserves a medal. There aren't any easy answers here. If you plan to get to the reckless-abandon stage, where sexual high jinks will be frequent and involved, she simply must feel secure and trust you without reservation.

Guide to a Love Connection

Capricorn and Aries

Both are domineering people who are constantly jockeying for position. Capricorn's coldness and controlled feelings drive Aries crazy. Aries wants drama, intrigue, and spontaneity. Capricorn is too busy with career, organizing everyone's life, and staying in the serious mode. Aries looks at Capricorn as a bore. Capricorn sees Aries' behavior as bizarre. Even in the bedroom, Capricorn's reserved nature doesn't allow for too much creativity, and Aries won't sit still for this attitude. The shouting matches get more intense. Even though Aries readily forgives and forgets, Capricorn is not amused. And when Capricorn is miserable, so is everyone else.

Capricorn and Taurus

This couple is made for each other. They have lots in common. Capricorn is a homebody and so is Taurus. These two are devoted to each other and this makes possessive Taurus a happy camper. Both are career-minded. Capricorn is a little more obsessive about work goals than Taurus. But that's okay because Taurus plans to have a serious nest egg by retirement. Both are loyal, steadfast, organized, and practical in their approach to life in general. Regarding money matters, Taurus may be a little cheap, but Capricorn appreciates Taurus's conscientious approach to money. Sexually, there won't be any kinky, freaky, and unconventional sex, but it will be a satisfying encounter on the part of both. Hey, what's not to like here? Go for it!

Capricorn and Gemini

Forget it! Well, let me explain. This pair is no pair, at least not in the same relationship. Capricorn's interest in a rewarding career, security, and standing in the community will get on Gemini's nerves. Gemini sees this behavior as obsessive. Gemini takes pains to maintain a good image, but the twins see Capricorn's approach as much too anal-retentive. Gemini wants spontaneity, daring, and creativity in life. Capricorn is a little too serious for Gemini. And in the bedroom, the same things apply. Gemini's creativity and sense of adventure in bed are a turnoff for Capricorn, who is into conventional lovemaking. Capricorn sees Gemini's casual and distracted behavior toward the relationship as annoying. Maybe a short-term affair, but never a long-term commitment.

Capricorn and Cancer

Yes, I know you spotted each other at work or across a crowded room and each wondered who the other was. Cancer approached first because Capricorn remained in deep thought about whether to move. I know you want it to work—and it does for a while. But you two are opposites. Cancer won't be able to stand up under the close scrutiny of Capricorn, the serious-minded goat. Cancer is far too sensitive for the biting tongue of Capricorn. Capricorns don't intend to hurt feelings; they simply don't know how to relax and ease up. So they try to make people into their own image. In short, Cancer ain't having it! The crab simply wants an all-consuming relationship with an occasional tryst and walk near water and the full moon suspended in the sky.

Capricorn and Leo

This couple admires each other's qualities, like being well dressed, leadership ability, and the conscientious way they approach most things. But that's where it ends. Both are domineering and want to run the show. Leo wants to be the star of the show, while Capricorn is annoyed by Leo's high-maintenance attitude. Capricorn spends money wisely. Leo spends money. During the midnight hour, Leo's aggressive, over-the-top sexual behavior and the need to dominate create tension between them. Both are sociable people with many friends. Capricorn's idea of a great evening is creating it at home. Leos must make the party scene with full regalia and drama. Their public is waiting, you know. Long-term union or marriage is a no-go.

Capricorn and Virgo

Once these two meet, they breathe a sigh of relief because finally they've found someone to whom they can relate. They have so much in common, it's scary. Virgo and Capricorn are both earth signs, which means they're grounded, practical, and sensible people. Capricorn's focus on career and financial security enhances Virgo's nose-to-the-grindstone personality. These two are so busy working hard, they will need to be reminded about playtime. Although both have friends and acquaintances (Capricorn more so than Virgo), they would rather retreat to their safe abodes. Each has to curtail the criticism of the other if there's going to be some romance looming. Sexually, they could use a few enhancements, like toys or videos, to get the flame lit, not to mention burning. These two will have a comfortable relationship.

Capricorn and Libra

Capricorn is impressed by Libra's charm and magnetism. Libra loves a well-dressed, self-assured man, but Capricorn, the earth sign, and Libra, the air sign, just can't seem to get it together. Libras thrive on attention, including candlelit dinners at expensive restaurants, luxurious surroundings, and a lavish lifestyle. That's fine with Capricorn, too, but who's going to pay for all of this? Conservative and sensible Capricorn is not the one! Sparks will fly, initially. But skip the moonlight walk on the beach under the full moon. The bedroom scene will be very frustrating: Capricorn will hold back and not exude enough sexual excitement and Libra will make the grand entrance to the ho-hum attitude of the goat. This liaison will need work that this duo is simply not willing to give.

Capricorn and Scorpio

This is earth and water at its best. These two make beautiful mud together. These two have common goals of having mo' money and security. Capricorn's organizational skills work well with Scorpio's intuitive powers and fierce determination to succeed. Capricorn is goal- and career-oriented and Scorpio supports all along the way. Scorpio's sensuality awakens some dormant feelings in reserved

Capricorn. Sexy Scorpio takes the lead in the boudoir and that's fine with the goat. Capricorn's strength and confidence can easily handle Scorpio's jealous rages. Capricorn is a homebody, and Scorpio must know the goat's whereabouts at all times. It's about total possession, you know. If these two domineering signs can give a little and give up some control to the other, they will have a long relationship.

Capricorn and Sagittarius

Maybe this relationship could work in another life. Capricorn must be in full control. Sagittarius couldn't care less about controlling, but won't be controlled in the relationship. Capricorn simply can't get used to Sag's fly-by-the-seat-of-the-pants attitude. And Cap wonders, "Why is Sag so happy all of the time? Doesn't she understand the turmoil that the world is in?" Serious Capricorn's need for a systematic, methodical life will drive sassy, daring Sag into a rage. Capricorn would be livid if any kind of outbursts occurred in public. Sag is not bothered by all of Capricorn's requirements of a companion. They will realize about two weeks into the relationship that it ain't happening. They will both seek refuge elsewhere and quick!

Capricorn and Capricorn

You definitely must be worthy of a Capricorn's attention to get it in the first place. It takes a lot to catch a Capricorn's eye. When Capricorns find someone like them who is well dressed, career-oriented, and a class act (if they do say so themselves), there's an automatic attraction. The relationship of these two could die of terminal boredom. Capricorns are conservative and rigid in their approach to most things. The drill sergeant mentality will spill over into the relationship and everything will be put on a schedule, including the sex. They do feel safe with a partner like themselves. But what's needed is a partner who has qualities they don't have, and vice versa, to promote more of a balance in their lives. Get out now, while you still can. Ho-hum.

Capricorn and Aquarius

There's a meeting of the minds with this twosome. They can sit and talk engrossed in conversation for hours. But that's where it ends. Capricorn wants to be in total control of the relationship. But

that's hard because Aquarius is always elusive and must have freedom. Capricorn is grounded and predictable. Aquarius is unpredictable and goes with the flow. Aquarius's approach to sex is
similar to the rest of her life, meaning push the envelope and let's
see what happens. Reserved Capricorn is embarrassed by the quirky
bedroom antics of Aquarius. Capricorn is too baffled by Aquarius's
personality, and Aquarius is too indifferent about the whole matter.
All in all, each needs to set the other up with a blind date.

Capricorn and Pisces

One thing's for sure, Pisces will keep Capricorn interested and
intrigued. Capricorn's cold reserve will be melted away by Pisces'
mystery, romance, and passion. Capricorn is the strong-willed, no-
nonsense type who's always in the take-charge mode and in control.
That's fine with Pisces, who loves to be led and guided. But in the
bedroom, Pisces takes over, leading Capricorn to new heights. Although Cap tries to maintain a cool, calm exterior, Pisces knows
that the goat is history. Both enjoy fine dining, luxurious surroundings, and the better things of life. Capricorn's financial planning allows amenities to be enjoyed without worry. A steamy affair
or a long-lasting marriage.

ROMANCE AND THE CAPRICORN

If you're trying to get a date with a Capricorn or, better yet, something going for the long haul, you need to be impressive. With the
female of the sign, to get this date off on the right foot, bring flowers or scented candles. Candy is out because the Capricorn sister is
forever watching her weight and trying to eat healthier.

Rule number one: Capricorns are not interested in public displays of affection. It's okay to hold hands or exchange a light kiss
occasionally, but bumping and grinding and deep soul kissing will
have to be saved for the boudoir. Actually, if too much is going on
that are turnoffs beforehand, you won't see the boudoir.

If you're planning a date with a Capricorn, there are several tidbits you need to be aware of. First and foremost, try to be ready on
time—not CP time. Otherwise, you may not have a second chance to
make a first impression.

If you're dating a Capricorn brother and you're into spandex and boa-constrictor-type clothing, that hoochie-mama look will never work with a Capricorn man. The brother enjoys girl watching, but does not want his date to be the object of the gawkers' attention. He's conservative, and he will expect his date's outfit to have an understated elegance. Capricorn men are most meticulous when it comes to dating. They will definitely make the date memorable and it will be a class act, just like this brother. If you're not sure what to wear, you need to go shopping and ask a salesperson.

If you're going on a date with a lady Capricorn, leave all the gold chains at home. A gold bracelet or one gold chain will do nicely. If you have gold teeth, I suppose there's nothing you can do about it (on the first date), but try not to grin too much. Impeccable dress is always an attention getter with both the men and women of this sign.

Having a good sense of humor will help to break the ice. Capricorns are so rigid and serious, they can always use a good laugh or joke. Actually, Capricorns have a great sense of humor, too.

If you want to take a Capricorn out on a date, you need to wait until you can afford it. And you'll need that sense of humor if you only have a two-for-one coupon for White Castle burgers. Not that you'll be expected to have $200 or $300 handy. But a quality date for a Capricorn is more important than the frequency of the dates. A Capricorn sister from Connecticut remembers a date that definitely got her attention. "Well, first he sent a car for me and there were flowers in it when it arrived (so was he!) and then dinner and then romance. It was great!" The point here is, long before you and your Capricorn companion end up in the bedroom, you must be able to stimulate her mentally, too. "He's got to drive me crazy before we get to the bedroom, but I love a man who knows what he's doing and is doing it because he's with me," said a Capricorn sister.

A Capricorn sister who's twice divorced and back in the dating game explains one of her pet peeves: "A turnoff for me is a guy who's cheap. I want to be taken to a nice place to eat, instead of going to get some chicken and bringing it back home." Capricorns are not going to be cheap dates.

However, sometimes big bucks don't have to be spent to get

Capricorn's attention. "Going out with someone I truly care about, riding around, talking, sitting by the river, a walk in the park, or back-to-nature stuff is important," said one Capricorn female. Romance with a Capricorn is synonymous with class. Granted, there may not be a lot of money, but putting time, effort, and creativity into the date is what counts. By the way, there's no creativity in going to a movie, but a moonlit picnic under the stars is another story.

Capricorns are interested in the total package as well. You must have something going on in your head if you're considering dating a Capricorn brother. The Capricorn brother definitely can relate to the body-beautiful concept. You must read, know about current events, and have a good head on those broad shoulders. (And I don't mean during sex!)

If by chance you get the attention of Capricorn, who has a dubious and cautious approach to most things, you obviously have put time and effort into the date and subsequent relationship. For example, a female Capricorn barber recalls the most memorable approach to romance: "My boyfriend asked me to meet him outside of my job instead of coming up. That bothered me but I went out, anyway. He handed me a single yellow rose (my favorite color) with a card that said, 'A single rose for the one woman who holds the only key to my heart.' I was sold!"

A Capricorn sister from Oakland, then a college student, remembers her most memorable date. Her potential partner prepared a candlelit dinner; he played Donald Byrd in the background and later read from Gibran's *The Poet*. "It blew my mind," she said.

Capricorn sisters are proud people and have a sense of who they are and what they expect from a mate. Even though Capricorns want to find love, and enjoy the chase and the whole idea of the love bug biting, they won't tolerate impropriety on any level. For example, a Capricorn attorney explained a sticky situation in which she found herself: "A man I admired professionally had a little too much to drink at dinner and made a pass at me. I simply untangled myself from him, told him another time, and avoided him for three months. He finally got the picture."

One Capricorn woman ended a relationship with her Aries companion after she learned that he was lurking in the bushes of a nightclub that she went to with some coworkers. When this earth sign mentioned that she had gone out, the ram wanted to know who the man was who walked her to her car. Of course, Ms. Capricorn was mortified, but Mr. Aries would only admit that he was merely passing by the club at the exact moment she came out. Hmmm.

Although it may take a considerable amount of time for the Capricorn to open up, intimate talks are very important in a relationship. Also, taking trips together is important to the Capricorn because she can't truly unwind until she's away from familiar surroundings, someplace where no one knows her name and she's not expected to be "on." Then she can truly relax.

When all systems are go and he can take the time from his busy schedule to accomplish this goal, you'll be the winner. Nothing is more delightful than a Capricorn who is relaxing among friends and truly enjoying the moment.

Sometimes it's just the little things. A Capricorn nurse commented that after she and her Aquarian companion decided to marry, a minor comment that he gave no relevance to touched her. "I'm coming home," her companion said after they had decided to marry only days before. These two both had separate homes. Unbeknownst to the Aquarian, that comment definitely set the stage for romance.

SEX, SEX, AND MORE SEX

GETTING THE GROOVE ON . . .

Capricorns feel that in order for the love and romance to commence, you have to gain their trust. And this earth sign will have to be turned on way before the sex starts.

Like other areas of their lives, control is important in the bedroom, too. They definitely will want to run the show. These earth signs might appear cold and removed, but that's only a defense mechanism. Once they are aroused, their sexual gratification is the most important thing. This is not to say that they are not good lovers, because they definitely can be. But the goal for them, from a sexual standpoint, is to reach the highest peaks of sexual gratification, and they work toward achieving their goals, in life and in the bedroom. A Capricorn can stand toe-to-toe with any other sign of the zodiac, so you need to get your rest.

Turn-ons for the Capricorn include intimate talks before and after sex. Intelligence rates high on the list of a Capricorn. They firmly believe after sex is over, you have to talk about something, and Capricorn will want the subject to be of substance. And yes, right up to the sex act itself, you'll feel that you're being interviewed. Before the night is over, your goals, aspirations, classiness, and sassiness will all be uncovered.

Capricorns must be comfortable to truly relax and enjoy the moment. Hopefully, the location is neat, with semiluxurious, aesthetically pleasing surroundings. Also, cleanliness rates very high in their book. Taking a shower and a bath in the Jacuzzi is always a good idea with a Capricorn. Sex for them can't be rushed, so relaxing beforehand helps them unwind. If you're the type who wants to rush things, you can skip this encounter. For example, a Capricorn woman ended a relationship with her Leo companion because he was always in a hurry. "I hate it when a man wants to take me to bed first thing. With my friend, he would get out of his clothes, get in bed without any foreplay. He didn't know how to make love to a woman."

Also, with many Capricorns, kissing is an important part of the process, and if you don't want to or know how, then run out and take a crash course. Find a Cancer person. This expert will be glad to show you. Capricorns do their homework when it comes to assessing the strong and weak points of a potential or current lover. And if you're coming up short, well . . . "I dated this man who didn't know how to kiss and he had saliva all over my damn face and would miss my lips. I asked him one day, 'Damn, when are you going to learn how to kiss me?' When I take the time to show him how, next thing I know he's all over my mouth." For this Capricorn, the bottom line was "I like to kiss. If a person doesn't want to kiss me, we can't deal."

The Capricorn sister will want to have sex included on her calendar. Don't despair, this move is simply a carryover from the rest of her methodical, systematic life. And you will also find yourself being led by her between the sheets. She knows exactly what she wants in and out of the bedroom, and she doesn't like to be surprised in bed. For the most part she can be pretty conservative. She wants to know what to expect because she will need time to contemplate the whys and wherefores of an agreement regarding sex toys, costumes, and even videotaping. You're more than likely to get a positive response if you're married to a Capricorn or you've been dating for maybe ten years.

If you're married to a Capricorn, you'll find yourself inundated with sex. You'll have all you can handle and then some. One tip: When Lady Capricorn is not around, get some rest, because sex with this sister will be long and often.

For the Capricorn woman, cut the chatter when it's time to "get busy." Questions like "Whose stuff is this?" or "Do you want some more?" will be met with a coldness you won't believe. The attitude of the Capricorn woman is "Show me." And brother, you need to be busy performing, not talking. You're wasting time. The missionary position is preferable, because Capricorns are traditionalists for the most part. But oral sex will be considered with a lot of reluctance. Of course, they are definitely more receptive to receiving head than giving it. If you get the Capricorn brother to perform cunnilingus, congratulations! Even in a casual conversation with a Capricorn, you might get an air of disdain or the look of a bitter taste in his mouth when the subject of oral sex comes up. The Capricorn brother will admit to a woman performing oral sex on him, but whether he'll admit that he's gone down on a woman is another matter. If it happened, the woman had to be sworn to secrecy for the rest of her life.

Sex with the Capricorn man will be scheduled as well, and put on the calendar frequently. Of course, he will expect you to be ready, willing, and able whenever the notion hits him. He's definitely turned on by the undressing process. He will want to enjoy the whole thing. He will slow-dance to some Luther, Maxwell, or Ojays as he discards one piece of clothing at a time, while kissing your body in the newly unwrapped area. The Capricorn sister can be a little intimidating because she will want to run the show as well. Lady Capricorn must be in control, or at least *think* she's in control. You might hear commands like "Move to the left and don't move too fast. You're not running a race, you know." But hang in there, the

Capricorn sister can be quite erotic once she gets going.

Don't present him with any surprises in the bedroom, like bringing in a third person or coming up with role playing. He's not the one! He's too dignified for that. She may be prone to a little kinkiness because she wants to heighten her sexual pleasure. Her symbol is the goat climbing to the top of the mountain, and sexual gratification is simply a part of reaching the top in every aspect of her life. The key here is to tell her about any new developments in advance.

Lastly, if you really want to arouse both the male and female of the sign, take your time and don't rush the moves to try to get to the bedroom. You'll be aroused enough. The "outercourse" of not being preoccupied with sex is the way to Capricorn's heart. If you can wait, you'll be pleasantly surprised. Once you win the Capricorn's heart, it's on, like a pot of neck bones.

A Capricorn remembers the best sex she ever had; it was because the sex was put off for six months. "First he took me out to eat. We went to his place, listened to music, and laughed and talked. We had dated for about six months and he hadn't ever approached me sexually. He said, 'I just want to show you I want you for you and not for sex.' That got my attention. He was the first man I've ever been with who made me see stars while I was making love. I forgot I was on this planet." Well, now!

EROGENOUS ZONES . . . SOME PHYSICAL, SOME NOT

According to some Capricorns, there's this thing about the underarm area that really gets them going. Some male Capricorns shave their underarms. They feel it's more sanitary and leaves room for his mate to caress, touch, and even kiss the armpits, which drives some Capricorns wild. Go figure.

Another erogenous zone is the knee area. Rubbing the knees or kissing the knees, along with an intense body massage, will have this goat kicking up his hind legs. Any caresses or kisses to the stomach area, including sticking the tongue directly into the navel, is all the arousal Capricorns need to get this party started.

A Capricorn female says, "Seeing the naked body of someone I love who's tall, dark, and handsome, lots of foreplay, sitting on it, and doggy style are moves that get me aroused."

The Capricorn woman will also expect you to compliment her body once the clothing is discarded, because she prides herself on eating properly and staying in shape. A Capricorn woman said what drives her wild in the bedroom is when her man releases an "Oh, s—t!" like he can't believe how good it is or when he rubs her body like he's not sure if she's real.

The Capricorn man prides himself on being able to satisfy a woman. He will definitely take the lead with any bedroom maneuvers because he must be in control at all times. And he wouldn't want to give the impression that he doesn't know what he's doing in the boudoir, even if he doesn't.

With brother Capricorn, it doesn't take much to arouse him. Start with slow, seductive music, soft lights turned down low, and semilavish surroundings. He can also be sadistic, so watch out for those whips and chains. Just kidding!

A Capricorn day care director related a story of true romance: "When I was seven months pregnant, my mate went out in a snowstorm (five feet of snow) on my birthday and bought me flowers and candy." Obviously, the effort on his part scored points, and he scored that night, too.

If by chance you're living with a Capricorn and you're wondering why the hot, torrid sex is now a thing of the past, there are probably several reasons. Lingerie and looking alluring even when you're headed for bed are important to this earth sign. A Capricorn brother from New York City put it this way: "When I first started dating this woman, we would have sex damn near every night. And each night she would have a different sexy nightgown or garterbelt with thong panties. A year later, she's wearing plaid nightgowns or long johns or flannel pajamas to bed. I know it's cold where I live, but I ask her all the time what happened."

For the Capricorn, visual effects are just as important as touching. The Capricorn wants all of the senses to be titillated and stimulated. Speaking of titillation, a Capricorn woman described her night to remember. "After we arrived, had a few drinks, I straddled his lap, facing him. He put a sheet over us and all I could do was concentrate on him and not the surroundings.

He kissed me, and the rest is history. He had a French tickler on the end of the condom."

PLAIN OL' SEX AND NOTHING MORE: WELCOME TO THE FREAK SHOW

Of the twelve signs of the zodiac, there are the participants of the freak show, those who watch from the sidelines, and the stars. Capricorns watch from the sidelines.

I seriously doubt if your Capricorn will buy into trying over-the-top sex with someone he just met. For Caps to even consider such leanings, the two of you would probably have to be out of the country, and you would have to be sworn to secrecy. This approach would never work unless they could blame their behavior on some-one or something: for example, "I was contacted by a sex therapist who asked me if I would consider participating in a sex survey and I reluctantly agreed." Of course, there would be no truth to such a notion, but it would certainly allow Capricorns to save face or es-cape the knowing stares of those who thought them to be of such high moral character. That's the problem. Capricorns can't truly en-joy the experience for worrying about who may find out.

Such was the case for a Capricorn sister who was on her honey-moon with her Pisces husband. The Capricorn describes what she says was a disastrous romantic encounter. "My husband and I made love on our honeymoon outside, underneath the arch in St. Louis," she said. Most would say, "So?" But although she went along with the idea, you can bet it didn't originate with her.

In short, the same scenario holds true with the freak show. You must gain the Capricorn's trust—and that ain't easy!

MONEY MATTERS

Capricorns are very conservative when it comes to money. Pru-dence and money are synonymous for this earth sign. The underly-ing motivation for Capricorn is that he plans to be a force to be reckoned with in his career and in his community. She will con-stantly strive to upgrade her status or social standing, and one sure way to achieve this is by having money.

Money for the Capricorn means power. Consequently, saving money, spending it wisely, and investing it are all a part of the plan. There won't be any involvement in harebrained get-rich-quick schemes with this practical person. He's patient and readily understands the implications of investing for the future. As Capricorns grow older, their approach to life becomes less serious, and they want to have more fun, including traveling, a vacation home, and sometimes expensive hobbies.

Even if they command six- or seven-figure salaries, their obsession about overspending is ever-present, sometimes to the point of being miserly. These patient, methodical people plan to live large one day. And they understand very early that one of the sure ways of achieving this goal is to put off buying the toys or gadgets until later. They know readily that the dividends from their investments will pay off later. And these practical creatures have the patience, the drive, and the motivation to put immediate gratification on the back burner.

If you happen to notice travel brochures, books on travel, or travel videos lying around the Cap's home, this earth sign is planning to take you to exotic places: Africa, the Great Wall of China, Paris, France, places that most only dream about. But you must have patience. You'll definitely not be able to buzz-saw through their carefully collected and invested nest egg. It ain't happening here. Capricorns don't miss a trick when it comes to money. Your spending habits will be observed. Capricorn's money won't be the cash that's being spent, not for a long time, anyway. Get the picture?

If you have a Capricorn spouse, companion, or friend, you will even be lectured on the money that you spend "needlessly." Of course, your reply might be "Who asked you?" No matter; this earth sign doesn't like to know about money that's being wasted. Of course, he definitely enjoys the finer things of life—fine wines, expensive clothing, and lavish surroundings. But his purchases are, most of the time, made very carefully and thoughtfully. Early in life, he understood that quality outlasts quantity, so most of the purchases the Capricorn makes will last for years. Besides, he believes that as hard as he works, he deserves some measure of satisfaction through his purchasing power.

If you're married to a Capricorn and a baby is on the way, by the time it's born, the financial portfolio will already have been put together. All the while you're pregnant, he will be creating a "present" of his own for the new arrival. Capricorns are always thinking and planning ahead for their next move.

PAMPERING TIPS FOR CAPRICORN

- Taking charge of a Capricorn's life to pamper the goat is no small task, but be persistent. A well-executed plan is the key.
- Prepare an elaborate meal, including china, candles, and wine, then take it to her. She'll love it.
- Plan a surprise weekend getaway, even if it's simply to a motel. The Capricorn is always superbusy, and this gesture will be a welcome respite.
- Taking the children for a day or helping with an elderly relative will score major points. Capricorns take on the role of leader and are usually the responsible ones in such matters.
- A full body massage and a soak in the hot tub as the two of you drink champagne and listen to your Capricorn's favorite music will work. You may be in for a long night!
- Little things like dropping the kids off at school, picking up the dog at the vet, or cutting the lawn are all the pampering that's needed sometimes.
- Planning a major trip out of the country or a cruise must have your Capricorn's input. Outline the plan and do your homework because she won't be able to truly relax if you don't.
- A quiet trip to the country to enjoy the rolling hills and streams, the crickets and smell of honeysuckle, is the bomb! The key is to leave the cell phone, pager, and laptop computer at home.
- Register for a self-help, relationship, or business seminar the two of you can attend together. Your Capricorn will be able to relax and at the same time absorb some valuable information.
- Breakfast in bed on the weekend will work. But the key to

getting the job done is to get crankin' before your Capricorn mate awakes. How about 6 A.M.? Or you may have to chain him to the bed.

Gift Ideas for Capricorn

❋ If you've got champagne ideas with beer money, well, skip the gift until you can afford quality. Instead, offer to keep the children for a day or baby-sit the dog.

❋ Capricorns love books on how to invest wisely, retire early, or do self-improvement. Books or books on tape are sure bets!

❋ Get your Capricorn a signed, numbered print that would be of value one day.

❋ An engraved watch for him or a locket for her would be ideal. Capricorns look for quality and love personalized items.

❋ A hand-carved chess set would be to his or her liking.

❋ The practical nature of Capricorn dictates practical gifts, too. A lawn service contract, a set of tennis rackets, or a gift certificate for a car tune-up works as well.

❋ Buying stock in a new company for your Capricorn is an attention getter. The idea lets her know you're thinking about the future.

❋ An expensive bottle of perfume or cologne works well and also suggests a certain intimacy in the relationship.

❋ Season tickets to spectator sports or the theater will work. Capricorns love sports and the arts.

❋ And speaking of the arts, you can't go wrong with a piece of original artwork—signed, of course.

Aquarius

(January 20 to February 18)

SYMBOL: THE WATER BEARER

Positive love traits: Kinky lover, confident partner, unselfish; one of the stars of the freak show.

Negative love traits: Unpredictable, perverse lover; a penchant for ménages à trois.

Ruling planet: Uranus is associated with independence
and humane initiatives.

Word to the wise: Control freaks, beware: You won't be able
to control these air signs because they will simply disappear.

Trying to have any type of relationship with an Aquarian will
have you constantly wondering what's up. You won't really know
where you stand in the relationship (if there is one) because nine
times out of ten, the Aquarian won't be able to tell you either. You'll
be constantly watching him, trying to figure him out, all the while
never sure if you're in a courtship. Save yourself some time and energy and go with the flow. You have no choice; you pretty much
have to take it or leave it.

Aquarians are air signs, which means that they are independent, aloof, analytical, intriguing, and very hard to keep up with.
Like air itself, air signs cannot be contained, harnessed, or backed
into a corner. If either happens, the Aquarian will simply disappear.

And you will definitely be intrigued because they're charismatic, charming, intelligent, and creative types. There is simply
something about them that you won't be able to ignore. Part of the
Aquarians' charm is that they don't understand how charming they

really are. Unlike the Leo, who thrives on attention, the Aquarian rarely seeks attention and tries to avoid it. But they find themselves in the limelight most of the time because they are constantly thinking about others and working in areas to help people either directly or indirectly.

An Aquarian brother agrees. "You have to be concerned with other people, other than just yourself. From the elderly to children, the whole nine yards. You're not on the planet by yourself."

Aquarians are also loners because these mental people can entertain themselves very effectively. The few friends that they do have are usually childhood or college buddies. One of the first things you notice about Aquarians is their aloof demeanor—friendly but distant. That look of being somewhat removed is genuine because they are constantly thinking about the future—not next week or next year, but the next millennium!

Once the Aquarian gets his head out of the clouds or the stratosphere long enough to notice you and consider you a friend, your patience will be tested to the limit. The friendship that you're hoping will blossom into a relationship may take an eternity. What with all of their many projects, interests, and humanitarian efforts, an uptight, out-of-sight hookup will be held up indefinitely.

What the Aquarian is thinking about now, the average person will realize or conceive ten years later. For example, twenty-two years ago an Aquarian machinist presented his companion with a business approach to marriage, a prenuptial agreement of sorts, long before it became popular. "I told my wife when we got married that if it didn't work after ten years, we would go our separate ways without the hassles usually involved in a divorce, and she agreed." Aquarians don't like to feel boxed in.

Aquarians are usually the ones with the latest haircut, clothing style, car, or electronic gadget. Enhancements like hair weaves, toupees, contacts, or multiple body piercings are not a concern for them. In fact, they may be the ones who are wearing them. These air signs usually have slim builds because they are constantly on the go. They're usually walking briskly, head in the air, with a preoccupied look of confidence on their faces. Some people may perceive Aquarians as "I know I'm all that" types, and Aquarians must constantly fend off snide remarks from jealous people. It's simply

not true! Aquarians are caring and warm and have a genuine interest in your well-being.

They may give you a warm hello as they rush to the next appointment, but more than likely they could not pick you out of a
lineup if you mugged them. There is simply too much going on in
their heads and too much ground to cover to remember a face in
the crowd. Besides, they have a terrible time with the names of
bosses, coworkers, even family members sometimes. They may call
Susie instead of Sally or Horace instead of Herman, or they may
just shout out, "Hey, you."

Aquarians are always intrigued by the new and different. By the
time they complete a project or end a relationship, they will be off
and running in another direction, looking for the next adventure.
You'll find them off the beaten path, not in the mix with crowds of
people. Yes, they can hang out at a party and be dressed in the latest
hip-hop getup or elegantly dressed at a black-tie function with the
"right" people, but they would rather be at a play, taking in a live
jazz concert, or reading a good book. Any activity that mentally
challenges and entertains is good to go with this futuristic sign.

THE AQUARIUS MAN

Love matters with the Aquarian brother will move at a snail's pace.
This independent brother must weigh all the pros and cons of a
relationship and the long-term effects on his well-being. The
song "Don't Fence Me In" had to have been written by or for an
Aquarian.

Falling in love for this air sign is a giant step, and a step he
doesn't take lightly. His need for adventure, spontaneity, and variety
is ever-present in his life. And for him, life's grand without the
emotional entanglements, the dependence of another, or upsetting
a great lifestyle. He's charismatic and smart and is getting plenty of
play. The way he sees it, he can't get to all the potential honeys *now,*
so why would he consider settling down *forever,* with one person?

Consequently, love matters in the case of an Aquarian will be
slow-going, but not impossible! Even though, initially, finding the
way to this air sign's heart will be an uphill climb, the journey will
be worth it. Once an Aquarian enters your life, you won't ever be

the same. You won't be able to help yourself. There's something about this man that attracts most people. When he walks in the room, full of self-confidence and dressed to kill, all eyes are on him, including yours. But he rarely notices.

The Aquarian brother keeps up with the latest styles and trends, and he may even set a few of his own. His dress is usually mild but distinctive. Physically, Aquarians are quite appealing, with sensuous eyes that seem to sparkle, nice buns, big juicy lips, and no Jheri curls. But now that you're in the "Wow" stage, the reality check needs addressing.

If you're trying to get next to this elusive creature, you must be a friend first and he must respect your intellect before all the up close and personal stuff starts. In fact, intellect is usually more important to the Aquarian brother than physical beauty. For example, an Aquarian reporter was touring a manufacturing company for a news story when a factory worker came up to him. "Is you married?" the woman curiously asked. "Yes, I is," he replied.

Another Aquarian agreed, "Physical things—that's important but not an end-all. It's not imperative that a person be a knockout or gorgeous. I'm looking for a beautiful person on the inside and outside, with high moral character, intellect, brains, but that's like trying to find a needle in a haystack." There is always an exception to the rule, however. As one Aquarian commented, "I'll screw a dumb '10' and a smart '2' won't get the time of day."

Intrigue and mystery gets this brother's attention quicker than answering your door with nothing on but your garterbelt. After all the sex stuff is over, your Aquarian will expect some stimulating conversation about current events and the burning issues of the day.

Aquarians make life happen! They don't sit like a bump on a log and wait for paint to dry. They hate being bored. In fact, they consider it a terminal condition. Therefore, with an Aquarian, there will be lots of fun, frolic, and foreplay, foreplay, foreplay. But before you decide to ask this man to marry you, consider this: You might be dancing close all night with this brother, and he might be nibbling your ear and kissing your neck, but that doesn't mean this is the beginning of a relationship. The brother is always interested in seizing and enjoying the moment. The next morning you may be back at square one!

In addition to emotional issues and revering their independence, a bad relationship will make an Aquarian reluctant to take the plunge again. "I got hurt once really bad. I guess you could say the hunter got captured by the game. Her mother liked me but decided that I was too young, so instead she introduced me to her daughter. The daughter was 17 and I was 22. I thought, this is the one. I taught her some things and got her ready for somebody else. She went off to college, and the courtship eventually ended," an Aquarian firefighter said. And for the next twenty years, any effort to get close to this brother was a waste of time.

For the Aquarian, your personal appearance speaks louder than words. Aquarians notice minor details that few men would pay attention to. "I notice hands that look like a man's and chipped nail polish. I notice lips first, and feet. I like pretty feet. I don't like feet with corns." Go figure.

So make sure all of the i's are dotted and the t's are crossed. An Aquarian brother went on and on about a would-be relationship that fizzled before it began. "I can't stand it when a woman doesn't keep herself up. Comb your hair, for God's sake, and brush your teeth. You're going outside, you've got rollers in your hair, house shoes on, what's up?"

And if you expect to get to know this humanitarian, cut the crap. He's not interested in who you know; he's more interested in what you know. "I don't like people who mock other people. If you're going to say something to the person, you should try and help them." In other words, you're going to have to come down off of your high horse if you expect to hang with this brother. Another Aquarian brother agreed: "I don't like people with an uppity personality, people who have something more and who think that they're better than the next person."

Although this brother is down to earth, he can converse intelligently about most things. And above all, he doesn't like the snobs of the world. He will get to know everyone, from the janitor to the president of the company.

An Aquarian brother who is a Muslim is resisting the inclination to date women who are members of the organization. "I want somebody to be able to make decisions, based upon their individuality. There is some conformity that takes place when you're a part of something, and sometimes that stifles the person."

For example, an Aquarian brother ended a relationship abruptly when his girlfriend declared she wanted a baby by him. "That person was lazy and she didn't have any ambition about progressing as a person. She told me she wanted a baby. . . . I didn't understand it. I just didn't get it. That's why I ended the relationship."

Although Aquarians are generous, pace yourself when talking about your needs. "I don't like women to beg. The first day I meet you, you're telling me about your problems. 'I don't have this' or 'I need that,' " this Aquarian brother said. This brother has a remedy, however. "My philosophy at one point was to beat them to the beg. I would start out with my problems first. Then they'd think, 'He ain't got nothing 'cause he's begging too.' "

THE AQUARIUS WOMAN

If you're considering dating an Aquarian woman, I hope you have a good sense of humor; you'll need it. The Aquarian woman is elusive, charismatic, and exciting, and you'll be totally charmed by her. Now, whether she'll be charmed by you is another story entirely, but you'll get an A for effort even if the relationship doesn't blossom into a "Baby, please, baby, please don't go" kind of thing.

When you meet this woman, you will be thoroughly entertained, interested, and intrigued. This air sign will have you breathless and you'll think to yourself, "I've died and gone to heaven!" She is warm and definitely has a sincere interest in your well-being. She's the humanitarian of the zodiac; therefore, she doesn't discriminate. This Aquarian sister is like that with everyone. She has a unique approach to life, love, and the pursuit of happiness, and she's like no other sign of the zodiac.

Like the man of the sign, the Aquarian woman will want to know you as a friend first. She'll have to respect you as a human being before any hot-to-trot romance can take place. And read the newspaper and pay attention to what's going on so that the two of you will have something to talk about. Although Ms. Aquarian is a chatterbox, she will expect you to jump into the conversation with something pertinent to say.

But bragging or being self-centered is a no-no. "I don't like men who brag a lot. They're trying to impress you; so they go on and on about the material things they have or their position in life," an Aquarian technical specialist said.

And if you're bragging too much, she will use her intuitive powers to see right through the front. For example, an Aquarian ended a relationship with a companion when she found out he was on crack cocaine. "There were warning signs. He used to brag, but he still lived with his mother. When you're at a certain stage in your life, you should have accomplished certain things. He never admitted it, but I'd go to sleep and he would sneak out in the middle of the night. Every week there was a new story for why he didn't have any money!"

Ms. Aquarius has definite ideas about relationships. And although the encounter was magical, don't assume that you are in the first phase of a long-term liaison. Aquarians guard their independence. Being an air sign means being a magician—now you see her, now you don't. Don't take it personally. It's just how she operates. For example, an Aquarian operating room technician had a casual affair with a man whom she had met through a mutual friend. The brother wanted a relationship and said so. But she moved, had her number changed to an unlisted one, and lost touch. Two years later the Aquarian sister just happened to be at the mutual friend's house at the same time the brother was. He was so overwhelmed by seeing her again that he cried. That's the kind of effect these charismatic divas can have on a brother.

This air sign is usually slim with long, shapely legs and hair either cut short or worn at shoulder length in a variety of styles. She's a trendy dresser and always stylish, even in blue jeans and T-shirts. And she'll expect *you* to be neatly dressed. Don't show up in the polyester pants or shoes that are so worn they turn up at the toe. Aquarians are forthright and honest, and you will be told about your appearance. Aquarians don't have a lot of tact, and they like the direct approach. So if your feelings get hurt, the best approach is to tell them immediately. Don't let the wound fester until it's almost gangrenous. If you wait too long, by the time you do mention it, your Aquarian will have no idea what you're talking about.

She will expect her mate to be close and connected; consequently, her companion will be expected to understand and know her needs before they can be verbalized. Sounds demanding? She is! But she gives back 150 percent in any relationship. If or when she gets married, her mate will be in heaven. But she may not stay that way—married, that is.

The ruling planet is Uranus, which is associated with independence and humane initiative. The humanitarian projects are rampant and there's usually not a lot of cuddling time. Here's a suggestion: Volunteer to help the Aquarian in one of her many projects and during the breaks try to sneak in some quality time with her. With Aquarians you've got to seize the moment and make it count. (But I would skip the marriage proposal in this setting.)

An Aquarian woman will always be full of surprises. She might tell you to meet her at your place and have dinner and a bubble bath waiting. Or she might want you to meet her at a sex shop to see the latest gadgets. For example, an Aquarian woman entered an erotic fun shop to show her companion a vibrator that was made to straddle or sit on. She walked over to the shelf where it was supposed to be located and asked the salesclerk to show it to her. The salesclerk got loud on her: "Ma'am, we can't keep these vibrators in the store, but they're on back order. I can put your name on the list and call you when it comes in." Undaunted, Ms. Aquarius put her name on the waiting list.

Aquarians are very comfortable being single. "I've been by myself so long, I just make my children the most important thing in my life. And a lot of guys I meet don't like that. I don't think they value their children as much as they should," an Aquarian woman from Milwaukee said. One Aquarian woman had difficulty convincing potential companions that all she wanted was occasional sex with no strings attached. "That sounds like something a dude would say," one guy told her. But what may be impossible for some is very plausible for the Aquarian. An Aquarian sales manager had a similar experience. "I dated an insecure, low-self-esteem man strictly for sex. It was a no-win situation otherwise. I finally just said no more, it's over."

Above all else, if you're trying to connect with this woman, you need to have a life. Aquarian women don't want men who are constantly around. You need to have a life apart from hers. Yes, this woman is charming and intelligent and she definitely has it going on. But with all of her humanitarian efforts, the likelihood of being sidetracked with an uptight, up close, can't-do-without-you relationship for the rest of her life is very unlikely.

GUIDE TO A LOVE CONNECTION

Aquarius and Aries

These two are hot to trot. Yes, ma'am! It doesn't get any steamier than this. These two souls are very independent, Aquarius a bit more than Aries. Aries will try to dominate, and that's fine with Aquarius. But when Aquarius gets tired of the ram's ranting and raving, demanding all of the attention, Aquarius will simply disappear temporarily to recoup. Both are imaginative in bed and neither has a problem participating in the freak show. Both love spontaneity and striking out on a trip impulsively to see where the road leads. Aquarius is more laid back, while Aries must be the life of the party and the center of attention in any social setting. Over the long haul, these two could enjoy a lifetime commitment—but who's going to handle the checkbook?

Aquarius and Taurus

We all know that opposites attract, but with these two, that's taking things a little far. Airy Aquarius wants a meeting of the minds, while Taurus wants to meet with . . . well. Aquarius is too busy with all of her many projects to give Taurus all of the attention he requires. Actually, a little conversation and a nice dinner at home are all that the bull wants. Aquarius frowns on most forms of domestic life and doesn't see what all the commotion is about. Both enjoy sex, but unlike Taurus, staying in bed for days on end is not Aquarius's idea of bliss. These two are fixed signs, which means they are blockheads and neither will budge. So get out now before it's too late!

Aquarius and Gemini

Aquarius is intrigued by Gemini's dual personality. (Gemini is the sign of the twins.) Gemini is impressed with the intelligence of Aquarius. Both are social and party animals, Gemini a tad more so than Aquarius. Both love impromptu adventures. When it comes to money, Gemini is a bit more cautious. Aquarius will spend money, period, be it hers or his. Sexually, these two have no qualms. They can both be the freak of the week! The indifference of Aquarius regarding Gemini's disappearing acts delights Gemini. Neither is jealous of the other because both have lives apart. These two are air signs; therefore, independence and space to do their own thing are key. But when they get back together, the bliss, harmony, and deep affection for each other continue like it never stopped.

Aquarius and Cancer

The two of you have definitely passed this way before. But the question is, Why?! Aquarius is aloof, independent, elusive, tactless, quirky, and misunderstood. Cancer is moody, insecure, a whiner, emotional, and better suited to a companion who can deal with these traits. Aquarius has no patience, so why are these two having drinks and deep conversations, and on the edge of their seats with each other? Charisma, sexual energy, tension, and the like are definitely in the air. What's working here is that each admires the traits of the other. Once they meet halfway and fall into bed, it's on, like a pot of neck bones, but after Aquarius gets over the notion of wanting to take care of Cancer, reality sets in. Trying to coax Cancer out of his cocoon of insecurity will be a lost cause. Move on, Aquarius, and give him a long kiss good night.

Aquarius and Leo

When they meet for the first time, they will feel like they have struck gold. The conversation will be stimulating. The physical attraction that these two opposites of the zodiac experience have both anticipating all the sexual peaks. But the valleys await as well. For conventional Leo, sex with an Aquarian is a bit over the top. The Aquarian, independent and aloof, doesn't understand or deem necessary all the royal treatment that this lion wants. Leo will take Aquarius's demeanor as a lack of interest and feel rejected. Both love the social scene—Leo a bit more than Aquarius. The mental masturbation that this pairing must endure should be avoided.

Aquarius and Virgo

The sexual tension between these two is quite evident to both, but that's about the size of it. Aquarius wants freedom. Virgo wants total devotion and accountability. Aquarius, with her many projects, likes to be surrounded by people. Virgo wants a small group of friends and prefers entertaining at home. Both are intelligent and can talk for hours about current events and issues of the day. Trouble is, these two are better at challenging each other intellectually than at romance. Both are aloof and analytical when it comes to relationships. Sexually, Aquarius can definitely take Virgo to the next level, but Virgo's prudish attitude about some areas leaves Aquarius frustrated. Both should consider other relationships. This union is a no-go!

Aquarius and Libra

These two air signs have lots in common. Both guard their independence and freedom. Both love meeting new people. Both are highly intellectual and can converse for hours on a variety of subjects. All systems are go in the boudoir. Aquarius's freaky and daring sexual behavior delights Libra, who loves to experiment. Libra's indecisiveness will drive Aquarius batty. Aquarius's mental agility will push decisions to resolution, and that's fine for Libra. Libra is a flirt, the charmer of zodiac. But Aquarius is not turned off by such behavior. If Aquarius can stay put and not wander off into the stratosphere, these two could have a charmed life together.

Aquarius and Scorpio

These two will spend most of their waking hours in the bedroom. Aquarius is an air sign; freedom and independence are all-important. Scorpio's jealous and controlling nature sends Aquarius running for cover and hiding. After this duo emerges from the bedroom, there won't be much to hold them together. Scorpio's controlling nature will be a turnoff for Aquarius; he's involved in so many projects that he simply won't have time to check in three times a day, much to Scorpio's dismay. The demands of Scorpio will have aloof, distant Aquarius looking for other outlets. If Aquarius is boxed into a corner, he will simply disappear. And Scorpio, you can't control what you cannot find. The two of you are better as friends than as lovers.

Aquarius and Sagittarius

There is no limit to what this pair can do in a relationship or in any other endeavor. Aquarius is ahead of her time in her outlook on life, and Sagittarius is always looking to the future and keeping pace with any new technologies. Both are intellectual sorts and share many intricate ideas and concepts with each other. In the bedroom, their attitude is "Whatever goes on behind closed doors between consenting adults is nobody's business." Just imagine. Both are independent and must have freedom to explore and do their own thing. Sag is the flirt, but Aquarius is not insecure about such leanings. Sag needs to control the purse strings because the Aquarian's philosophy is that money is to be spent, not hoarded. Hey, this can work!

Aquarius and Capricorn

Okay, the vibes and the energy are there—now what? These two will find out very early that energy and attraction don't make for a long relationship. Aquarius is too far into the stratosphere to even address Capricorn's down-here-on-earth needs. Aquarians must have freedom and control of their lives. Capricorns are homebodies and can't understand why the Aquarian wouldn't want to be under the thumb of the goat. Aquarius can be a homebody, too, but when it's time to go and hang out, it's time! Aquarius has no regard for money except to spend it. If you're married to an Aquarius and you're the Cap, get separate accounts! While you're getting a separate account, how about a new and separate relationship?

Aquarius and Aquarius

These two are connected mentally even before the physical contact begins. Aquarians agree that having a relationship with another water bearer is like looking in the mirror or making love to themselves. Huh?! This relationship could definitely work, provided these two stay around long enough to enjoy and take part. It's just that they're friendly and engaging, but kind of removed from most situations, including the in-love approach to romance. And they are oh-so-busy with their many humanitarian projects. However, when they finally decide to hook up, the encounter is like they've never been away. They're not even put off by tactless comments because they both love the direct approach and are not prone to licking their wounds. This match has possibilities.

Aquarius and Pisces

The duo keeps pace with each other more in the bedroom than outside. Aquarius and Pisces will seek new heights of lovemaking that have both believing that the relationship will work. But Pisces' emotional demands and insecure approach to the relationship have Aquarius feeling boxed in and hassled. Aquarius is an air sign and must have freedom of movement and independence. Pisces is water and simply wants to spend most of her time with the loved one at home. Aquarius is the humanitarian and has to roam, explore, and get involved with community concerns. Pisces feels left out. Aquarius doesn't have the patience or the inclination to make Pisces feel needed. While Pisces is left at home licking her wounds, Aquarius has disappeared and left the building.

ROMANCE AND THE AQUARIAN

For those of you who think romance isn't important, think again. If you're dating an Aquarian, you're going to have to spend some time and money, and create some spontaneity and intrigue about the date. In other words, don't plan on running by the convenience store and picking up the lastest *TV Guide* and a six-pack for a quiet evening at home. It ain't happening!

A frustrated Aquarian commented about her dates, or lack thereof. "You meet these guys who just want to come over, drink your wine, eat your food, and have long conversations on the phone. They think that's a relationship. The best relationship I had was with a man who would come over, bring wine or a present, and bring my two kids a gift, too."

Aquarians are not interested in what you do on an everyday basis. You've got to be responsive and creative when it comes to romance because Aquarians are creative and spontaneous and will expect the same from you. One thing the Aquarian won't tolerate is boredom. An Aquarian wants your undivided attention—not one eye or ear on her and the other on the basketball game on television. "An intimate evening for me is just the two of us—where I have his total attention and affection from dinner to sex to sleep, where he's planned everything from start to finish," said an Aquarian from California.

An Aquarian woman who has a live-in Gemini companion reports that "sometimes he wants me to be the aggressor and be creative. Other times he wants to believe that he is the only man I've had sex with and if he didn't teach it to me, where did I learn it," an Aquarian from California said.

Hey, guys, this thing of coming over to your companion's house to watch the football game while you swill beer is not going to work. Ms. Aquarius is not the one! And before you put your feet up and reach for a cold one, you'll be told in no uncertain terms that the two of you are going out. The conversation will go something like this: "Uh, uhnnn! You won't be looking at Michael Jordan slam-dunk tonight! I already have seats reserved at the Playhouse Theater and we are going!" "But baby, this is the last game of the play-offs!" "Tuff, set the VCR and hurry up, I don't want to be late!" Oh, well. From the Aquarian's point of view, you're trying to kill two birds with one stone. To her this isn't an official date, anyway; you're simply watching the football game.

The point with romancing this unique person is creating a unique date, a date that you wouldn't consider in your wildest dreams. That kind of date your air sign is interested in. Outings like poetry readings, visits to the art museum, live music, daytime parties, tennis tournaments, and taking trips together to places neither has been.

For example, taking the Aquarian sister to the mountains and roughing it would suit her just fine. But make sure you have plenty of games, gadgets, or books to stimulate the mind. Once you're in seclusion, the physical stimulation from your woman will begin instantly. She will definitely want to show her appreciation for planning this off-the-beaten-path date.

When an Aquarian wants something, money is no object. It's

no problem because he will spend your money as readily as he spends his own. But if there is little money available for travel, being creative with the resources available is also an attention getter. For example, camping in the backyard under the stars will be the perfect backdrop to making love all night. Driving up the highway to wherever the road leads is a great date for this sign. As one Aquarian woman put it, "Having candles lit during a back rub was one of the most romantic experiences I've had."

Another Aquarian remembers one of his most memorable but inexpensive dates: "A walk in the park by the river, a blanket, a game of chess and a game of backgammon, a little wine, and just enjoying each other's company, talking and exchanging ideas."

Aquarians love surprises and spontaneity on dates. Although you might have planned and made reservations at a particular restaurant, it's okay if you suddenly change the plans. Aquarius loves spur-of-the-moment kind of stuff. For example, a drive down the highway may not seem very exciting, but for one Aquarian brother it ended up being one of his most romantic dates. "We got together and just got in the car, drove, found a spot, talked, and made love in that spot," he said, adding that the spot wasn't necessarily secluded.

If you're planning a date with an Aquarian, double-check the particulars. These airheads, excuse me, air signs, aren't noted for remembering dates and times. For example, an Aquarian invited his girlfriend to a party at a hotel that his company was giving for a coworker. The brother was partying down and after three hours wondered why his mate hadn't arrived. When he called her to see what the trouble was, she said, "You never gave me the location and address!"

An Aquarian commented that the best way of creating romance, sensuality, and intimacy for him is the little black dress. "There is something about a woman when she wears a black dress, black sheer stockings, and high heels. That's superchic. And not everybody can wear that little black dress."

Stimulating conversation is a sure winner for a romantic evening. An Aquarian wants to know your opinions and ideas about everything. This is all part of the process, and, hopefully, your comments will be substantive. "People need to know about current events. I don't like talking over people. When I talk about far-reaching subjects, a lot of people look at me like I'm crazy and say, 'You think you know everything,'" said an Aquarian brother from Wisconsin. "My friends and acquaintances tell me all the time, 'Man, you're way up there in outer space somewhere. What are you talking about?'"

True to the symbol of the humanitarian, another Aquarian described the date from hell. "Every now and then I like to expose the Duh-ruh ladies (those who lack intellect) and take them to an expensive restaurant. I suggested prime rib and my date ordered it. When the waiter brought it, she commented, 'These ain't no ribs' at the top of her voice. 'I ordered ribs! I thought we were talking about the ribs that's got the bones.'" The only thing his date got that night was a deliberate nudge out the door.

SEX, SEX, AND MORE SEX

GETTING THE GROOVE ON . . .

Like the relationship, sex with the Aquarian can't be rushed, either. By now, you're licking your chops, waiting for the magic moment when the two of you meet between the sheets. But you need to move slowly in this area. Too much planning can sometimes spoil the whole encounter. Aquarians love spontaneity. They do expect props, like the right music, the favorite wine or champagne, the scented candles, and maybe a costume as a surprise.

Most Aquarians believe you need to pick up the vibe on the possibility of any romantic or bedroom antics. The key with an Aquarian is going with the flow and paying attention to the innuendos and the signs that she throws to let you know that all systems are go. For example, an Aquarian was sunbathing topless on the balcony of her hotel during a vacation in Florida. When her husband came in, he asked her if she wanted to make love. She wanted, instead, for him to initiate kissing, touching, and sex on his own. A definite no-no is to enter the room with a checklist, for Christ's sake! You're not planning a workshop or presentation!

The trouble is, you've waited so long to finally get to this point, you're trippin'. Just chill. Let the mood and the moment dictate what's to come. But I want to warn you, when it comes to bedroom matters, Aquarians can step toe-to-toe with you. Just pace yourself. Obviously your Aquarian feels comfortable with you, which is a tall order. Now you can expect the experience of a lifetime!

Aquarians are in the no-holds- or no-holes-barred category. These air signs are stars of the freak show. Their inventive and creative nature in bed has the recipient of their lovemaking proposing marriage, declaring that she is in love and that this air sign is definitely the one! But for the Aquarian, it's just another day at the factory. No biggie, in their view, it's just simply normal behavior. Take this to the bank! Aquarians do everything a little bit better than most. Now that that's addressed, we can move on to the next phase of the program.

The element of surprise and spur-of-the-moment play is a favorite of Aquarians. An Aquarian surprised her mate after they met at a hotel. When her mate asked if he could take her coat, she complied and revealed a white lace teddy and jacket with the booty out! Homeboy just fell back against the wall, blown away.

Your approach for any impending sexual relationship with an Aquarian is to be open. For example, a Gemini sister explained how erotic the sexual liaison would get with her Aquarian: "My Aquarian lover was the best I ever had. I would pick him up with only my coat on and we would make love in the car in the garage. He had a house and I had a house."

The sexual experience with your Aquarian might begin with an erotic short story that he's written and will read aloud. For the Aquarian brother, talking dirty, along with explaining on a situation-by-situation basis what's to come, gets him easily aroused. "I don't want a shrinking violet, but I want someone to push the envelope. And talk to me! I can't stand the nonverbal woman who lies there like a bump on a log!" Are you listening, ladies?

Aquarians will do anything to please their lovers, even setting their own pleasure aside. In fact, foreplay is their forte, so much so, they forget about the "play." Don't be squeamish about asking for what you want. The Aquarian is into pleasure. If they are pleasing their partners, then they are also pleasing themselves at the same time.

Aquarians are also voyeurs. For example, an Aquarian doctor had a date with an Aquarian woman at a work-related conference and was staying at a hotel. The woman invited the doctor to her room for drinks. The doctor, who didn't want to drive home after drinking, spent the night in the hotel room. The couple played around a bit but nothing happened. The next morning, as the woman came out of the shower in her robe and proceeded to curl her hair as she sat in front of the mirror, the doctor started to masturbate and fantasize about what was underneath the robe. The Aquarian woman, though amazed, was not turned off by what she witnessed.

There are no real sexual positions that the Aquarian is into. Again, she likes any position that enhances the pleasure and eroticism of her partner. The 69 position or the wheelbarrow (partner's head on the floor, legs and feet around the partner's waist) is good to go, too.

The sexual turn-ons run the gamut for the Aquarian. Variety is what they seek in all that they do, sex included. As a woman from North Carolina put it, "Gentle touching and sucking my fingers drive me crazy in the bedroom!" Yet another Aquarian female has this to say: "Slow, tender touching and caressing of breasts and vagina and oral sex!" Just like the Scouts of the world, you must have an open mind and be prepared for whatever!

For example, an Aquarian brother found himself in what he thought was an embarrassing situation for this partner: "I was with this woman and we were in the throes of passion, she was turning her head from side to side, and her wig stayed in place and the wig ended up covering half of her face. I didn't realize she had a wig on. She said forget it, took it off, and got back in the groove and she didn't miss a stroke."

An Aquarian sister recalled a romp and rendezvous that left her salivating. "I went on a trip to St. Thomas in the Caribbean. After the sun went down, my partner and I left the other couple we were with and went for a swim in the ocean. I took my top off and when we started going at it, I heard my friends calling out for me," she said. "I didn't answer and couldn't answer!"

Another Aquarian brother was turned on by seeing his wife in the nude. "The act of her taking off her clothes is a turn-on for me. To watch her go about her normal routine in the house, while she's nude, is a turn-on for me."

Both the men and women of the sign are highly experimental, and will add bisexual and homosexual encounters to their repertoire. "I want to go in the natural flow. If you're not erotically in tune, it won't work," an Aquarian brother said.

One Aquarian man commented that he didn't really need an experienced lover, but he did have one request: "As long as she knows the front from the back of the body, I'm cool!"

EROGENOUS ZONES . . . SOME PHYSICAL, SOME NOT

The calves of the legs are erogenous for Aquarians. Try massaging the calves as the Aquarian lies on her stomach. Then place some ice cubes at the bend of the knee and allow the cold water to slowly travel down her leg, titillating each artery. Believe it! You'll get that smoldering volcano to erupt!

For the Aquarian, who is so advanced on several sexual levels, this sensation will be an illuminating, erotic experience. Most Aquarians don't realize that their calves are their erogenous zone, in part because this area is a part of the lower extremities. They're usually so impatient that they never explore down that far. Their sexual pleasure comes from giving pleasure. If you're into oral sex, then you can bet the Aquarian will take it a step further by massaging your butt, genitals, or anus all while the oral process is going on.

The bottom line for most Aquarians, aside from the enhancements like lingerie, music, sex toys, and the like, is knowing how to give good head! That statement is the anthem for most Aquarians. And it's not a bad idea to learn to reciprocate.

If you want to arouse this air sign, don't be boring or routine in your approach to sexual matters. Actually, mental and verbal stimulation is a huge turn-on for the Aquarian. Foreplay for them starts at the dinner table or in the bubble bath as you anticipate all that's to come. "I love highly suggestive talk which translates into

what's going to happen in my head, then moves down to my genitalia," an Aquarius from Mississippi said. These mental creatures
have great imaginations, so talk, talk, and more talk is "good head"
for them as well.

The erogenous zones that turn the Aquarian on include the
works. An Aquarian brother said that when his mate has on lingerie, it is more enticing than the naked body. "When my companion is partially nude, my imagination is more effective than what
the eye is looking at. Half-clad is more of a turn-on than completely
nude. I prefer someone to leave something to be desired," he said. "I
don't mind an aggressive woman at all. In fact, I enjoy it."

An Aquarian female marketing director enjoys the multitouch-
ing experience. "I love to have intercourse and my lover puts his
finger in my ass simultaneously." By now you're getting the picture
that this air sign wants you to be performing more than one maneuver. Their philosophy is, you've got two hands, two feet, and a
mouth. All of the extremities should be in use.

Another Aquarian is attracted to minor details that few would
notice. "When I see a doll baby [southern term for a pretty
woman], I'm instantly attracted. I like the wispy hair that falls se-
ductively on the neck when a woman's hairstyle is pinned up in
the back," he said. "I like looking beyond the surface of things."
Also, "various skin tones drive me nuts, from the dark cocoa to
the café au lait and the smoothness of the skin gets my attention,"
he said. Sounds like all you have to do is show up with this
brother! He's turned on by hair. "I'm a stickler for hair. I like to be
able to run my fingers through your hair. If your hair is nappy, go
to the beauty shop on a regular basis. But I don't like hair weaves
because I don't want a roadblock when I'm running my fingers
through your scalp. I don't care if it's long or short as long as it's
well kept."

"Sincere sounds of passion from my mate and my mate's complete satisfaction are what drives me wild in the bedroom," said a
native of Jacksonville. "I want her to call somebody [Mom] and ask is
it possible that this man is from a different planet." Folks, the answer is yes!

PLAIN OL' SEX AND NOTHING MORE: WELCOME TO THE FREAK SHOW

Well, now, so you want to freak with the Aquarian. Well, you're in for a high ol' time! There are twelve signs of the zodiac, and of those signs, there are the stars, the participants, and the onlookers of the freak show. Aquarians are the stars. They are in that no-holds-barred category. Whatever goes on between two consenting adults is fine with this air sign. Timing is everything. If you approach them about having sex for its own sake and they're in a good mood, you might be challenged right then and there to get on it. But while you're hemmin' and hawin,' your Aquarian love child will be gone. Their futuristic attitude carries over to the bedroom as well. So whatever is presented in the way of bedroom aerobics won't turn them off. In fact, your Aquarian bed companion will put his own creative spin on the matter. The woman of the sign will be the first person to allow you to come in her mouth, for two reasons: She wants to determine the taste and have the experience, and she wants to please you as a partner.

With the Aquarian, visual stimulation is also key. Generally, they like to be enticed by some sexy nightie or G-string. "I don't want a physically overweight person. That's a health problem. I ain't with the big weather girls, two tons of fun," an Aquarian brother said.

The Aquarian brother will allow you to put on your costumes, including the spike heels, simply to have the experience. And that's the key here. Make the encounter fun, creative, like never before, and the Aquarian will be at your beck and call at a moment's notice. Just remember, once you initiate this over-the-top sex, you can't go back. "I was just playing" will be met with dismissal and you'll be expected to perform or get the hell out of Dodge City! So don't start something you can't finish!

MONEY MATTERS

An Aquarian with money is a dangerous thing—even more so if it's your money! But before we jump to conclusions about how your humanitarian will deal with or handle money, you must consider the source.

First and foremost, Aquarians are suckers for a sob story. If by chance you've given your companion, spouse, or loved one money to hold for you, keep, or deposit, you may never see it again. Of course, when you gave him the money, he had every intention of carrying out your orders, but somewhere along the way, his intentions got overshadowed by the needs of the moment: A relative needed help on his rent, or a next-door neighbor needed formula for the baby and food for the household.

Save yourself some time, effort, and frustration; realize who you're dealing with and act accordingly.

Aquarians have little regard for money except to spend it—or enjoy all the comforts of having it. They have the notion that your hard-earned money can be spent just like theirs. This air sign doesn't discriminate.

If by chance you're married to an Aquarian and there never seems to be enough money, that's par for the course. Aquarians spend it like it's going out of style. They can't even spell the word budget, let alone be frugal or penny-wise. As far as they're concerned, these are simply words children learn to spell in school. They simply can't relate to such musings.

Aquarians are very smart and they know firsthand about stock options, mutual funds, 401(k)s, education funds, and all that jazz. But whether or not they have the patience to enjoy the fruits of years of saving and investing is another story entirely.

He will sometimes even borrow large sums of money and forget that they owe you. Once you remind him in a tactful manner about wanting to get paid, he might declare that he thought it was a gift that you decided to donate to his humanitarian cause.

Keep the lid on, if you can, and carefully explain the scenario to your ex-friend, excuse me, friend, as tactfully as possible. Aquarians see nothing wrong with spending your money. After all, you're a friend. And if the shoe were on the other foot, she would gladly give you her cash. Trouble is, she rarely has money to loan.

Aquarians are stubborn, too. And the best way to get them to see the importance of saving is to set the example. But don't give them the account numbers and access! If by chance they can benefit from financial planning, then they might listen. Otherwise, keep

your Aquarian spouse, companion, mate, sibling, or friend away
from the cash.

For example, if she's running some sort of after-school program
for pregnant teens and supplies are needed, she will spend her own
money rather than wade through the bureaucratic red tape to purchase the items. The way she sees it, the teenagers need the supplies and it's only money, you know. Oh, well, there goes the rent!

PAMPERING TIPS FOR AQUARIUS

- An impromptu trip out of town gets the Aquarian's attention. They're always looking for that great escape.
- Rent a hotel room (upscale, please, not the Motel 5.5) with a
  Jacuzzi, champagne, and room service.
- A back rub and foot massage, along with scented candles, a
  reading of your poems or spoken-word creation. Then enjoy
  your appreciative Aquarian.
- Aquarians are turned on by scents and aromas. Prepare a
  soul-food meal at your place with all the trimmings. You'll be
  dessert!
- Take a ferry or rent a sailboat and explore some uncharted
  waters. You'll enjoy the motion of the ocean and all that that
  implies.
- Create a movable feast, to be sent to his place—and he will
  deliver.
- A camping trip with some music and some sleeping bags is
  all that's needed for your Aquarian, who loves the great outdoors.
- Honest communicating with and listening to the Aquarian,
  who is often misunderstood, are a form of pampering. Aquarians love the direct approach.
- Companion's day out will always work. Once you take charge
  and take care of everything for 24 hours, your Aquarian will
  be putty in your hands.

GIFT IDEAS FOR AQUARIUS

❋ When it comes to what Aquarians want, they spare no expense. But in receiving gifts, it's the uniqueness rather than the cost that works for them.

❋ Gifts like handmade jewelry, hand-carved statues, or woven fabrics from arts and crafts shows strike an Aquarian's fancy.

❋ Have a sketch made from a photograph of her and have it framed. Major brownie points.

❋ Books on spirituality, metaphysics, science, or any futuristic publication are a sure bet. Books on tape are good if his schedule is too busy.

❋ Season tickets to the theater or favorite sport also work.

❋ How about a piece of original artwork—signed, of course.

❋ A spa membership will have her singing your praises.

❋ Antique furniture is always a winner. Aquarians appreciate the history and artistry of such pieces.

❋ Any personalized gift: Write him a poem, have it written in calligraphy and framed, and he'll be deeply appreciative.

❋ Any souvenir from out of the country—such as an African mask, jewelry, or fabric—will be treasured.

Pisces

(February 19 to March 20)

SYMBOL: TWO FISH SWIMMING IN OPPOSITE
DIRECTIONS

Positive love traits: Passionate, romantic, imaginative,
and sensitive lover; one of the stars of the freak
show.

Negative love traits: Kinky; prone to masochistic sexual
behavior; may like threesomes.

Ruling planet: Neptune is associated with illusion,
glamour, mystery, and deception.

Word to the wise: Pisces people shy away from aggressive
types. It will take forever to really know a Pisces.

You can save yourself some energy in trying to figure out what
makes the Piscean person tick. Understanding these complex people
is going to be a slow process because they don't quite understand
themselves. They will only allow a select few in their private domain. These water signs are complicated, emotional people whose
feelings and concerns about life and loved ones run deep. The ruling planet of Pisces is Neptune, which is associated with illusion,
glamour, mystery, and deception.

Of course, Pisceans want very much to dwell behind a facade.
They want to be looked upon as mysterious but alluring, objects of
curiosity. Also, they want to be perceived as people who have it going on in every aspect of their lives. But this has larger implications. The facade is a protective shield against those who want to
discredit, harm, or look down on them. They simply cannot bear to
be perceived as weak or vulnerable by onlookers or the general

masses. A Pisces writer recalls the most embarrassing situation for him: "I was visiting the parents of a girlfriend and mistakenly ate the dog's food. I laughed it off." The point is, it was an honest mistake, but the Pisces was mortified.

Actually, they may be perceived as nose-in-the-air, above-it-all type of people. Really, all this illusion and mystery is merely a smoke screen for their insecurities and need for support, love, and attention.

One of the reasons that they're hard to know is because you will rarely see them out meetin' and greetin' unless there is some specific purpose, like a church, community, or work function. You won't find these people in the middle of huge crowds. Most Pisceans are loners. The men of the sign will have friends, but they'll be mostly female. And the Pisces sisters will have more male friends than female. They guard their privacy fiercely. The bar scene is not really their cup of tea. But once they're dressed and out, they can definitely be engaging, fun-loving, and very accommodating people.

They're confined to quarters, you know. Their home is their sanctuary because that is where all the pretense and games and being on guard can be put aside. In fact, their key word is confinement. They don't have to leave home as long as they feel safe and have the necessities—good book, bottle of wine, and some soothing music—at their disposal. Then all is right with the world.

Pisces is a water sign, and most people are drawn to water signs. They enjoy sitting by and swimming in lakes, rivers, oceans, and ponds. Water signs are reassuring, emotional, intuitive, soothing, and nonthreatening.

The symbol for Pisces is two fish connected by a string and swimming in opposite directions. One type of Pisces is like the fish that swims upstream against the current, against the odds, eventually attaining his goals. These are the ones who have a sense of structure to their lives. The other type of Pisces is like the fish that swims downstream with the current, taking the easy way, going with the flow. This Pisces lacks ambition and direction and is even lazy, simply wanting to be left alone, writing poetry or a song now and then, earning just enough to make ends meet.

When you first meet them, they will be impeccably dressed. Even if they're in a jogging suit, it will be some designer brand.

Most Pisces are very conscious of their image. The women of the sign are the ladies of the zodiac and have a Ms. Manners demeanor. The Pisces men are usually the quiet, sensitive types who definitely know how to treat a lady. We're talking high-maintenance activities like dinners, trips, and attending all of the right social functions.

Pisces are usually small in stature, and their faces are usually oval. Most Pisces are attractive, but have unusually large eyes that project inquisitiveness and surprise. Their complexions are smooth and blemish-free. Later in their lives, Pisces people usually have weight problems because they enjoy being confined to quarters, where physical activity is at a minimum.

Pisces people are the dreamers of the zodiac. They look at the world through rose-colored glasses. Generally, they want to be left alone to dream their dreams and not deal with the real world. Pisces people are the consummate laid-back sisters and brothers.

These creative water signs are people of the arts, usually directing plays, teaching needlepoint, painting, and writing, or putting together a proposal for funding an underprivileged children's workshop. Pisces people are interested in endeavors that have broad implications. They're spiritual, with an innate sense that they are here on this earth for a higher purpose. And they're *very* intuitive. When a Pisces speaks, you better listen.

THE PISCES MAN

Any relationship with a Pisces man will be slow going. This is a brother who takes his time. This brother simply will not make a move on you until he's ready. If he feels the time is not right to do the wild thang, you can stand in the room in your birthday suit and he'll barely notice. He's got to do the background check (ask his friends if they know you). He's also got to determine if you're who you claim to be. I know that this sounds bizarre, but Pisces people are the mystery people of the zodiac. They guard their privacy and they must be in control, or at least think they are. So they're not going to run off half-cocked and jump into a relationship without further study. You may be thinking, now, is this a relationship or a medical research project? But to the Pisces, that's simply how important the process is.

And if by chance you think that you're all that with this brother, don't be too aggressive and pushy. He will simply shrug it off in his most disinterested, matter-of-fact, oh-well manner. His philosophy is simple: Just like you, Ms. Thang, there will be others who will come a-callin'.

For example, a Pisces brother from Memphis had such a relationship. "After dating this sister for two months (no sex, we Pisces take our time), we had an intimate dinner and, at her suggestion, proceeded to the hotel. On the way, she ended the relationship but wanted a screw to remember me by. Too bad it was Elvis Week; no room at the inn, oh well."

The Pisces brother has charisma and style and is curiously attractive to the opposite sex. He is the dreamer, the romantic of the zodiac. Romance is this brother's middle name. He's definitely into creating the rendezvous that dreams are made of. Trouble is, we have to wake up sometime, and there may be trouble when reality sets in and the dream is forgotten. For example, you may have had a glorious out-of-town trip with sand, sun, and sea, a favorite spot for the Pisces. But when the two of you arrive back home, you might not hear from this brother all week. Don't despair; he has trouble digesting the real world, so contact with his lady love may be low on the totem pole. There's work, meetings, family feuds, and other matters that need his attention right now. Besides, you're his fantasy world and he'll soon be back to you once again, trying to escape all of the hustle and bustle of the real world.

Now for the good part. This brother is definitely worth the wait in the romance and sex departments. This brother put the R in romance and the X in sex, X-rated, that is. Once you gain his trust, after about two months of dating (that's a pretty long stretch by today's standards) and intimate, heart-to-heart talks, your patience will be rewarded. Now, with all of this big buildup, you're probably wondering what's not to like here?

Seriously, you'll have an easier time cultivating the relationship because the stage of closeness and honesty will be set. Pisces men love women who are intelligent, have a working knowledge of the arts, and have a strong spiritual base.

These engaging, sensitive people are easy to talk to. Women who are interested in the Pisces brother will pour their hearts out, explaining how some dude jilted them—and all the while the Pisces offers atmosphere, tissues, and music. In a relationship with a Pisces brother, you'll get a clear sense that he is interested in you as a person. Of course, sex is a high priority, but he'll need to know you before knockin' the boots commences. As one Pisces brother put it, "What I find intriguing is how a woman's life circumstances have affected her way of thinking."

Enhancements such as hair weaves, dreads, toupees, color contacts, or body piercings are no big deal for Pisces people; you may find them using or wearing such enhancements as well. Being well groomed for the Pisces brother is an absolute must. For the most part, they are neatness freaks. So if you're inviting a Pisces to your house, you need to wash the miniblinds, vacuum, remove the cat litter box from the walk-in closet, and get the cobwebs out of the corner. He won't miss a trick.

If you fall for this brother, you'll be whipped, and there is no solution because of their easygoing nature. There will be very few confrontations, disagreements, and mood swings. This relationship will probably suffer because Pisces in many cases is too good to be true, and potential mates have a tendency to take Pisces' kindness for weakness. He's so intuitive, he'll know if you're telling a lie or even embellishing the truth, so you might as well come clean. If the deception continues, this brother will go along with the program for a while. But let's not take too much for granted, because when they're fed up, they will pull up stakes and move on. For example a Pisces computer technician realized during the courtship phase that his relationship with a control freak (Ms. Take-charge) wasn't going to work. "I remained unavailable for three weeks, then called to say hello and have a nice life, friend!"

The problem is, Pisces has a tendency to fall for the wrong companion and for the wrong reasons. His idealized view of marriage and the realities of the union are rarely in sync. A marriage with a Pisces only has a 50-50 chance of survival. And if by chance he wants to end the relationship, you probably won't get all the specific reasons.

What you'll observe, however, is that the Pisces brother can be moody, quiet, and introspective, constantly wrestling with his motivations and overall purpose in life. And that purpose may not include a relationship with you. A Pisces brother who loves his wife dearly says, "The relationship works on a friendship and parenting level, but not so on a romantic level."

The romance part of the relationship is all-important to the Pisces and is a large part of what he may live for. But the realities, all too often, put a damper on his hopes and dreams, creating a sullen, unmotivated, and self-indulgent Pisces who's hard to reach and connect with.

THE PISCES WOMAN

This sister is a master at getting what she wants from a man, in and out of bed. Although Pisces women are not as slow about moving on a relationship as their male counterparts, they maintain that checklist of what they're looking for in a man.

The Pisces sister's needs are simple. She wants a strong, supportive, and confident man whom she can spoil and surrender to fully. With that philosophy, the line forms at the left. On the other hand, the Pisces career woman knows exactly what she wants out of life, but needs companionship to make her feel complete.

The Pisces woman has the ability to draw men right to her. She's a soft-spoken, alluring, gentle, and caring water sign, which makes the male species stand up and take notice. And when the brothers start paying attention, for the most part, it's instantaneous; of course, they won't be able to pinpoint what the deal is. It doesn't matter—it's on.

For example, a Pisces woman from Ohio recalled that during college, she had more men than she could handle at one point. The campus was at a major university in the South with a 4 percent black population. "I got the big head in college. It was weird; all these guys were attracted to me. My girlfriends were egging me on, saying take advantage of it. At the time, I was seeing one guy, then another guy came along I liked, and then there was a third. Well, two of my boyfriends ended up at the same party. I came with one and the other showed up. The third found out about it the next day. It wasn't my intention to hurt any of the them. I wasn't being callous, I was being careless. If I could take anything back, it would be that."

Pisces women don't miss much when it comes to appearances. Image is everything, you know. They are into their own appearance, with having the "look," and they will expect you to be neat and clean even if your suit is from JCPenney. And if your appearance is suspect, if you have soup stains on your tie and poor hygiene, you might not be called back for a second impression. For example, one Pisces woman has telltale signals to determine if a brother bathes regularly. "When you're going out, check the person's collar. Look at his hands, his neck, and, if you can, his feet. If these details are not attended to, there are going to be problems." She added, "Everybody can have a little ring around the collar from sweating, but when the collar looks it's got ink on it and it's indelible, then something's wrong."

If you plan to enter into a relationship with a Pisces sister, get the dictionary and look up the word "romance." Before long, you'll become intimately acquainted with that word, because romance is the prerequisite for any long-term liaison with this mysterious and ultrafeminine woman. One Pisces professor had her complaints about the dating game. "I don't want him to be boring. A person who is an academic but knows nothing else but his subject is a bore. These academic types look good and dress well, but when you get past their subject matter, they don't have anything to talk about."

Yes, the Pisces woman does thrive on romance, but romance alone is not enough. They love to be able to feel totally secure around a man. Pisceans are not too hung up on your occupation as such, but you do need to have a job. Regarding what she's looking for in a man, a Pisces woman commented, "It changes with time. I'm looking for someone who can offer me security. I plan to work, but I don't want to have to worry that if I don't go to work the bills won't get paid. I want someone who has the energy to enjoy life."

Class, image, and home training are areas in her life that are important to her. For example, even though a Pisces teacher was divorced, she took pains not to allow the baby-sitter to see her and her friend in a compromising position together. "A baby-sitter came early once, my car was outside so I had to let her in, but my friend was in my bedroom. Since both of the apartment doors were on the same side leading to the porch, my friend left through the window because I didn't want the teenager to see my friend."

And loud, boisterous, aggressive behavior will get you nowhere but a quick trip out of Ms. Pisces' life. There won't be anyone in their lives to reflect negatively on the Pisces persona. For example, a companion of a Pisces was intrigued by her independence and straightforward personality at first, but when the Pisces reporter wanted to be alone and had to cancel a date because of work commitments, her companion couldn't hang. "I'm real honest and upfront. Life is too short. I don't like playing games. I have these crazy hours. I'm a moody kind of a person, and I don't want a person occupying all of my time. I like to be alone sometimes," she said.

When this leap year baby was called on an assignment about two hours before she and her date were supposed to go out, he went off. "He was upset, accusing me of being with someone else, demanding to know, How long did you stay out? and Who were you *really* with?"

Pisces women are compassionate and caring people. One very sharp weakness is that they don't know how to say no. For example, a Pisces day care center director agreed to go on a blind date at the urging of a friend. When she arrived at the bar, her blind date weighed 400 pounds. The Pisces approached the man, pretending to be a friend of the Pisces instead of the real date, talked a while, had a drink, and left.

Although they may seem to be pushovers and cream puffs, Piscean women have an inner strength that may not be apparent to those on the outside looking in. These women will be supportive, attentive, and excellent homemakers, creating a haven you will not want to leave. They will affect you subtly—like you're being run over by a truck, only in slow motion, a little at a time. And you won't know what hit you.

The Pisces woman is highly intuitive and perceptive. She knows the effect that she has on a potential companion. This water sign will strip you naked with her sixth sense, so don't play games and perpetrate. You'll have to come clean. She has the ability to read you before you even realize what you're going to say or do. If the coupling ain't working, you'll get the heave-ho, and she'll retreat back to her fantasy world for a minute. A Pisces woman from Boston had this to say about being alone: "I've had good times in bed. I mean, I can live off the memories. During this dry spell, they sustain me because I can conjure up all these good memories. I need more than good sex now."

Guide to a Love Connection

Pisces and Aries

Sex is the glue that holds these two together. And I mean they are sticking and staying in the bedroom so much that the reality of whether this union will last hasn't hit yet, at least not for Pisces, anyway. Once these two surface from under the sheets, reality sets in. Pisces only feels safe at home and when the strong ram is or-chestrating their lives together. That's okay for a minute, but Aries wants adventure, fun, and living life to the fullest. Pisces' key word is confinement, meaning a safe abode, a companion he trusts, and someone to understand his need to be appreciated. Aries' philoso-phy is that life's too short to sweat the small stuff. If it's going to work, Pisces will have to give in much more than the ram.

Pisces and Taurus

If Pisces is willing to focus on the devotion and security of hav-ing a bull around, then the bull is satisfied to be the devoted com-panion. While Taurus works long and hard, Pisces would rather be home being fed grapes one by one with champagne chilling on ice. That's when Taurus orders a reality check for Pisces. Taurus pro-vides the security that doubtful and insecure Pisces is constantly plagued by. There's no problem in the bedroom, except that they rarely want to exit. Pisces loves to be at home in the rich, comfort-able surroundings that they create and so does the bull. A lot of ifs are at work here. But if each of these two pays attention to the needs of the other, this could be one of the most fulfilling relation-ships of the zodiac.

Pisces and Gemini

Pisces are the mystery people of the zodiac and Gemini keeps secrets. Both come to the table with issues. Pisces sees Gemini as too flighty and noncommittal about the relationship. Gemini is too busy running from pillar to post to sit at home with Pisces and watch the paint dry. Pisces is romantic and passionate about the relationship. Gemini wants to enjoy it for what it is and then move on to the next phase of his program. Pisces is insecure and lacks direction. Gemini is a jack-of-all-trades and master of none. Both need stronger companions as support. If you're a Pisces or Gemini reading this section, you already know that the relationship ain't working. But I'll verify it for you. Give it up, so you can both be out of your misery.

Pisces and Cancer

These two do a lot of crying in their beer about what might have been and what didn't happen. But once the self-pity action is over, this duo has plenty of potential. These two are emotional wrecks but support each other like there's no tomorrow. Pisces, who goes back and forth in terms of what she really wants in the relationship, finds Cancer simply waiting in the wings. Pisces is insecure, but so is Cancer. But Cancer is the nurturer of the two and propels Pisces to heights never thought possible. Cancer will make the home warm and comfortable for stay-at-home Pisces. Although both love friends and family, being at home is where these two feel safest. Once they end up in bed, the encounter solidifies all fantasies. A match made in heaven.

Pisces and Leo

This duo will have to work overtime to make a go of it. Pisces is a dreamer. Leo is a doer. At first, each will be intrigued by the other. Pisces will write poetry and lavish attention on Leo, which she craves. Both love a lavish lifestyle and spending money. But Pisces' goal is to stay home and create a romantic setting there. Leo's public is waiting. The lion must make the sets, the parties, and the like. Pisces doesn't have enough get-up-and-go for the energetic lion. Leo sees Pisces' lackluster lifestyle as boring, and says so. Pisces feels rejection. Although both are passionate and highly sexed, Pisces' freaky behavior annoys Leo. Don't bother with this one. It's not going to work.

Pisces and Virgo

These two opposites of the horoscope are seemingly made for each other. But looks can be deceiving. Pisces' mysterious and secretive approach to the relationship doesn't sit too well with Virgo's reserved but straightforward nature. Pisces' insecure, tentative personality annoys Virgo, who is systematic and knows exactly what she wants from life. Pisces wants to dream dreams but may not always be able to actualize them. Virgo is a workaholic and cannot understand Pisces' lethargic state. Both love to create a comfortable setting at home. Sexually, these two come together nicely. However, Pisces, the more creative and passionate of the two, keeps Virgo on the run with some of her freak-show antics. An affair maybe, but marriage is doubtful.

Pisces and Libra

Both are charming, charismatic types and instantly attracted to each other. Pisces is a loner, happy to be just with Libra. Libra is an air sign and must have freedom of movement. Pisces loves being at home and away from the madding crowd. Both love lavish surroundings and romantic settings. Libra is a social butterfly who must flit from one person to the next. Pisces is left sulking in the corner. Pisces' emotional surges annoy Libra, who sees such behavior as confining and troublesome. The sex is freaky and over the top, which is fine for both. If these two could exist solely from a physical standpoint, the liaison could remain happy. But when reality creeps in for Libra, she will be the first to let go.

Pisces and Scorpio

Water means tears and high emotion. These two water signs resolve to be devoted to each other forever more. Yeah, yeah, yeah, everyone wants to know what the commotion is all about. Here's what's going on here. These two are devoted, passionate, and so sensual it's scary. Scorpio is the money manager who exercises prudence in building the nest egg for the future. Pisces is mysterious, over the top sexually, and romantic. Scorpio is highly jealous and possessive, and only wants a relationship that can be dominated, controlled, and pushed to the next level. Always the dreamer, Pisces wants to be left alone to dream dreams and seek new heights of pleasure and wealth untold. In short, these two will climb to the top of a mountain, look over the edge, and dare to dream the what-ifs of the world.

Pisces and Sagittarius

These two are operating on totally different frequencies. Pisces wants Sagittarius's undivided attention. That's impossible for Sagittarius, who can't sit still if her life depends on it. Pisces is emotional and expects love, devotion, the whole nine yards. Sag's thirst for knowledge, understanding, and the unexplored has Pisces upset. Pisces cannot relate and simply wants Sag to put away his toys and stay home. The sex is so awesome they don't want to give up on the relationship. Pisces is a dreamer, while Sag is a man of action. Sag will complain about Pisces' whining and lack of motivation; this hurts Pisces' feelings. While Pisces licks her wounds, Sag is long gone, flirting with his next honey.

Pisces and Capricorn

Pisces planned this union long before Capricorn knew what hit him. And with this fish, it's only a matter of time until the catch is reeled in. You see, Capricorn was working late as usual. Methodical and systematic Capricorn needs to throw caution to the wind. And Pisces, with a poem in one hand and champagne in the other, is just the person Capricorn can get buck with. The latter won't happen too often, but if anybody can create a wild streak in Capricorn, it's a Pisces. They both have a great sense of humor, love travel, and are really stay-at-home types. But what they do behind closed doors is another story. And Pisces is the culprit. With Pisces' creativity in the boudoir, this pair may never leave home. There are computers and faxes, you know. Enjoy!

Pisces and Aquarius

Both are creative types. Pisces is more on the artistic side and Aquarius has more of an intellectual bent. Pisces simply wants Aquarius to remain at home and understand the hidden treasures of all that Aquarius can benefit from. Aquarius's friendly but distant demeanor leaves Pisces frustrated and feeling unloved. The relationship starts to unravel as Pisces demands more of elusive Aquarius's time and attention. And Aquarius begins to feel closed in and trapped. From a sexual standpoint, experimental Aquarius sends Pisces into space. Both are stars of the freak show. Once intuitive Pisces realizes that aloof Aquarius is not involved for the long haul, it's over. Move on!!

Pisces and Pisces

These two could simply dream their lives away. But reality has to set in and therein lies the rub. Pisces people are the romantic types. Each needs a strong, determined, and focused companion to help offset the fish's dreamlike state of mind and lack of motivation. Romance and bedroom matters are never a problem with these two, but sooner or later, the blinds must be opened and a reality check must be taken. They need direction, they need a strong support system, they need to be loved without question. But of course, they lack the wherewithal to provide these elements to each other. In short, two needy and high-maintenance types shouldn't be in a relationship. Maybe these two could be friends.

ROMANCE AND THE PISCES

One of the most important things to a Pisces is the emotional, spiritual, and romantic character of the relationship. The Pisces brother will read you his favorite poem, write a poem, or even put the poem to music "just because." For starters, he's an emotional, spiritual, and hopeless romantic. Flowers, fun, drama, intrigue, baths together, full body massages, and glorious sexual encounters will all come with the territory of the Pisces' personality. After one romantic night with this brother, you may propose marriage to him.

The Pisces woman loves to entertain at home by preparing an intimate, classy candlelit dinner with champagne or wine. If you're invited to a Pisces' home, bring a good bottle of wine—you can't miss. If by chance you're lingering around the Ripple, Boone's Farm, or Wild Irish Rose, think again. You must give the impression that you know what you're doing. If you don't know, ask the clerk.

Pisces women love surprises and thoughtfulness, meaning going beyond the call of duty to create a warm, romantic, and inviting evening. If extra effort is put into the evening, extra attention is definitely paid to the companion. For example, a Pisces woman describes a most memorable evening: "A friend I once dated (who had a key to my apartment) was at my place when I got home. He had left a trail of love notes through the apartment, wine, candles, food. He had also picked up my toddler from the sitter, had fed him, and put him to sleep." Wow!

A Pisces woman postal clerk said that after knowing her new beau for only two months, she got the surprise of her life: "I was presented with a diamond ring."

Any setting near water is always a winner with these signs. A Pisces woman describes a simple but romantic date: "I enjoy having a lazy day with a nice light meal. I am a true water person. When I was in Florida, a romantic setting for me would be to beach-hop and stroll on the beach at night, hearing the water crash against the shoreline and seeing the waves rushing in and out." A Pisces brother, a development director, said that his idea of a romantic date is "building a fire on the beach." Then some serious cuddling.

A Pisces woman recalls a date at a swimming pool she managed that almost turned into disaster. "After we closed the pool, we had a party for employees and friends. My boyfriend had set up a little table with my favorite fruit and wine, but he couldn't find me. I ended up sitting at the bottom of the pool, enjoying what looked like a laser show from lights around the pool that were refracting through the water. I almost drowned in the pool. I was sitting at the bottom, I could feel myself drinking water. I had been smoking marijuana, and I shouldn't have been." Both were lifeguards, trained in lifesaving techniques. Her smoking days came to a screeching halt.

By the way, if you're planning to have a long-term relationship with a Pisces, by all means get rid of the Jheri curls and polyester clothing. Polyester farms have gone the way of the dinosaur. If you don't, you won't be able to get past the first date. Wet, greasy hair and romance don't mix with the Pisces.

A Pisces accountant from Houston was instantly turned off by a Virgo companion who was more intrigued with his own watch than with her. In his efforts to explain the time in different parts of the world, the Virgo held the watch so close to Pisces' face that she was looking at it cross-eyed.

Pisces people oftentimes find themselves being socialites or attending black-tie functions; they love this sort of thing. Your Pisces will expect you to be dressed for the part and provide him with an impressive armpiece and other amenities to complete the look. Read the newspaper and check out the news, so you can converse, not conversate!!! (There's no such word!)

And once the stage is set and all of the do's and don'ts have been worked out, my, my, my. Or should I say, my oh my! The romance is so intense that the girlfriends or guy friends will have to be told. In short, you'll be giving all the details of what the commotion is about as you look dreamily off into space, not forgetting a single detail. Say, it's all a part of the plan. Many times, Pisces prefer the dream or the fantasy to the real world. So creating a date as close to what their dreams are made of is what they seek.

A Pisces college vice president describes her perfect date: "My dream of a romantic date is to be invited two months ahead of time to some opening night, a play or the symphony. We really have to dress up—a fabulous dress, hair, massage, and everything will be done. We stop and have a glass of wine. I've made reservations for dinner after the event, and everything my date wants will be just right for him."

Intimate talks, taking time with children, remembering a birthday, and attending family functions are all top priority for Pisces people. Ironically, they are so secretive and mysterious that it will take some time to get to the intimate talk level. Pisces people have that sixth sense, and for them intimate talks with a companion help to peel back the layers of the personality so that understanding and intimacy will occur. Trust is all-important to the Pisces.

A Pisces woman describes the most romantic man of her dreams. Even though the two never had sex, they were in the relationship for almost two years. Her dream man had contracted AIDS from his wife, who had died a year before his courtship with the Pisces began. The Pisces learned of it only three months before he died. "He wouldn't touch me. We would be on the brink of going into the bedroom and he would say, 'No, I think I'd better go.'" His explanation for keeping the secret was that he couldn't bear to hurt the one he loved. "This man [the vice president of a bank] shared all of my dreams: I love to go to the ballet, I love to go to the symphony,

I love the finer things of life. He opened doors, literally and figura-tively. He knew how to walk with kings and didn't lose the common touch."

A Pisces woman remembers that the most memorable approach to romance was when her fiancé proposed marriage. A companion lured her to a hotel on the pretense that he had to attend a work function. He later apologized, saying he had gotten the day wrong. He ushered her to the restaurant and suggested that they have din-ner. After he excused himself, the waiter came over flirting shame-lessly and even gave Ms. Pisces a rose. Her Scorpio boyfriend finally showed up as people started to fill the room and the landing above her head. "He took out this ring and then proposed as more than a hundred people looked on. I accepted. Of course, the waiter was in on the whole thing. I was totally blown away."

SEX, SEX, AND MORE SEX

GETTING THE GROOVE ON . . .

Pisces people are water signs. Consequently, any water-related activities, sexual or otherwise, like hanging out in hot tubs or Jacuzzis, near the ocean or lake, or having sex while bathing, are just hunky-dory with Pisces and will get the groove on!

They love the melodrama of the buildup to sex. In creating a ro-mantic setting, Pisces people are hard to beat. The Pisces woman, who is usually quiet and demure and the epitome of womanhood, can become a tiger in bed. And at some point you might find your-self with a tiger by the tail. Pisces women enjoy sex to the fullest. Both the male and female will do just about anything short of death to please their partners.

These types are what romance novels are made of. They proba-bly wrote the book on romance and eroticism. With Pisces, the ro-mance and foreplay begin long before any thoughts of bedroom aerobics.

The Pisces brother will write erotic love poems while acting out the fantasies in the poems. He'll whisk you off to some deserted place for a secret rendezvous and titillate, touch, and taste every area of your body, bar none, all along the trip. In the car on the road, while sitting in your seat on an airplane, or even while you dine with others, it's on. As long as there are two consenting adults, that's all that's needed to romp, play, and dance the night away.

The women of the sign want intrigue and creativity in the bedroom. You'll be pretty amazed at the ease and creativity of any sexual encounter with a Pisces. Pisces people are sexually liberated types who love to give pleasure just as much as they receive. As a Pisces sister put it, "I'm willing to engage in some pain, but when I say enough, I want you to respect that, that's what I expect. I will get up and walk out."

The women of the sign love to dress up in costumes to complete the look for the freak show. Sexy teddies, edible underwear, cat suits, spike-heel shoes, dildos, vibrators, and videos can all be a part of the show to enhance, prolong, and experience the total package and total buildup.

One Pisces female performs an intricate and detailed striptease for her mate before the foreplay begins. She calls this maneuver "marinating the meat." She starts with music that is slow and ends at a fever pitch, much like what she expects in the bedroom. By the time she is down to her G-string, the boy is all over her. She believes it makes their sexual encounters much more erotic and passionate. Yeah, I guess so!

Although the Pisces brother is patient when it comes to ending up in the bedroom, once he finally makes it, he expects moans of delight and quick responses to his antics in bed. For the most part, Pisces brothers are not turned on by naïveté. As one brother put it, "There's no pleasure in teaching."

These brothers love to lick their partners' genitalia. Pisces wrote the book on oral sex. They knew at an early age that they would master the technique, and they have! These water signs, in the spirit of cooperation, can sometimes find themselves in threesomes or orgies. You just never know with them. Not only will the Pisces swing from the chandelier, he will hang upside down and stroke your body at the same time. There's that fantasy thing again. Pisces people prefer the traditional man-on-top position, but 69 is what they prefer during oral sex.

You're in for a very long night, or day, or weekend, or whatever! Good sex can't be rushed, you know? A Pisces female describes the biggest turnoff in the bedroom: "hurried, mechanical lovemaking and a quick trip to dreamland." As in falling asleep?

But a Pisces brother had to stand up and take notice after his companion set the stage for the most memorable approach to romance he ever witnessed. They took a vacation day from their respective jobs. Upon entering her house, love note number 1 directed him to brunch in the kitchen; love note number two directed him to the den to select music of his choice; love note number three sent him to flowers and incense in the living room; love note number four sent him to the foyer for a gift basket of oils, scented soap, and men's loungewear. The fifth and final love note included special requests for a day in bed. How's that for foreplay, outercourse, and sexual stimulation? Are you taking notes out there? She undoubtedly took her cues from a Pisces.

A Pisces woman from Ohio remembers a fantasy-filled evening with her Aquarian lover, which started off with fine dining, followed by a penthouse hotel room and champagne. The dessert was chocolate—not the Godiva variety, but chocolate syrup that Ms. Pisces purchased before arriving without telling her partner. Her lover began by pouring chocolate on her nipples, followed by all of the other areas that required sucking, licking, kissing, and lapping. "It was wonderful. We carried out all my fantasies." I wonder what the hotel maids thought the next day?

EROGENOUS ZONES . . . SOME PHYSICAL, SOME NOT

The erogenous zone for Pisces people is the feet. Pisces love to have their feet massaged and toes sucked. Actually, what you need to do is start from the tip of their head and travel to the feet. But they love mates who are in the no-holds-barred category.

Pisces men are definitely foot men; suck his toes and massage his feet, and watch that fish tail flip. Even before the massage begins, buy a footbath that your Pisces can soak in, complete with the vibrating element. This serves as a great aphrodisiac for these water signs.

Long and deliberate foreplay is always a winner. Pisces people love to cuddle before sex. Even if you don't know the erogenous zone at this point, cuddling rates right up there with kissing. A Pisces sister described prolonged foreplay with her new husband: "I like prolonged foreplay, and it may start with a telephone call." The Pisces woman explained that prior to a party where the couple ended up, she had only talked to her husband once and they hadn't seen each other. But after she arrived and they greeted each other with a kiss, all during the night they were giving each other these erotic glances. "I can feel him without him physically touching me. What was nice and sensual to me is just watching him interact with other people and every now and then, spying glances," she said.

Crass behavior won't get you to first base and certainly not a home run. Pisces people are pretty conservative when it comes to home training, having manners, and a devil-may-care attitude. When you have an intimate evening with a Pisces, discretion is the law of the land. "I had sex with someone and afterward I asked myself why. He disrobed and I thought wow, nice body and all. Then he farted and kept right on going, oblivious to it. It ruined everything for me. It was like we were in this helium balloon and somebody just put the pin in it."

A Pisces woman said what drives her crazy in the bedroom is gentle persuasion. After that, show time begins, and usually it's of the Academy Award caliber.

If the television is on, especially if it's football or basketball, I suggest that you turn it off so that you can concentrate on your Pisces, period, end of story. "Glancing at the game on TV while engaging in the act makes me feel like I ain't all that. But I know better," a Pisces postal employee declared. While you're watching TV, your Pisces is planning her next strategy, which will probably be how to get you out of her house so that she can get on with the next phase of her program (probably with a suitor who's a little more attentive).

Pisces are turned on by the slow and deliberate unfolding of events, leading up to intercourse. One Pisces woman explained it this way: "After our date, back to my place for good talk, good touching, taking it very slow and deliberate, enjoying every minute. The ultimate sexual act is very thorough and lingering. Then, ride me like a horse and anything you want to do is fine with me." Well, all righty, then.

These water signs are voyeurs and exhibitionists, too. They have an affinity for the arts, the theater, ballet, and such. And their musings are transferred over to the bed with all the pomp and circumstance they can muster. Melodrama is their key word. Costumes, role playing, and fantasies are all part of the mix. To keep them in the zone, or the erogenous zone, just be flexible.

If you're conservative, you need to be aware that anything goes with a Pisces. It's all part of the fantasy world that they prefer to live in. Besides, as one Pisces put it, fantasy is much more interesting and enjoyable than real life. "In my fantasy, I do exactly what I want without any judgmental, pious, or narrow-minded approaches to what suits me."

PLAIN OL' SEX AND NOTHING MORE: WELCOME TO THE FREAK SHOW

Of the twelve signs of the zodiac, there are the participants in the freak show, those who stand on the sidelines watching, and the stars. Pisces is one of the stars—maybe one of the creators of the show. Although it will take a while for him to expose himself with that over-the-top anything-goes approach to lovemaking, this water sign is worth the wait.

If you're thinking of approaching a Pisces about attending and participating in a freak show, keep several things in mind. First and foremost, she will have to trust you completely and feel that you, too, will have just as much to lose if the impromptu encounters are uncovered. Once she feels safe and confident that this can be enjoyable sex with lots of eroticism and a little S & M thrown in, you can sign her up on the spot.

Both the male and female of the sign will be eager, willing, and able to fulfill your wildest dreams in the sack. And they're not intimidated by experienced and aggressive lovers. For example, a Pisces brother commented that he's definitely not turned off when a woman shows him a move in bed that he hasn't seen before. "Please show me something I haven't seen in bed, the bathroom, kitchen, hall, garage, hood of my sports car, or out in the countryside," he said.

Both the male and female of the sign are sexually liberated. They will endure bondage, wear outrageous costumes, and create a fantasy world with sex toys and videos that you won't want to leave, ever. In short, a Pisces will do just about anything short of death to please a partner. By now, you're in search and seizure of the Pisces vixen or Pisces stud. Good luck!

MONEY MATTERS

First and foremost, the Pisces member of the family or business should *not* be in charge of money matters. Money means very little to Pisces; they simply want it for what it can buy. You won't find a Pisces trying to conquer the world and make millions.

These water signs are the dreamers of the zodiac. And they would like nothing better than to invest in some get-rich-quick scheme that some businessman with a mail-order degree hands them. Many of Pisces' ideas are totally impractical. And in his head, it's all worked out until a rational, thinking person enters the situation, pointing out the need for a feasibility study, a business plan, and financing options. Pisces is not a pushy person, and will readily agree if pertinent info is omitted from this foolproof endeavor.

Like Libras and Leos, Pisces love a lavish lifestyle, including the furnishing, the designer-name brands, and the minimansion to house all this luxury. Trouble is, who's going to pay for all of this stuff?

Saving, investing, and spending wisely are usually not part of the Pisces' makeup. They work hard, but they play hard. At home after a hard day, he will want all the trappings of success. Never mind that he probably only has enough money to cover the house note, two car notes, and credit card bills. The Pisces woman will still go and charge a $500 suit in a heartbeat if she has to go out of town for a meeting or speaking engagement. You may argue that she has three other off-white suits just like the one she bought. And Ms. Pisces will reply, "But I've worn those and I can't be seen in the same outfit again in one month!" Huh? You can't be seen by whom, the mirror?! This is an out-of-town trip! Image is everything to Pisces. Pisces people must present the illusion of success with all the material things even if they are almost destitute and can barely pay for all the stuff.

This argument is an exercise in futility, and one you'll never win, so here's the deal. If you're married to, dating, or living with a Pisces, you need to control the purse strings. Even if you don't think you're capable, any planning of the finances or balancing of the checkbook is a far cry from what many Pisces can or want to do.

On the other hand, there's also that fish swimming upstream against the current: the hardworking, diligent Pisces who uses his instincts, ability to ask pertinent questions, and thirst for knowledge to plan a well-thought-out financial future for himself and his family.

For example, a Pisces will research the pros and cons of buying a lot and building a house as opposed to buying a new house already built. Of course, most people would want the convenience of the latter, but the Pisces would see the value of the former, saving a sizable sum that could be used to buy more stuff, you know.

Aside from the dreamy state Pisces are most often associated with, they do want the best for their companions and families. And with that in mind, they have the wisdom and intuition to hire someone to do the financial planning, an area in which they have very little interest.

PAMPERING TIPS FOR PISCES

- Read aloud to your Pisces—including poetry, prose, or the Bible. Your Pisces will love it.
- Bathe your Pisces in milk or some expensive and exotic bathbeads by candlelight with soothing music in the background.
- Pisces, the water sign, must be near water. An extended stay in a hot tub or Jacuzzi sipping champagne with the companion close at hand works wonders.
- Plan a getaway to an isolated area like a cabin in the country or a beach house. Don't forget to include oils, candles, incense, and the CD player. Then get to work—on each other, that is!
- Pisces people have a vivid imagination. Kidnap your Pisces, turn the phones and pagers off. Play soothing music, including sounds of summer rain, thunder, and nature sounds. His imagination will do the rest.

✳ Surprise your Pisces with a meal. After dinner clean the kitchen. Then the two of you can enjoy dessert!

✳ A foot massage and a back rub after a long day at work will have your Pisces moaning with delight.

✳ A gift basket that has everything from chocolates to gift certificates for a manicure, facial, and massage makes a creative gift idea and provides a little pampering too.

✳ Pisces people love their companions to take charge of a situation. If there's a plumbing problem, a family crisis, or even a problem with the children, simply handle it. Your Pisces will be forever grateful.

✳ Plan a retreat indoors, without benefit of phones, computers, or e-mail. Supply your Pisces with all of the necessities: food, booze, music, and you!

GIFT IDEAS FOR PISCES

✳ Pisces people love gifts that have meaning such as framing their favorite poem and sketching them in the nude and having it framed.

✳ Keepsake items like pictures organized in a leather folder of the two of you on vacation together.

✳ Pisces love jewelry. An aqua birthstone ring or pendant is ideal for the female. Try cuff links or a bracelet for the male.

✳ Bright colors of coral, turquoise, emerald, and blue will work. For your Pisces beau, a silk tie and scarf in any of these colors works best. Try scarves or blouses for the woman. But polyester fabric is not an option!

✳ Pisces people love the arts. Books of poetry or season tickets to the symphony or theater are the bomb!

✳ Metaphysical paraphernalia like crystals and pyramids always pique the Pisces' interest. Having the Pisces' astrological birth chart done is a great gift idea, too.

✳ A spa membership with sauna and hot tub may work wonders for your Pisces, who has a tendency to lead a sedentary life. This gift is a welcome alternative to the usual offerings.

  ❋ Flowers, balloons, cards, and teddy bears are all romantic ges-
     tures the Pisces man or woman reveres. But don't forget the
     love note outlining what's to come later!

  ❋ A memento denoting some special event or an original piece
     of artwork for your creative Pisces works, too. He'll love it.

  ❋ Treat your Pisces to a cruise, preferably for at least ten days.
     You'll see a side of your Pisces that you haven't seen before.

About the Author

THELMA BALFOUR who works as a stringer for *USA Today*, has studied and practiced astrology for over twenty years. What was initially a hobby for Thelma soon became a major interest, culminating in the publication of her first book *Black Sun Signs*, and an astrology column in *Heart & Soul* magazine. Thelma now frequently presents workshops on astrology and relationships, and appears on radio talk shows. She also maintains a website where she answers a different astrological question every week. She is a native of Memphis, Tennessee, and lives there now with her husband and two sons. She can be reached at www.thelmabalfour.com.